DIRTY BERTIE

AN
ENGLISH KING
MADE IN
FRANCE

Also by Stephen Clarke

For more information on Stephen Clarke and his books,
see his website at www.stephenclarkewriter.com

Read Stephen's tweets at @sclarkewriter

DIRTY BERTIE

AN ENGLISH KING MADE IN FRANCE

STEPHEN CLARKE

CENTURY

Published by Century in 2014

2 4 6 8 10 9 7 5 3 1

Endpapers map and map on p.vi-vii of the prelims by Darren Bennett

First published in Great Britain in 2014 by
Century
Random House, 20 Vauxhall Bridge Road
London SW1V 2SA

www.randomhouse.co.uk

Addresses for companies within
The Random House Group Limited can be found at:
www.randomhouse.co.uk/offices.htm

The Random House Group Limited Reg. No. 954009

A CIP catalogue record for this book is available from the British Library

ISBN 9781780890340 (hardback)
ISBN 9781780890357 (trade paperback)

The Random House Group Limited supports the Forest Stewardship Council®
(FSC®), the leading international forest-certification organisation. Our books carrying
the FSC label are printed on FSC®-certified paper. FSC is the only forest-certification
scheme supported by the leading environmental organisations, including Greenpeace.
Our paper procurement policy can be found at www.randomhouse.co.uk/environment

Typeset by Palimpsest Book Production Ltd, Falkirk, Stirlingshire
Printed and bound in Great Britain by
Clays Ltd, St Ives plc

To Paris, which will always turn you into a Parisian . . .
if you have any sense.

And to N. and the Crimée Crew.

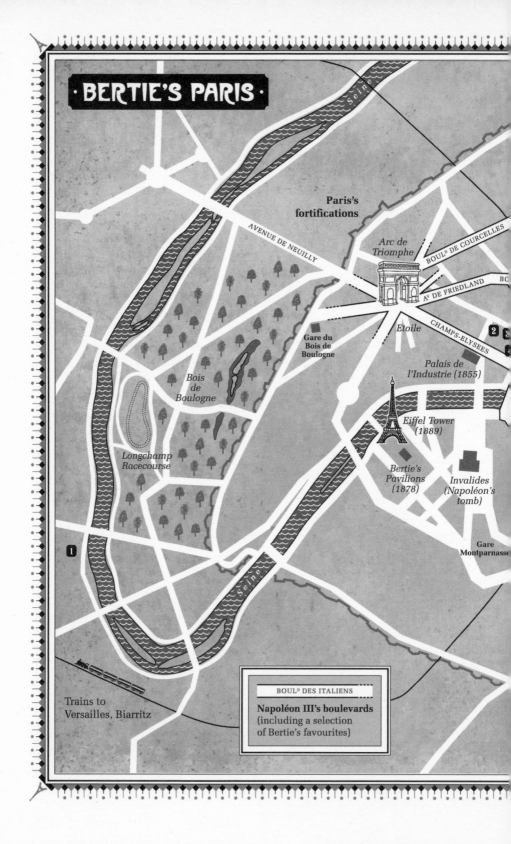

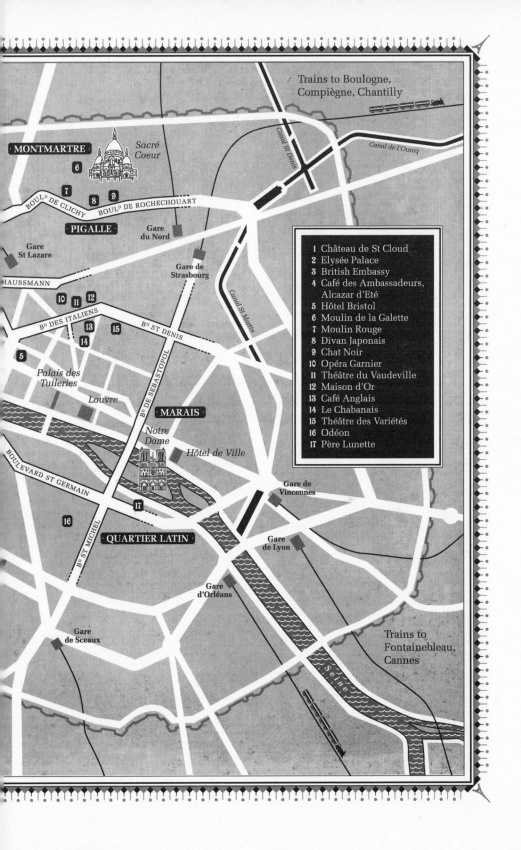

Contents

PREFACE

◆

'Edward VII reigns in London, but he rules in Paris.'
Émile Flourens, French Minister of Foreign Affairs

If DNA tests had existed in the early twentieth century, they would certainly have confirmed that King Edward VII was of soundly Anglo-German stock. His father Albert was pure Teuton, with morals as stiff as a Kaiser's moustache. His mother Victoria was at least half-German. And he was born at a time when 'French' was listed in every English-language thesaurus as a synonym of words like 'devil', 'mortal enemy', 'loser' and 'cad'.

Strange, then, that Edward, or Bertie as his family called him, grew up to be a Frenchman. Although in theory there should have been no one in England more Victorian – with all the hypocrisy and self-denial that that implies – than Bertie, he was a fun-loving, smooth-talking, serial seducer who would nip across the Channel for champagne dinners, can-can dancing and a spot of *amour* whenever he could. Anglo-German by birth, by nature he became completely Parisian.

While researching Bertie's escapades for my book *1,000 Years of Annoying the French*, I was surprised to find that most of the history books had skirted over this vital French part of his life. Whole weeks in Paris would be dealt with in two or three lines – although we all know how much fun you can cram into a week in Paris.

I found lots of euphemisms about 'adult pleasures' and frequent complaints from Victoria about 'horrid Paris' and its 'rottenness'; there were lists of louche-sounding names of the people Bertie met, and a few bawdy anecdotes, but very little detail. I couldn't work out why.

Perhaps these writers thought that Bertie's Parisian excursions were too frivolous for serious history? Or that his guilt-free sexual exploits in France were merely a side-show compared to his long-term affairs with famous English mistresses like Lillie Langtry and Alice Keppel (the great-grandmother of Camilla Parker Bowles)?

This lack of French details was a shame, I thought, because Bertie was a semi-permanent fixture in Parisian life during probably the most exciting, creative period in the city's history. The second half of the nineteenth century was a time when can-can dancing, Impressionism and the boulevards were born; when Montmartre, the Champs-Élysées and Parisian café culture came into their own; when prostitutes were everywhere, and adultery was practically an obligation for high-society men and women.

Bertie was an active participant in it all, and it made him the jovial, amiable man he became. He danced at the court of Emperor Napoléon III, agonized through the siege of Paris and was the very first guest to climb the Eiffel Tower. He fraternized with the most extreme French royalists and republicans, and was admired, respected and loved by all of them – as he was by almost everyone who met him, whatever their gender or nationality. Even the half-deranged Kaiser Wilhelm of Germany would calm down when he was with Bertie.

With this book, I have tried to tell – for the first time – the full, uncensored story of how the French taught a future King of England to seduce a whole planet.

Stephen Clarke
Paris, January 2014

1

1855: *AMOUR* AT FIRST SIGHT

~

'You have a very beautiful country. I would like to be your son.'
Thirteen-year-old Bertie to Napoléon III,
Emperor of France

I

Why do we modern Brits want to be friends with Europe? We disagree with most of the politics practised on the continent, and, if we're honest, we also disapprove of much of the natives' behaviour, from bullfighting to using kilograms, to refusing to let us win at sports we invented.

Yet, despite all this, we want to be *amis* with the continental Europeans, and our motive seems to be shamelessly selfish – we love to go there. In fact we always have loved to go there, but in the past, our visits were often received with arrows and cannons.

1

This is why, nowadays, we are careful to conduct our wars in far-flung, desolate places where no right-minded civilian would want to buy a holiday home or take a cookery course. What we *don't* want is to repeat the errors of history and be excluded from the beaches, ski slopes and vineyards of places like France, Italy, Spain or even Germany.

Queen Victoria's eldest son, Albert Edward, known to his family as Bertie, understood this at a time when most of his fellow countrymen were calling for 'splendid isolation', and when many Europeans wanted revolution in their own country and/or war with their neighbours.

Like us today, the future King Edward VII was much more interested in tourism than warfare. He loved what all of us love about mainland Europe – the spas, the food, the perfume of exotic sex. He was a thoroughly modern European. He could even speak their languages.

He was such an ardent admirer of continental pleasures that he earned himself the nickname Dirty Bertie in the English press, and spent much of his time until he became king running away from British public opinion. But what we shouldn't forget is that Dirty Bertie – a man who, if loyalty cards had existed in the latter nineteenth century, would have earned platinum status at Paris's louchest cafés and grandest brothels – eventually matured into a great diplomat: possibly Britain's greatest ever.

It was Bertie who almost single-handedly kept Europe at peace at the turn of the twentieth century. It could even be argued (and this book will argue it) that if he had smoked a lot less and lived a few years longer, Europe would not have gone to war in 1914.

More than military threats and official alliances between countries, it was Bertie's ceaseless round of get-togethers with his European friends and relatives* that dissipated the clouds of war. A state visit from Bertie's royal yacht or private train, some light banter over cigars, a few chummy dinners with the generals, and potentially explosive disputes about maritime supremacy or border manoeuvres were forgotten – at least until the next crisis.

And it was France that taught Bertie this *bonhomie*, this sunny, reassuring nature that made him popular with almost everyone he met, including the cuckolded husbands of his lovers and the almost permanently angry Kaiser Wilhelm.

It was the French who created one of the most successful seducers and most gifted diplomats that Britain has ever produced. The question is: how did they perform this miracle, on the son of Queen Victoria of all people?

II

Everyone needs a role model, and Bertie seems to have had two. In terms of European diplomacy (which, as we have seen, mainly involved keeping in touch with the

---

* Kaiser Wilhelm II of Germany and Tsar Nicholas II of Russia were Bertie's nephews, Alfonso XIII of Spain was married to a niece, Frederick IX of Denmark and Gustav Adolf VI of Sweden were married to great-nieces, Alexander of Greece was a great-nephew, Haakon VII of Norway was a son-in-law, and Bertie had family connections almost everywhere else in Europe except Austro-Hungary, which was ruled by his old friend the Emperor Franz Joseph, and France, where he was loved as an adoptive local.

extended family) it was probably his mother, Queen Victoria, although in later life she was too much of a hermit to be an inspirational figure. As far as his personality was concerned, it was definitely a Frenchman, the short-lived Emperor Napoléon III – a man who applied his uncle Napoléon Bonaparte's battle tactics to the bedroom, and whose ambitions lay less in ruling over a continent than in ruling under a continental quilt.

If Napoléon III inspired Victoria's eldest son to follow in his footsteps, it was because the French Emperor didn't let a squat body, large nose and puffy eyes get in the way of a life of seduction. It was at the highly impressionable age of thirteen that young Bertie first saw Napoléon III in action.* Despite his lack of classically good looks, the Emperor was the archetypal smooth-talking French lover, forever roaming his palace in search of new conquests amongst his beautiful courtiers. On one occasion, at a masked ball, he was in such a rush to consummate a new acquaintance that he instantly ushered his prey into a side room, only to be informed as he fought to undress her that the *mademoiselle* was in fact a *monsieur*.

Yet Napoléon III was no brutish boor. When a married Englishwoman, famed for her prudishness and for having slept in the same bedroom as her mother until the age of eighteen, visited him in Paris, she confessed that she was 'tickled by' his flirtatious ways. She wrote that:

---

* Bertie's first impression of Napoléon III's appearance wasn't promising. In his diary he noted drily that 'the Emperor is a short person. He had very long moustachios but short hair.'

I have seen him for full ten days, from twelve to fourteen hours every day – often alone . . . I know no one who puts me more at my ease, or to whom I felt more inclined to talk unreservedly, or in whom involuntarily I should be more inclined to confide . . .

Surely we are only a few sentences away from the ripping open of a bodice? As if to confirm this, on arriving back home in England, the same lady wrote to Napoléon in French saying that she had felt 'penetrated and touched' by his welcome, and that when she said goodbye to him it was with a 'swollen heart' after their 'beautiful and happy days' together. 'You said "au revoir" on the boat,' her letter reminds him, 'and it is with all my heart that I repeat it.' She closes with 'tender friendship and affection'.

The love-struck words of a passionate woman. All the more surprising, then, to realize that they were written in 1855 by a 36-year-old Queen Victoria. Yes, even she could be 'penetrated and touched' by a Frenchman.

History has been slightly unfair to Victoria. The old Queen, stiff-lipped and corseted in her widow's weeds, usually gets the blame for everything prudish and hung-up about nineteenth-century Britain. We only have to picture her and immediately our brains are cleansed of anything remotely erotic. She is the antidote to sex.

But as the above French letter (no pun intended, *bien sûr*) shows, Victoria was a woman like any other. And as an ageing widow, she shocked her children, including Bertie, by becoming very intimate with two of her

male servants, Scotsman John Brown and Indian Abdul
Karim – one man from a nation famed for its lack of
underwear, the other from the country that gave us the
Kama Sutra.

Whether Victoria ever indulged in physical relations with
either servant has never been reliably established, and she
almost certainly restrained from divan diplomacy with
Napoléon III, but as her son Bertie was to prove, tight
corsets and multi-layered petticoats never stopped anyone
in the nineteenth century enjoying a healthy sex life,
monogamous or otherwise.

In fact, the morally confused, sexually inhibited society
that we generally call Victorian wasn't totally Victorian by
any means. It was also very Albertian. England's famous
prudery of the time originated largely from the Queen's
husband, Franz Albrecht Karl Emanuel von Sachsen-
Coburg und Gotha – or Albert for short.

Prince Albert was the disciplinarian father who tied the
straps on his eldest son's moral straitjacket so tight that
when they broke, the resulting sense of liberation sent him
philandering across the whole of Europe (and especially
France). It was Albert who tried to create an angelic Prince
Albert Edward and spawned Dirty Bertie.

And the breaking point came during a royal family visit
to Napoléon III's court in Paris in 1855.

III

Being both a snob and a monarchist (theoretically the two
can be separable), Victoria's initial reaction to Napoléon

III was unfavourable to say the least. For a start, he was the nephew of England's arch-enemy, Bonaparte. Furthermore, he had originally been elected President of France after the expulsion of King Louis-Philippe in 1848,* and had then staged a coup d'état and declared himself Emperor Napoléon III on 2 December 1851, the forty-seventh anniversary of Bonaparte's own investiture.

In Victoria's eyes, whether Napoléon III was an emperor or merely a president, he had originally come to power by removing a king, and was therefore a danger to Europe's (and Victoria's own) stability.

Victoria would also have known about Napoléon III's decidedly racy past. His mother, Hortense de Beauharnais, was the daughter of Napoléon Bonaparte's first wife, Joséphine. His father Louis was a younger brother of Bonaparte – legally, at least. When the child was born in 1808, Louis suspected Hortense of having been unfaithful, and only acknowledged paternity after pressure from big brother.

From the age of seven, the violent tides of early nineteenth-century French politics swept the future Napoléon III into exile in various countries, including two years, from 1846 to 1848, in London. It was here that he learnt conversational English while living in sin with a young actress called Harriet Howard, who had climbed England's social scale in the classic fashion, by running away from home at the age of fifteen, taking a wealthy lover, bearing him a child

---

* For more details of the British involvement in the 1848 revolution and the unfortunate Louis-Philippe's fate at the hands of his English hosts, see *1,000 Years of Annoying the French*.

and then inheriting his fortune. When King Louis-Philippe fled France in 1848 and the future Napoléon III crossed the Channel in the other direction, it was largely Harriet Howard's money that financed her lover's presidential campaign and subsequent coup d'état. She moved to Paris and remained Napoléon III's mistress until he found a suitable wife, leaving him with a lasting sense of gratitude and affection for all things English.

Sadly for him, the feeling wasn't mutual. When he came to power thirty-six years after Waterloo, Anglo-French enmity was alive and well and living in Britain. In August 1853, Victoria took eleven-year-old Bertie on an outing to the Solent for the Royal Naval Review, a show of strength that was specifically designed to remind Napoléon III of Trafalgar and the dangers of provoking his neighbours. It was the first event of its kind since 1814, the year before Waterloo, and the lead ship in the British fleet was a brand-new 131-gun warship, the *Duke of Wellington*, which had been hastily renamed after the death of the national hero who ended Napoléon Bonaparte's career. Even the old *Victory*, Nelson's flagship at Trafalgar, was present at the 1853 Review to give a salute to its young successors. Perhaps the only false note in this display of naval might was that Victoria and the royal family watched the proceedings from a yacht called *Fairy*.

The Brits weren't the only people trying to put France's new emperor in his place. The French upper classes were also being decidedly unwelcoming. The 'real' aristocracy – those whose family had been ennobled by a king rather than an emperor – saw Napoléon III and his Spanish wife, the Empress Eugénie, as *parvenus*. Meanwhile, other branches of the Bonaparte family were jealous of their cousin, and refused to join his court.

Struggling to gain legitimacy for his Second Empire, Napoléon III looked outside France and tried to strike up personal relations with his fellow European sovereigns. But when he sent out the first feelers towards Victoria in 1854, he received a predictable putdown, despite the fact that since October 1853, the two countries were, for the first time in centuries, fighting on the same side in a war – Crimea.*

Anglophobes in Paris were quick to say that Victoria's standoffishness was typical of the Brits – they didn't mind accepting France's help to support their interests in the east, but they were too snobbish to invite their new ally to dinner. A close associate of Napoléon III, Horace de Viel-Castel, wrote sniffily in his memoirs that Victoria had refused to issue 'a personal invitation to the Emperor and Empress of the French', as if their titles alone should have been enough to win them a ticket across the Channel.

Canny Napoléon did not give up, though. He intimated that he wanted to come and deliver a personal invitation to Victoria and Albert to attend the 1855 Exposition Universelle that was being planned in Paris. He must have known that Albert was fascinated by all things scientific and industrial, and had been one of the prime movers

---

* Not everyone in Britain felt comfortable with this sudden Anglo-French alliance – Sir James Graham, the First Lord of the Admiralty, called it 'unnatural'.

behind the 1851 Great Exhibition in London, at which, annoyingly for Napoléon, members of the deposed French royal family had been guests of honour.

The ploy worked, and an invitation to visit London was duly sent.

In April 1855, the French imperial couple sailed to Dover (into a dense English fog that they may have seen as a bad omen), to be met not by Victoria but her husband. Other sovereigns might have seen this as a snub, but Napoléon and Eugénie were on a charm offensive, and immediately set about seducing the dour Albert. The two men had something in common, because Napoléon spoke with a strong Swiss-German accent, thanks to one of his foreign exiles after the fall of Bonaparte. So conversation was slow and Germanic – rather like England's rail service at the time – and the train journey to Paddington apparently went very smoothly.

Waiting at Windsor, and no doubt rehearsing the level of condescension she could show the French upstarts, was Victoria, whose attitude to the French visit was evident in a letter to her Secretary of State, the Earl of Clarendon, in October 1854: 'His [Napoléon's] reception here', she wrote, 'ought to be a boon to him and not a boon to us.' She was deigning to meet him as if he were a poor relative begging for a loan.

But if Victoria was at first somewhat cold towards her French visitors, the ice very soon thawed out. Little Napoléon was not a handsome man in comparison to the grand Albert, and sported a straggly goatee and an absurd moustache that was permanently waxed into two long, needle-sharp points, but he was an innate charmer. As Jacques Debussy, a biographer of Empress Eugénie, noted, Napoléon 'showed no delay in winning the affection of the Queen [Victoria], as he did with anyone he wished to seduce'.*

Napoléon may not have been trying to bed Victoria, but reading between the lines of her descriptions of the state visit, we can see that the Frenchman deployed all his Gallic seduction techniques. The Emperor was, Victoria told her friend Sir Theodore Martin, 'so simple, naïf even, so pleased to be informed about things he does not know' (we can almost hear Napoléon telling the Queen, 'Oh, madame, you are fascinetting, please tell me more about ze ideal diet of Corgis') and 'so gentle, so full of tact' ('do not worray, Your Majesté, your secret detestation of your Prime Ministaire is safe wiz me') and 'so full of kind attention towards us, never saying a word or doing a thing, which could put me out' ('yes, mah dear Victoria, I absolutely *adore* boiled pheasant'). This was a French *séducteur* on his best behaviour, devoting as much care and patience towards his female prey as a fisherman reeling in a prize trout.

To complete this atmosphere of heady eroticism, Victoria awarded Napoléon Britain's highest honour: appointment to the Order of the Garter – the order of chivalry founded in the fourteenth century by King Edward III after he had danced so energetically with a lady that her garter slipped off. He picked it up, put it on his own leg, and declared

---

* This is *séduire* in the French sense, which can mean win over, as well as charm into bed.

(in French): 'Shame on anyone who misinterprets what I just did,' probably implying: 'If you assume I'm going to be removing the rest of the lady's clothes afterwards, it's just your dirty mind.' This of course became the Order's motto: 'Honi soit qui mal y pense'. Investing Napoléon as a so-called 'Stranger Knight of the Garter' was his due as a visiting head of state, but his highly charged relations with Victoria must have added an extra French *frisson* to the ceremony.

After a week of public and private functions, there was still a hint of English condescension in the air – Victoria wrote to her uncle Leopold that 'our Imperial guests . . . behave really with the greatest tact', as if surprised that the French heads of state held their knife and fork correctly and didn't wipe their mouths on the tablecloth. But the two couples had overcome their differences to become firm friends, and a return visit was arranged.

IV

Before thirteen-year-old Bertie was informed, to his delight, that he would be accompanying his parents to France, his childhood had been one long bout of Albertian oppression. In an attempt to mould him into a perfect Anglo-German prince, Bertie's father had subjected him to a régime of discipline, loneliness and violence.

A series of adult tutors were instructed by Albert – with Victoria's approval – to drill the boy for six hours a day, six days a week in German, French, Latin, arithmetic, history, more German and even more (mainly royal) history.

To avoid immoral influences, Bertie was kept away from all other children except his closest siblings, and after falling behind his younger brother Alfred, Bertie was declared retarded and banished to educational solitary confinement, relieved only by a few short, stilted visits from Eton boys who were considered worthy company for a prince.

Young Bertie was ordered to write essays for his father, each one of which provoked a paternal report to the effect that they were below standard and that he needed to study even harder. When the frustrated boy rebelled with foot-stomping, furniture-throwing tantrums, he was given a sound flogging by Albert. In short, Bertie's young mind and body were being force-fed a diet of failure and humiliation.*

Even the ten-year-old Prince's French teacher, a certain *Docteur* Voisin, said that the boy was being made to do too much intellectual work, which was a bit like a Viking military instructor complaining that the curriculum contained too much pillaging.

'Make him climb trees! Run! Leap! Row! Ride!' Voisin urged Bertie's main tutor, a dull 29-year-old barrister called Frederick Waymouth Gibbs. But this and other pleas to grant the boy something approaching a normal childhood were ignored by his parents.

It wasn't entirely Victoria and Albert's fault that they were so rigid. Albert had endured a disturbed childhood himself:

---

* Incidentally, failure and humiliation is a model still used today by the French education system, which is principally designed to prove – unnecessarily one might think – that teachers know more than their pupils.

when he was five, his mother left home, married her lover and never saw her children again before dying of cancer aged only thirty. Albert's father, a renowned lech, then married his own niece and turned his back on his offspring. It was perhaps natural that these dysfunctional beginnings should spark a yearning in Albert for stability at all costs.

Victoria meanwhile was haunted by the fear that her male children might inherit wayward genes from the Hanoverian side of her family. Her grandfather was 'mad' King George III, the first royal to talk to trees, and her uncle was the dissolute George IV, of whom *The Times* newspaper said on his death: 'There never was an individual less regretted by his fellow-creatures than this deceased king.' Not the kind of DNA that was going to preserve the British monarchy. And Victoria had been a staunch monarchist since childhood – according to Lytton Strachey's playful biography, her favourite tune as a young girl was 'God Save the King'.

When baby Bertie was only a few days old, Victoria wrote to her uncle, King Leopold of Belgium: 'I hope and pray he may be like his dearest Papa.' A month later, she wrote again, repeating herself more emphatically: 'You will understand how fervent my prayers are . . . to see him resemble his angelic dearest Father in every, every respect, both in body and mind.' In short, from the start, Victoria was begging God to make sure Bertie would grow up as a fun-hating German prude who didn't understand cricket.

It was, of course, entirely thanks to this tyrannical upbringing that Bertie would later rebel and turn into exactly the kind of gambling, philandering playboy that his parents abhorred. But then a very similar pattern was being repeated for most upper-class British males at the time, so Victoria and Albert were only applying an extreme form of current educational thinking.

Before his first visit to France, Bertie's sole relief from tedium came when Albert took him shooting at Windsor and Balmoral, a form of release that Bertie would embrace for the rest of his life. And he also enjoyed a temporary feeling of self-worth when he was allowed to accompany one or both of his parents to official functions such as the sombre funeral of the Duke of Wellington in 1852, the Naval Review of 1853, and long ceremonies at which his mother pinned the newly created Victoria Cross on the chests of soldiers returning from the Crimea. His childhood was never exactly electrifying.

So when Bertie was told that he would be going with Victoria, Albert and his sister Vicky to Paris, he must have been as thrilled as any schoolboy who is told that there's a class outing coming up – no lessons for ten whole days! Even the news that he would have to wear his uniform – the kilt – probably wouldn't have bothered him, because he had no classmates to warn him that the French might laugh at a teenage boy in a skirt.

But probably the most exciting prospect of all about the trip to Paris was that he would be seeing the Empress Eugénie again.

Like Napoléon III, the Empress had climbed to the summit of French society by exploiting all her natural attributes. Whereas most of Napoléon's female targets gave in immediately to his charms and status, she had forced him to court her for over two years, and eventually marry her. The writer Prosper Mérimée, author of the original story of *Carmen* and an old friend of Eugénie's from her pre-Empress days, wrote a none-too-subtle couplet about the imperial couple:

> The Emperor is there because of an election,
> Eugénie because of an erection.

She was not a classic beauty, but everyone seems to agree that she emanated a powerful sexual charm.

Bertie had spent some time with her during the French couple's visit to England, and had written in his diary that she was 'very pretty' – a daring entry given that the diary was one of the writing assignments inflicted on Bertie by his father, and was far from private. During her brief stay at Windsor Castle, Eugénie, who longed for children and had suffered several miscarriages, had lavished her attention on the boy in a way that Victoria and Albert had never done, and it is easy to imagine the effect that the voluptuous French lady would have had on the loveless teenage prince.

In short, if the Channel steamer had broken down during the British royals' crossing on 18 August 1855, the feverish heat of Bertie's anticipation would probably have powered the engine right up the Seine to Paris.

V

Victoria and Albert's state visit to France was one of the most successful family holidays in history.

According to all accounts, including those of Queen Victoria herself, mother and children were in permanent throes of ecstasy, and, to use the French idiom, even the staid Albert temporarily removed the broomstick from his *derrière*. Those ten glorious summer days in France were packed with more thrills than young Bertie had known in his entire life.

Even though he had been out in public with his parents before, the welcome they received in Boulogne-sur-Mer must have been an eye-opener. A contemporary painting of the occasion by Louis Armand, which now hangs in the Château de Compiègne near Paris, gives an idea of what it all must have looked and felt like for a teenage boy.

The harbour is teeming with boats that have taken to the water to greet the royals. Out in the bay, a fleet of warships is letting off cannons in salute (either that, or the French and English captains are holding a small fiftieth anniversary re-enactment of Trafalgar).

The new royal yacht, *Victoria and Albert*, a majestic gold-prowed steamer, has docked, and its deck is packed with French dignitaries doffing their top hats to the arriving guests. Eugénie, pregnant again and fearful of another miscarriage, has stayed at home, so Napoléon III has come to Boulogne alone, and he is proudly leading Victoria down a wide, red-carpeted gangplank towards a line of horse-drawn carriages waiting to take the guests to the railway station.

Meanwhile, as far as the eye can see, hordes of spectators are jostling to get a glimpse of Bertie and his family. Many of these onlookers are chic women in silks and crinolines, holding parasols to protect their fashionably pale skin. A veritable army of bayonet-touting imperial guards and mounted cavalry has been mobilized to keep the ladies at bay.

There is nothing half-hearted or condescending about this reception. If Napoléon had wanted to pull rank, it would have been customary for him to wait for Victoria to step on to his soil. On the dockside, there is a small marquee with a pair of thrones suggesting that the original plan might have been to hold the welcoming ceremony on land. But Napoléon has gone on board to take Victoria's hand and invite her personally to come ashore. It was a friendly, and apparently spontaneous, gesture.

After his successful trip to England, Napoléon III was clearly out to prove two things: first, that he was a true European sovereign and understood the historic importance of this trip. There had not been a state visit to France by a reigning English monarch since Henry VI in 1431, and that had not been a particularly happy occasion for the French because Henry came to Paris to be crowned King of France. Now was Napoléon's chance to erase the memory.

Secondly, he was determined to show that he was the kind of man who returns hospitality. Napoléon wanted everyone, both in England and France, to see that he really knew how to throw a party.

As Bertie was driven through the admiring summer crowds to the railway station, he must have begun to suspect that this was not going to be like one of the formal state occasions that his mother and father organized. Back in England, onlookers had usually been showing due respect for his (or more precisely his mother's) royal status. By cheering the monarch, the people were almost cheering themselves as a nation. Here in France it was different: these people owed the British royals nothing but they were saying, 'Welcome *chez nous*, we're going to show you a seriously good time.'

Like the harbour, the railway station had been decorated, and a contemporary engraving shows the procession passing under an enormous archway draped with flags and flowers and inscribed with giant Vs. In the station itself, people are waving their handkerchiefs and hats in welcome. All along the route, the crowds had been so dense that the royal party were a couple of hours late boarding the imperial train, which didn't pull into Paris's Gare de Strasbourg* until dusk, at precisely 7.12 p.m.

In Paris, the excitement started all over again, not least because of the 101-cannon salute that marked the royal guests' departure from the railway station. The city's new boulevards (of which much more in a later chapter) were lined with thousands of spectators, watching the procession from behind an unbroken rank of soldiers standing to attention, or as close to attention as French soldiers get.

British history books usually describe the rapturous reception that the royal party received, with Parisians

---

* Now the Gare de l'Est. The Gare du Nord had been built in 1846, but that line went up to Lille and on to the Belgian border.

shouting 'Vive la Reine!'; however, less gushing French accounts, notably that of the historian André Castelot, ring slightly truer. To mark their arrival on the Paris fashion scene, Queen Victoria had put on a blue dress and grey silk jacket, and Albert had donned his field marshal's uniform, but, according to Castelot, their costume change went almost completely unnoticed. The light was fading fast, and the Parisians who had turned out to witness the procession could hardly see a thing. Many had given up waiting, and others had grown impatient. Consequently, according to French commentators, the crowds were not hugely enthusiastic – more curious than rapturous.

Even so, in Bertie's mind, a horse-drawn carriage ride through Paris by night, along wide new streets that had been specially cleared of traffic, would surely have made up for any lack of enthusiasm amongst the city's disgruntled citizens. The Champs-Élysées was in the final throes of its transformation from a rough track across marshland to a fully urban avenue, and it was now lined with the brand-new venues for the 1855 Exposition Universelle. All of these buildings have since been demolished, but on the site of the current Grand Palais and Petit Palais stood the immense Palais de l'Industrie, a 200-metre-long, 35-metre-high stone edifice with a gigantic domed glass-and-iron roof. In the centre of its façade was a triumphal arch topped by a sculpture modestly entitled *France Crowning Commerce and Industry*. On this summer evening, as Bertie was driven past it, with its transparent roof and 400 windows ablaze with gas lights, it would have been one of the most brilliant sights on the planet – second only to London's Crystal Palace.

Next, the royal party drove past the Arc de Triomphe, which was standing in the middle of the new place de l'Étoile, a hub for some of the city's swankiest new avenues, and into the darkness of the Bois de Boulogne, which was undergoing a spectacular makeover. The old royal hunting forest on the western edge of Paris, once so thickly wooded that aristocrats had hidden there during the Revolution, had been ravaged by occupying British and Russian troops after the Napoleonic wars, and had needed extensive replanting.

However, after seeing London's Hyde Park, Napoléon III had decided that a plain forest was too rudimentary for his showcase Paris, and had ordered the remodelling of the woodland into an urban park with wide avenues for prom-enading carriages, and even an artificial river, a facsimile of the Serpentine. Here, he would surely have been keen to flatter his English guests by telling them how their capital city had inspired him to refurbish his own.

What's more, in a homage to the 'sport of kings' imported into France by the Brits, Napoléon had also commissioned an addition to the park – Longchamp racecourse, which, although Bertie didn't yet know it, was to provide him with plenty of thrills in years to come.

As the procession crossed the Seine, Napoléon must have regretted that he hadn't managed to get the royal party to the Château de Saint-Cloud before dark. It was a jewel of French architecture, a mainly classical structure built by Louis XIV's brother the Duc d'Orléans and enlarged still further by Louis XVI as a gift for his bride Marie-Antoinette. The château overlooked the river and the distant city from its vast, terraced park, and had been chosen by both Napoléon I and Napoléon III as the venue for their investitures. It was the ultimate French status symbol, and now Victoria, Albert, Vicky and Bertie were getting only a partial view.

Inside the château, the reception that Napoléon had prepared was grand and intimate at the same time. We can get an idea of the atmosphere from a painting by one of his favourite artists, Charles Müller.

The picture, based on sketches that Müller made on the night, shows the reception hall crowded with finely dressed courtiers, the chicest gathering that France could muster. These were the imperial couple's friends, allies and confidants, including Napoléon's cousin and former fiancée, Mathilde, who was living openly with her aristocratic Dutch lover.

Decorating the staircase, like so many potted plants, Müller depicts a rank of soldiers in plumed gold helmets that reflect the light from the weighty chandeliers. And at the heart of this glowing scene are its royal and imperial stars. Most visible, given that he had commissioned the painting, is Napoléon, unrealistically slim and upright in a blue military frock coat and tight red trousers, his moustache as stiff as the hands of a clock face stuck at quarter to three. Beside him, elegant in a high-collared dress, Eugénie is looking kindly at a slightly dowdy Victoria, who is the only adult woman in the room wearing a bonnet, a sort of tight white nightcap. The Queen seems to be bowing to the French couple (Müller was French, after all), as if grateful for being invited into such a smart home. Albert, resplendent in a scarlet tunic, is standing to one side, perhaps so that his tall stature won't put Napoléon in the shade. With one hand on his sabre, Albert is looking thoughtful, as if asking himself, 'Is that Frenchie chatting up my wife?'

Müller has also taken great care over the portraits of Princess Vicky – a miniature of her mother, right down to the bonnet – and Bertie, who are standing between their parents. The young Prince is wearing a smart white shirt and dark jacket, his fair hair slicked down as though his mother had just forced him to comb it. Strangely, Bertie is the only person in the picture looking at the painter. It is as if a realization is dawning on him. He is in the centre of this scene, surely the most glamorous event that night in the whole of the western world,* apparently thinking: Amongst all these royal and imperial adults and these incredibly chic courtiers, that artist is drawing me. *Mich. Moi.* Am I *really* that important? Well, now you mention it . . .

VI

Over the next few days, Bertie had to rise to the challenge of constant attention, from the critical eyes of the public

---

* On the same day, an agreement was signed between the Vatican and the Austrian government, giving the Catholic Church control over marriage laws and education in Austria, but there is no record of a big party afterwards.

as he and his family were displayed around town, and the closer scrutiny of his parents, who would have been watching him keenly for any sign that it had been a bad idea to invite him along. Until they received proof to the contrary, Bertie was still a backward boy in need of constant bullying by his moral tutors. Here in France, he was off the leash and needed careful monitoring.

Some of the official events must have been hard going for a teenaged boy known for his lack of concentration – such as three hours trooping around the Exposition's art show featuring 5,000 works by 2,000 artists from 28 countries (although half of the art was French, of course). The show excited people like the notorious drug-taking poet Baudelaire, who wrote that 'the exhibition of English painters is . . . worthy of a long and patient study'. It sounds like the kind of exhibition that would bore a thirteen-year-old to tears.

Even so, there was one canvas that would almost certainly have caught Bertie's attention: German painter Franz Xaver Winterhalter's group portrait of Empress Eugénie and her ladies-in-waiting. To the modern eye, the pale, languorous women with their flat centre partings, drooping ringlets and enormously bouffant dresses look like a collection of human cushions, but to Bertie (and indeed everyone but the hardest-nosed Parisian revolutionary), the eight women posing in a rather damp-looking woodland clearing would have been a vision of almost divine loveliness, the perfect pallor of their skin and their shimmering gowns giving them an air of infinite self-assurance. And let's not forget those shoulders – each dress, including that of the Empress, is cut to leave the women naked from the biceps upwards, with their necklines hanging tantalizingly loose just above the cleavage. If any of them had crossed her arms, her dress would simply have fallen off.

The erotic undertone of the picture was like an advert for imperialism. A few decades earlier, the superior attitude of these aristocratic women would have got them dispatched to the guillotine, but now they shamelessly display their finery, mutely implying, 'Stick with Napoléon III and you too could have some of this.' In Bertie's case, a few years later the message would come literally true.

The tour of the art exhibition was followed by lunch, which apparently caused some confusion in Paris. The meal was announced in the official programme of the state visit using the English word, and 'lunch' was something that few French people had ever heard of. One journalist reported overhearing a Parisian man saying it must have been a misprint for 'punch' – the English royals were probably going to be tasting rum cocktails.

Bertie would have enjoyed his visit to the Palais de l'Industrie a lot more, because here was an exhibition featuring plenty of noise, steam and excitement. Visitors to the 1855 Expo could see brand-new or recent inventions like the lawn mower, the washing machine (not that any members of the royal family would be using either of those personally), the saxophone, Samuel Colt's six-shooter pistol, telegraph machines, electric clocks, a coffee machine capable of producing 2,000 cups per hour, a cement rowing boat, the world's biggest-ever mirror (5.37 metres high and

3.36 wide), and all kinds of machines that sliced, crushed, harvested, heated, cooled or transported any industrial or agricultural product you could think of. One of the most popular attractions was the stand giving away free samples of freshly roasted tobacco.

Some of the more stately occasions were just as eventful. On Thursday, 23 August, the British royals were guests of honour at a ball given by the city of Paris at the Hôtel de Ville. Amongst the other guests were some visiting sheiks, one of whom bowed before Victoria and, before anyone could stop him, lifted the Queen's dress and kissed her ankle, proclaiming, with an acute sense of English history, 'Honi soit qui mal y pense.'* It was a joke that could have got him skewered by Prince Albert for fondling the royal personage if Victoria had not reacted with a restrained laugh. Despite her prudish image, the Queen was apparently getting into the Parisian swing of things.

The day after the ankle-kissing incident, 24 August, is the one that most of Bertie's biographers† linger on. After a dusk review of 45,000 troops performing manoeuvres on the Champ-de-Mars (where the Eiffel Tower would later be built), Victoria insisted on taking Bertie to the Invalides to see the tomb of Napoléon Bonaparte. It was an impromptu visit, so when the small party arrived at what

* The sheik's gesture might have been a witty, topical allusion to the fact that Victoria had appointed Napoléon to the Order of the Garter when he was in England.
† For a list of the biographies I read while researching this book, see the Bibliography, page 365.

is, even today, a museum set around a residential home for injured soldiers, the reception committee was a modest but remarkable one – a group of torch-bearing veterans, including some old-timers who had fought alongside Bonaparte himself.

It was a dark, windy night, and the torches were flickering wildly as the visitors were led into the chapel by the limping veterans. The former Emperor's body was lying in state in the small Chapelle de Saint-Jérôme while his immense mausoleum was being built beneath the great dome.* The coffin was draped in a violet pall embroidered with honey bees – the Bonaparte emblem. As Victoria entered the shadowy, chilled chapel with Napoléon III and the old soldiers, she was overcome with the solemnity of the occasion, as she freely admitted in her diary:

> There I stood, at the arm of Napoléon III, his nephew, before the coffin of England's bitterest foe; I, the grand-daughter of that King who hated him most, and who most vigorously opposed him, and this very nephew, who bears his name, being my nearest and dearest ally! . . . Strange and wonderful indeed, it seems, as if in this tribute of respect to a dead and departed foe, old enmities and rivalries were wiped out, and the seal of Heaven placed upon that bond of unity, which is now happily established between two great and powerful nations!

* The tomb had been started in 1842 and would not be completed until 1861.

Victoria must have guessed that this declaration of a divinely approved friendship between Britain and France would not have gone down well with politicians back home, despite the temporary Anglo-French alliance over Crimea, but she decided to seal the moment for history. Turning to Bertie, the heir to her throne and to this new friendship, she ordered him to kneel before Bonaparte. The young Prince, dressed in full highland costume, including the sporran (or 'hairy bag' as André Castelot calls it in his account of the visit) obeyed, and as he did so, a lightning storm erupted outside, sending thunder crashing against the chapel walls. Some of the veterans interpreted this as a supernatural sign and began to weep.

To Bertie's young mind, it must have come as fresh confirmation that he was at the very heart of events. And in a very real way, this was the ceremony that formalized his lifelong bond with France. With a crack of cannon-like thunder, the spirit of Bonaparte himself was telling the boy: '*Bienvenu chez nous.*'

The following day, 25 August, saw Bertie yet again being committed to canvas. Joseph-Louis-Hippolyte Bellangé's painting *Royal Visit to Napoleon III: meet of the Imperial Hunt at the Chateau de la Muette, in the forest of St Germain, 25 August 1855** shows the French and British

---

* The painting appears to be slightly misnamed, because the Château de la Muette was on the edge of the Bois de Boulogne, not the Bois de Saint-Germain. The château was subsequently demolished and replaced by a more modern mansion, now the Paris HQ of the Organization for Economic Co-operation and Development.

first families enjoying a social gathering that was the complete opposite of the hunts Bertie had known until then, which were usually windblown slogs across the bleak Scottish moors.

In Bellangé's picture, a large pack of hounds is being held in formation by huntsmen in green-and-gold coats and red breeches, while the ever-present crowds of chic onlookers strain to get a look at the VIPs and are kept away by mounted guards.

The royal and imperial party stands in front of the château, with Albert and Napoléon in decidedly non-rustic frock coats and top hats, and Victoria in bright pink, looking uncharacteristically elegant. Actually, she looks exactly like the French *dames* watching from the château, so either the Queen had wholeheartedly embraced *la vie parisienne* or Bellangé was taking liberties with the truth. In fact the painting is generally more diplomatic than realistic, because Napoléon and Victoria are made to look as tall as Albert. Bertie, meanwhile, in long trousers and highland cap, is glancing up towards his father as if to say: 'These people are here to look at *moi aussi*, aren't they?' He was growing in stature every day.

The royal visit reached its culmination that same night when Eugénie and Napoléon hosted an immense ball at Versailles. Even by the lavish standards of the time, it was a spectacular event. One French observer, the photographer Caron de Lalande, wrote that the soirée 'would seem like an impossible fairy tale if the lucky witnesses of these wonders were not here to testify that they really saw and touched these unimaginable "sumptuosities", that they really smelled all the flowers reflected by floods of light in the infinite gallery of mirrors'.

Napoléon III was, like Albert, a champion of new technology, and Louis XIV's palace had been fitted with the latest gas lighting, and plenty of it. The state rooms were lit as if it were daytime, a magical experience for people used to shadowy candlelight. There were flowers and plants everywhere, in vases along the walls and hanging from the ceilings like coloured chandeliers. The guests were as luminous as the décor – a sea of silk, white breeches, bare shoulders and moustache wax. More than 1,000 privileged partygoers had been invited to dance to four orchestras, one of which was directed by the Austrian maestro of the waltz, Johann Strauss himself.

The pregnant Eugénie made a rare public appearance, coming out to receive the English guests as they arrived in their carriage from Saint-Cloud. The Empress met them at the top of a staircase, which, perhaps unbeknownst to Victoria, was a protocol victory and proof of Eugénie's status – making the Queen walk up to greet her.*

Victoria proudly noted in her diary that 'there had not been a ball at Versailles since the time of Louis XVI'. This, too, was an important step for Eugénie, who had now elevated herself to the status of Marie-Antoinette.

The night's festivities opened with a waltz, enjoyed by all the royals including Bertie, who joined in with the adults and acquitted himself admirably. The dancing was followed

---

* Napoléon, remember, had not done this in Boulogne, but had gone to greet Victoria on her ship.

by dinner in the Opéra Royal, Louis XIV's private theatre within his palace.

There are photographs of this soirée, as there are of most of the events of Victoria's state visit, but inevitably they are grey and static. Again, we are lucky enough to have a painting that captures all the glamour, colour and movement of the occasion. Eugène Lami's *Supper at Versailles in Honour of the Queen of England, 25 August 1855* depicts a scene that is less like a state banquet (elbows tucked in, be careful not to splash your soup over the Belgian Ambassador) than a massive, almost riotous, wedding reception. Instead of formal exchanges about the Crimean War and the trade deficit against a background of the polite clink of silver on porcelain, there must have been a roar of conversation and laughter.

The imperial couple and their guests of honour, including Bertie and his sister, are sitting at a long table up in the royal box. Below them, filling the stalls area, are 400 diners, who are not simply sitting down to eat – half of them are on their feet, wandering from table to table, saying *bonsoir* to friends, showing off their new outfits. And watching all this from around the stalls and up in the circle seats is an audience of less honoured guests, who have been invited to dance but not to dine. They are leaning over the parapets, pointing out celebrities, taking in the glittering scene.

Bertie had almost certainly never seen anything like it in his life, and the same might well have been true for Victoria, who wrote in her diary that it was 'quite one of the finest and most magnificent sights we have ever witnessed'.

After dinner, there were fireworks, including a pyro-technic tableau of Windsor Castle, then more dancing, which went on until three, although according to her diary, Victoria and her family left at two, 'the children in ecstasies'.

It is very easy to understand Bertie's ecstasy. Napoléon III hadn't assembled a royal court in the staid English sense of the word – he was living in a French carnival, an imperial-themed holiday camp. Bertie must have understood by now that there was much more to being a sovereign than waving to one's subjects and learning German grammar. You were also entitled to enjoy yourself, and if you had enough serv-ants, money, palaces and beautiful people at your disposal, the enjoyment was extreme.

It is hardly surprising, therefore, that next morning, the last of their visit, Bertie and Vicky went to beg Eugénie to persuade their parents to let them stay on. When Eugénie diplomatically replied that Victoria and Albert couldn't do without them, Bertie is said to have retorted: 'Not do without us! Don't imagine that. They don't want us and there are six more of us at home.'

As the royal party, accompanied by Napoléon, left from the Gare de Strasbourg later that day, one observer, the Comtesse d'Armaillé, wrote that Bertie 'kept looking around him, as though desperate to miss nothing of these last moments in Paris'.

After yet another review of the troops at Boulogne that Victoria described as a 'forest of bayonets' (perhaps Napoléon was giving her awaiting Royal Navy officers a subtle reminder that his coast was well defended), there was a final dinner, followed by emotional farewells. The children cried as their boat steamed away from France, and for much the same reasons as the teenage Mary Queen of Scots (who was half French*) had done almost 300 years earlier when she was banished from her cosy life at the French court to go rule over unruly Scotland.

Bertie may have been in shock that his French holiday was suddenly over, but he must also have felt the first stirrings of a conviction that he *had* to return to France at all costs, and that he would one day resume the fun where he had left off. Like some Dickensian waif who gets his first taste of cake, he had become aware that there was a better life out there somewhere. And thanks to Napoléon and Eugénie, Bertie knew that France was a place where he would be welcomed with open arms.

'Open arms' being the apt expression. Because it wasn't only the grand ceremonies that had made their mark on him. More important than all that, surely, was the huge dose of self-esteem that he had just received. After years of a stifled existence peopled almost exclusively by dry tutors and disapproving parents, of an education that consisted of being reminded at every opportunity that he was a waste of ink, in France he had been a success. People liked him, they wanted to paint him, they actually *admired* him. He had not only behaved regally in public, earning even his mother's approval and banishing all memories of his tantrums at home, he had danced well, made conversation with an

---

* See *1,000 Years of Annoying the French* for all the problems that dual nationality caused Mary (or Marie as she called herself).

emperor, an empress and their courtiers, and achieved something that he had never even come close to back in England – he had *fitted in*. He had been good company. He had been one of the gang.

What was more, no one in Paris looked askance at him for his German accent. All his life he would mispronounce the English letter R as a Teutonic clearing of the throat, but this only helped him speak better French.

He had also been treated like a valued adult friend rather than an imperfect heir. Napoléon had taken Bertie out for a personal guided tour of his capital, driving the small carriage himself. Afterwards, the two of them strolled on the terraces of the Palais des Tuileries,* chatting man to man. Like everything else during the Paris trip, this was a very new experience for Bertie – the worldly Frenchman taking time to show him around, talking to him about something other than schoolwork or the need to be less insane than Mother's ancestors.

It's not difficult to imagine the kind of things that Napoléon would have told his young protégé, the son he had been longing for, and trying for, ever since he married Eugénie. Napoléon was an opportunistic man who had got to his position in life thanks to his guile and determination as well as his Bonaparte blood, against fierce opposition from both royalists and republicans. Like all

---

* The Palais des Tuileries, originally built in the sixteenth century and adopted by Napoléon Bonaparte as his Paris home, was a château that joined the two wings of the Louvre. It was destroyed by Communard revolutionaries shortly after the fall of Napoléon III, in May 1871.

self-made men, he relished the pleasures he had earned. So it seems impossible that he wouldn't have shared a few tricks with the star-struck English Prince who had expressed such rapt admiration for everything he saw and did in Paris.

'One day,' the Emperor may have told Bertie, 'you'll have courtiers of your own. And believe me, *petit prince*, you'll be fighting the women off. Haven't you seen how they all want to talk to you and dance with you? In ten years – five, even – they'll be falling at your feet. You'll have your pick of the most beautiful girls in your country – no, in the whole of Europe. Look at me, I'm short, not that good-looking, but I can get any woman I want with a snap of my fingers. Of course, Eugénie isn't always happy about it, but I made her an Empress, so she's grateful for that. Your princess will be just as indulgent with you.'

This man-of-the-world speech would have been punctuated with nonchalant puffs on a cigar, which was also a novelty for Bertie because both his parents abhorred tobacco. Like Napoléon's womanizing, cigar-smoking was a badge of distinction that Bertie would go on to imitate all his life, until lung disease killed him.

If Bertie was the son Napoléon had always longed for, then Napoléon was the father Bertie would never have, and the boy apparently told his host: 'You have a very beautiful country. I would like to be your son.'

Eugénie also lavished attention and affection on Bertie, probably even more than she had done in London. Now that she was pregnant and absent from most of the public events, Bertie's contact with her was almost entirely in private, in the intimate setting of one of her *boudoirs*. A beautiful, broody woman in the company of an impressionable, affection-starved teenage boy – it's a powerful equation.

And Eugénie's attention was multiplied by the number of her ever-present companions, the ravishing *dames d'honneur* that Bertie had admired in the Exposition's group portrait. Unlike his mother's ladies-in-waiting, the Empress's female courtiers were chosen for their beauty and wit rather than their good blood or fondness for dogs.

Not, of course, that Eugénie or her erotic entourage would have deliberately set out to over-excite a thirteen-year-old boy. They had plenty of male suitors to keep them occupied. But they were chatty and charming, flirtatiously teasing, more like a group of girlfriends than a sovereign and her servants. And when, resplendent in their ballgowns at Versailles, the aristocratic French *femmes fatales* clasped Bertie to their chests and let him guide them around the dance floor in a twirling waltz, their bare shoulders and encouraging smiles would have been as intoxicating to the youngster as a magnum of champagne.

A French biographer of Edward VII, Philippe Jullian, whose other books include a volume of nineteenth-century nude photos, gives a resolutely French view of Bertie's sudden sexual awakening. In Paris, Jullian says, the young Prince:

> . . . breathed for the first time that *odor di femina* whose trail he would follow for the rest of his life. The beautiful,

perfumed women who kissed him (he was just a child, after all) also curtsied before him, and as they plunged forward, their *décolleté* revealed delights that were veiled at Windsor.

Writing in her diary, Victoria herself innocently high-lighted this perfumed trail that Bertie had stumbled on during his first trip to Paris: 'The beauty of the French capital, the liveliness of the French people, the *bonhomie* of the French Emperor, the elegance of the French Empress, made an indelible impression on his [Bertie's] pleasure-hungry nature.'

Of course, at that time the Queen didn't realize what kind of pleasures her son would be hungry for, or quite how big his appetite would very soon become . . .

2

THE ROYAL CHERRY IS
UNROYALLY POPPED

~

'The women whom he had kissed as a small boy were prepared
to give their all to the young man.'

Philippe Jullian, in his biography Edouard VII

I

So far, Bertie had only seen the champagne fizzing in
the glass and witnessed its effect on others. He hadn't,
as it were, popped a cork of his own. And for a long time
after the family trip to Paris, there was little chance that
Bertie would be returning to France for a second glimpse
of the earthly pleasures available there. Apart from one
short hop across the Channel with his parents in August
1858 to meet Napoléon and Eugénie in Cherbourg, the
delights of the French imperial court were off the menu.

The problem was politics. Napoléon III had apparently

taken a lesson from his warlike uncle and decided that the best way to keep a grip on power was to appeal to French patriots by annoying the neighbours. After the end of the Crimean War in 1856, he began meddling in Italian affairs, helping to 'liberate' areas of the country occupied by Austria, and thereby worrying England and Prussia that he would cause a Europe-wide war. And just a couple of years after fighting the Russians in Crimea, Napoléon began carefully leaked discussions with the Tsar about an East–West alliance that threatened to sandwich Prussia like a fat sausage, with France poised to slice off the west bank of the Rhine.

All this saddened and infuriated Victoria. She still sent Napoléon warm letters from his 'devoted sister', but to her ministers and her uncle Leopold, the King of Belgium, she poured out her exasperation about the French.

When Napoléon invaded Naples in May 1860, she wailed to Leopold that:

> *No* country, no human being would ever dream of *disturbing* or *attacking* France;* every one would be glad to see her prosperous; but *she* must needs disturb every quarter of the Globe and try to make mischief . . . and, of course, it will end some day in a *regular crusade* against *the universal disturber* of *the world!* It is really monstrous!

Leopold warned Victoria about French hypocrisy, saying that she should 'make every reasonable exertion to remain

---

* The Queen had obviously forgotten at least the previous five centuries of Anglo-French history.

on personal good terms with the Emperor' but that 'the French dislike the English as a nation, though they may be kind to you personally'.

In short, in the five or so years after Bertie's holiday of a lifetime in Paris, any subtle hints to his parents that he fancied a return visit must have been met with outraged splutterings about his failure to grasp the basics of world politics. This might also explain why Bertie later became such an accomplished diplomat – once he reached adulthood, he would steadfastly refuse to let politics come between him and a pleasure jaunt to Paris.

For the time being, though, he had to obey Mama and Papa, and his frustrated tantrums grew steadily worse until finally he was exiled to Richmond Park with a chaplain, his Latin tutor and three young men in their twenties (two majors and a lord) whose collective mission was to form his character. Prince Albert wrote out a detailed programme, requiring Bertie's new life coaches to ensure that the boy refrained from 'careless self-indulgent lounging ways, such as lolling in armchairs on or sofas, slouching in his chair, or placing himself in unbecoming attitudes with his hands in his pockets'. It was also essential that the young Prince of Wales should avoid 'the frivolity and foolish vanity of dandyism'. Albert might as well have said, 'Make sure Bertie doesn't turn out French.'

II

Unable to call on Napoléon and the *Parisiennes*, Bertie began to look elsewhere for his *éducation sentimentale*. In July 1857, aged fifteen, he was sent on an educational tour of the continent, accompanied by four carefully vetted boys of his own age – three young aristocrats and William Gladstone, eldest son of the Chancellor of the Exchequer of the same name. The plan was for Bertie to be based in Germany, at Königswinter on the Rhine, for three months, during which he would make small sorties across the border into Switzerland and France for healthy pursuits such as hiking and breathing fresh air. Paris was definitely out of bounds.

However, on the first night at Königswinter, Bertie let the freedom and the local wine go to his head, and kissed a girl. The event was considered so serious that Bertie's adult minders decided to omit it from their reports back to Prince Albert, no doubt because they feared that the whole trip would be instantly called off and their summer ruined.

In fact, it was very apt that Albert's son had surrendered to temptation where he did. After all, according to popular legend, just upstream from Königswinter the most famous Rhine Maiden of them all, the mermaid Lorelei, was perched on a rock overlooking the river, luring innocent men to their doom. At the time, she was the heroine of a well-known song, a setting of Heinrich Heine's poem 'Lied von der Loreley', which describes how 'the most beautiful maiden sits aloft . . . combing her golden hair and singing a wondrous, overpowering melody'. A boatman 'is enraptured and does not see the jagged rocks'. At the end of the poem, the poor man's boat sinks and he is swallowed up by the raging current.

Of course it wasn't quite so tragic in Bertie's case, but

from the reactions to his first snog, you might have thought that he had just dived headfirst into a torrent of debauchery. The young Gladstone wrote home to his mother with the shocking news that Bertie had engaged in pre-marital oral contact with a member of the opposite gender. Mrs Gladstone naturally passed on the information to her husband, who reacted with moral outrage, declaring that 'the Prince of Wales has not been educated up to his position'. He called the public kiss an 'unworthy little indulgence' which showed that Bertie was becoming 'wanton'.

All this, by the way, from the politician who famously took it upon himself to scour the streets of London for prostitutes, whom he would then ask to describe their wicked ways, before going home and whipping himself. Wantonness was a subject Gladstone knew a lot about.

On Bertie's seventeenth birthday in 1858, he may have thought that freedom was at last approaching. He received a letter from his parents announcing that they were giving him a personal allowance of £500 a year – a small fortune at the time. He was also being allowed to join the army as a lieutenant colonel, something that he had long wished to do.

Of course, with parents like his, the good news was too good to be true. Bertie was still to be under the constant surveillance of a moral guardian, one Colonel Robert Bruce, a forbidding figure who looked a lot like Albert, sharing his combination of bald pate, bushy whiskers and morbid seriousness. Bruce was instructed by Albert to 'regulate all the Prince's movements, the distribution of his time and the occupation and details of his daily life'. Most of all, the new surrogate father was told, Bertie needed to practise 'reflection and self-denial'.

His parents still seemed to consider him a lost cause. Prince Albert wrote to his eldest daughter Vicky, who had recently married the Crown Prince of Prussia, Friedrich (father of the future Kaiser Wilhelm II who would go to war with Britain in 1914), and made a rare Teutonic joke about Bertie's intellect, saying that it was 'of no more use than a pistol packed in the bottom of a trunk if one were attacked in the robber-infested Apennines'.

If the Italian Apennines were on Albert's mind, it was because, before letting Bertie go away to the army, he planned to send him to Rome to study the ancients at first hand, all attempts to teach the boy Latin from books having failed miserably. While there, in early 1859, Bertie was allowed to pay a visit to the Pope, though only under the watchful eye of Colonel Bruce for fear that the young Prince, if left alone with the Pontiff, might promise the dissolution of the Church of England. And in the event, Colonel Bruce hastily escorted Bertie out of the Vatican as soon as the subject of English Catholicism was raised.

Bertie did use his time in Rome to study art, though it wasn't all ancient. He visited the studio of the well-known English painter Frederic Leighton, where he admired a portrait of a sultry Italian model called Nanna Risi. The erotically charged painting had already been sold, but Leighton convinced the buyer to step down and let his illustrious English visitor have it. Perhaps for the first time, Bertie saw that his rank really could get him any woman he wanted.

While in Italy, Bertie met Edward Lear, the artist and limerick writer, who said of the Prince that 'nobody could have had nicer and better manners'. He also met the poet Robert Browning, who thought him a 'gentle, refined boy'. Just as he had done in Paris, Bertie was proving that he could fit in socially wherever he went.

Despite the fact that Bertie had resisted physical temptations while in Italy, Victoria was still in a panic about his morals. She wrote to her daughter Vicky saying that she trembled at the thought that the boy would soon come of age 'and we can't hold him'.

In October 1859, Bertie was sent to study at Oxford, but even this brought no loosening of the reins. Instead of joining his fellow toffs to celebrate their escape from the straitjacket of public school, Bertie was made to live out of college and attend private lectures. His only opportunities to sink into moral decline came when he managed to sneak away from the ever-present Colonel Bruce to smoke a forbidden cigarette.

In January 1861, Bertie went up to Cambridge, but was subjected to the same rigid régime. The French biographer Philippe Jullian casts doubt on this idea, asserting that while in Cambridge, Bertie was 'already tasting the pleasures that ought to have been the reward for a wise marriage'. Jullian mentions a rumour that a Cambridge girl found herself 'in a delicate situation'. But we can't be sure whether this is true. After all, Jullian is French, and therefore unable to imagine that a young man might be prevented from having sex at will.

It probably wasn't until later that year in Ireland, at the

age of nineteen, that Bertie would finally succeed in doing the deed and convincing his mother that further attempts at improving his character were useless. The only thing to do was to marry him off.

III

By 1861, Victoria had cause to feel more optimistic about her eldest son. At the end of the previous year, Bertie had returned from a triumphant tour of Canada and the USA, during which he had experienced again the thrills of an adoring crowd. Even the supposedly anti-monarchistic Americans had turned out en masse to cheer him and by implication his absent mother. In New York, a crowd of 300,000 took to the streets and paved the route of the royal procession with flowers. Wherever he went, Bertie delighted everyone, both his hosts and his newly promoted moral guardian, now *General* Bruce, with his innate sense of diplomacy, his tireless charm and his dancing. The Prince complained of having to waltz with the ageing wives of local dignitaries, but stuck obediently to the names on his dancing card and committed no public faux pas, not even when a good-looking girl polka'd into view, propelled by her ambitious parents.

The general conclusion after the tour was that Bertie had done a grand job of representing the monarchy abroad, and had even got the Americans singing 'God Save the Queen'.

Typically, Victoria and Albert didn't want to let all this international success go to their son's head. The Queen noted that after America he was 'extremely talkative' and had taken to smoking cigars. She grudgingly gave Bertie permission to smoke in England, 'but only on condition that he does not do so in public or in the house'.* And she began looking around frantically for a wife to take the Prince of Wales's morals in hand.

Albert, meanwhile, decided that the boy had a 'growing sense of his own importance' and needed the fun and public adulation drilling out of him. This was no doubt why he packed Bertie off to Cambridge. And now, after only a couple of months at his second university, faced with yet more evidence that his son was no scholar, Albert concluded that Bertie would benefit from a dose of army discipline with the Grenadier Guards in Ireland. It was a tactic that was to prove fatal, in more ways than one.

Although this was more than fifty years before the British army would be fighting to retain possession of Ireland, while in uniform Bertie was to be protected as if he were in enemy territory – the enemy in this case being the dissolute British soldiers. Because of warnings from General Bruce about the 'temptations and unprofitable companionship' of young officers, Bertie was billeted in private quarters, away from the other men, and his social life was restricted to four or five strictly regimented regimental dinners a week. On other evenings, he was allowed to 'read and dine quietly in his own rooms'.

---

* Victoria was so violently opposed to smoking that one foreign ambassador, when invited to stay with the Queen, took the precaution of smoking his cigars lying in a fireplace and blowing the smoke up a chimney.

Albert also instructed that his son be forced to learn the duties of every rank in turn, starting as an ensign – the lowliest commissioned officer. In short, the ten weeks spent at the Curragh Camp in County Kildare were designed to be as humiliating as the rest of Bertie's education.

Fortunately for him, the other soldiers saw Bertie's prison-like living conditions as a challenge, and organized a commando raid on his heavily fortified virtue.

Sources differ as to what happened on the evening of 6 September 1861. The most credible version seems to be that one night, after General Bruce had gone to bed, some of the officers sneaked a woman called Nellie Clifden into Bertie's quarters. Nellie was a good-time girl from London who had followed the officers, her best customers, to Ireland. So on that night a couple of months before Bertie's twentieth birthday, when the young Prince got back to his bedroom, there was a warm welcome awaiting him. Probably guessing that this kind of opportunity was not going to fall from the heavens every evening, Bertie took full advantage of the situation. He did so again three days later, and booked a third performance, too, either in his own quarters or by sneaking out to another room.

Nellie was by all accounts amusing company, both in and out of bed, and Bertie arranged to see her after he got back to England. Soon, she was trading on her famous conquest and styling herself 'the Princess of Wales' in London's dance halls.

It took a few months but eventually the gossip about Nellie broke through the class barriers and reached the ears of Bertie's father. On 12 November, Prince Albert heard the catastrophic news that his son had lost his virginity without parental permission. Worse, he had probably smoked a cigarette afterwards – indoors, too.

Albert had already contracted the illness that would very soon kill him, and was suffering from chronic insomnia and bouts of fever, but he took up his pen to express to Bertie 'the greatest pain I have yet felt in this life'. He spoke in typical Albertian terms of Bertie letting himself be prematurely 'initiated in the sacred mysteries of creation, which ought to remain shrouded in holy awe until touched by pure and undefiled hands', and said that if only Bertie had confided in his father about his 'sexual passions' (not a very credible idea), Albert would have explained 'the special mode in which these desires are to be gratified'. No, not cold showers, hiking up mountains or blasting a shotgun at wildlife, but 'the holy ties of Matrimony'.*

Both Albert and Victoria felt certain that this biblical fall from grace with Nellie was the ultimate symptom of their son's errant Hanoverian genes. Despite all their best efforts, Bertie was turning into the infamous George IV. Soon, they feared, he would be gambling away his money, recruiting a harem of mistresses and bringing the royal name into international disrepute. And they were, of course, completely right.

For the moment, though, there was a solution. Albert ordered Bertie to make a full confession to General Bruce. Bertie did this (although he refused to give the names of

---

* Luckily, Albert was unaware that three days earlier, on 9 November, Bertie had almost certainly smuggled a prostitute into Windsor Castle for a private birthday party.

the officers who had smuggled Nellie into his quarters), and sent a letter of sincere repentance to his father, who accepted the apology and offered forgiveness – on condition that Bertie agreed to take the only action that could save him from perdition.

He had to marry, and fast.

A potential princess had already been selected – sixteen-year-old Alexandra of Schleswig-Holstein-Sonderburg-Glücksburg, daughter of the heir to the Danish throne. Bertie had met Alexandra, but not been overwhelmed. His sister Vicky had witnessed the meeting and reported to her parents that 'he was disappointed about her beauty' and thought 'her nose was too long and her forehead too low'. Too bad. Bertie would have to redeem himself by tying the knot. He had committed one youthful indiscretion too many, and now his youth was over.

So, too, tragically, was Albert's life. On 25 November 1861, he made an unscheduled visit to Cambridge for a heart-to-heart with his son. There, he received Bertie's apology during a long, exhausting walk through an East Anglian storm, made worse by the fact that Bertie lost his way. Back at Windsor, Albert collapsed, and on 14 December he died – though not before giving his eldest son one last opportunity to disgrace himself.

Typically, on receiving a telegram summoning him to Windsor on the thirteenth, Bertie did not grasp the gravity of the situation (in his defence, the telegram was ambiguously worded), and arrived at his father's death bed at three in the morning, in high spirits after a London dinner.

Queen Victoria, who had lost her mother only nine months earlier, went almost insane with grief. And she blamed Bertie for this new disaster. She had always seen Albert as a cross between an angel, a prophet, a guru and a saint, and she had no doubt that 'that dreadful business at the Curragh' had destroyed her perfect husband. In Victoria's tearful eyes, Bertie had become the devil incarnate. She wrote to her daughter Vicky that: 'I never can or shall look at him [Bertie] without a shudder . . . [He] does not know that I know all – Beloved Papa told him that I could not be told all the disgusting details.'

Prince Albert had decreed that Bertie should marry, so marry he would. The Queen wrote to her uncle Leopold:

> I am . . . anxious to repeat *one* thing, and *that one* is *my firm* resolve, my *irrevocable decision*, viz. that *his* [Albert's] wishes—*his* plans—about everything, *his* views about *every* thing are to be *my law*! And *no human power* will make me swerve from *what he* decided and wished.

A quick wedding was to be Bertie's punishment, imposed by his father from beyond the grave.

Victoria felt morally obliged to inform the Danish royal family that the bridegroom-to-be was not a virgin, and was probably astonished by their very Scandinavian reaction: they knew all about it. Wedding plans were duly set in motion.

Meanwhile, the Queen had another duty to fulfil in her husband's name, and one that suited her own purposes, too. Before his death, Albert had planned an educational tour for Bertie, taking in Vienna, Venice, Greece, Egypt and the Middle East. Now the grieving Victoria wanted her son out of her sight and, less than eight weeks after Albert's death, Bertie was packed off abroad under the close moral guardianship of General Bruce and a chaplain.

Over the next four months, Bertie would meet the Emperor Franz Joseph of Austria and the Viceroy of Egypt, steam up the Nile, shoot (amongst other things) crocodiles, vultures, owls and lizards, and grow a straggly beard.

Predictably, the educational aspect of the trip bored Bertie – while the rest of his party explored the pharaohs' tombs, he stayed back at camp, smoking and reading a racy bestseller called *East Lynne*, about a married lady who elopes with her lover, bears an illegitimate child, and then returns in disguise to become the governess in her husband's new household. Much more exciting than old Egyptian stones. When faced with the prospect of visiting the temple at Thebes, Bertie objected, saying: 'Why should we go and see the tumbledown old temple? There will be nothing to see when we get there.' But Albert had decreed that the tour should be character-forming, so off to the ruins he had to go.

There was, however, one major compensation. Luckily for Bertie, his mother was so intent on following 'dear Papa's original plan' to the letter that, against her own better instincts, she rubber-stamped the final stop on the tour – a brief courtesy visit to the court of Napoléon III. Bertie was to spend a night at the British Embassy in Paris, then visit the French Emperor and Empress at one of their summer residences, the Château de Fontainebleau. The

Queen's only condition was that she didn't want to hear anything about the stopover in Paris, or 'Sodom and Gomorrah' as she called it. She wrote to General Bruce warning him that the Prince should not return with any 'worldly, frivolous, gossipy kind of conversation' because she at least was still in mourning. Not that Bertie would want to tell his mother the kind of things a young prince could get up to at Napoléon's court.

So, after landing at Marseilles on 10 June 1862, Bertie rushed northwards to Paris, knowing that at last, after all the emotional trials of the previous months, it was time for some unadulterated enjoyment. He was also going to get the chance to delve deeper into the tantalizing world that he had discovered with Nellie Clifden.

As with Bertie's childhood visit to France, most of his biographers accord only a few lines to this return trip as an adult, referring euphemistically to the more sophisticated pleasures he enjoyed there the second time around. This is probably because there is so little documentation surrounding his brief stay – it was not an officially sanctioned royal visit, so there were no group portraits, no troop inspections, no homage to an imperial tomb.

But Bertie's time in Paris in 1862 was so important to his development as a man that to ignore it is an inexplicable omission. The few days that he was now allowed to spend with Napoléon III and Eugénie must have been the realization of a fantasy, the achievement of an ambition kept locked away behind the façade of good behaviour that Bertie had been forced to maintain throughout his repressed teenage years, and even more so since his father's death.

Sitting on the French train as it rattled northwards from Marseilles, Bertie must have been reminded of his first journey from Boulogne seven years earlier, and smiled at his boyish crush on motherly Eugénie. Now he was looking forward to some altogether less innocent feminine company.

3

BERTIE AND THE 'PALACE DAMES'

~

'This futile court, so seductive on the surface . . . that thinks
only of pleasures and enjoyments.'

Marquise Irène de Taisey-Chantenoy, in her memoir
À la Cour de Napoléon III

I

Bertie had the good fortune to visit the Château de
Fontainebleau, seventy kilometres south of Paris,
during its heyday, the decade or so that it spent as one of
Napoléon III's *résidences secondaires*.

By the nineteenth century, Fontainebleau had been a
royal and imperial residence for around 700 years. The first
castle was built there in the twelfth century, and was visited
by Thomas Becket while he was in exile in France, just
before he returned to England to have his brains hacked

out in Canterbury Cathedral. The future King Charles II spent some time there in 1646 while his father and Oliver Cromwell were fighting over England's mode of government. Louis XVI and Marie-Antoinette used Fontainebleau as a venue for plays and concerts, and had only just finished redecorating Marie-Antoinette's sumptuous boudoir when the French Revolution put an end to the party.

Only the first Napoléon – Bonaparte – used Fontainebleau as more than a forest hideaway, and spent his short but busy stays there conducting politics, including the finalization of several European treaties as he redrew the continent's borders. It was there that he signed his abdication papers in 1814,* and in the courtyard that he bade an official farewell to his closest supporters before his exile to Elba.

Bonaparte's nephew Napoléon III had more frivolous plans for Fontainebleau, and even today the château's official website can barely disguise its disapproval. The *Histoire* section declares that the new imperial couple were only attracted to Fontainebleau 'when the idea of tourism began to develop'. Their holidays there 'became regular and increasingly lengthy', it states, and 'their entourage was much more relaxed than that of previous sovereigns', as though Napoléon and Eugénie were a pair of idle squatters.

However, Napoléon III gave the château an impressive

---

* His first abdication, that is. He was of course to return from Elba and retake power, only to lose it for the last time after Waterloo in 1815.

makeover, in what the website snootily describes as his 'characteristically eclectic style'. He ordered new furniture for many of the private and public rooms, commissioned a new set of imperial apartments overlooking the gardens and a spectacular 450-seat theatre inspired by the auditorium at Versailles. This was a veritable baroque temple to the arts, with a painted ceiling depicting an azure sky inhabited by angels and a semicircular sweep of columns and arches encrusted in gold leaf. The château may have been a country retreat, but under Napoléon III, its entertainment facilities were worthy of central Paris.

Every year, usually for four to six weeks in May and June, the imperial couple, along with 200 or so staff and their closest friends and family members, would move out to Fontainebleau for the ritual of the so-called *séries*. These were weekly house parties attended by fifty or sixty relatives, friends, courtiers, ambassadors, foreign dignitaries and leading lights of literature, science or high society. Every week, a new set of guests would arrive, replacing the previous group who had been graced with an imperial invitation.

To get there, the guests would usually take the train from Paris and be picked up by a fleet of imperial carriages that would drive them through the town and alongside the château's 1.2-kilometre-long 'Grand Canal' like a group of trippers on an upper-class package holiday. On arriving in the immense central courtyard, the visitors would be met at the foot of the sixteenth-century 'horseshoe' staircase and escorted to their rooms – or rather their apartments.

Each guest, including Bertie in June 1862, would be

installed in one of more than 200 private suites, assigned according to the occupant's rank. The more intimate or important the visitors were to the imperial couple, the closer their apartment would be to the social hub of the château. It was a set-up in which, as the château's website puts it, domestic arrangements were 'very supple' – an obvious euphemism for sexual comings and goings.

Unless you were a particularly honoured *invité*, the accommodation was not luxurious. Typically each suite consisted of a *trois-pièces* – a three-roomed apartment with a *salon*, bedroom and *cabinet de toilette* (bathroom and dressing room). Eugénie, who oversaw the decoration of the guest rooms, was aiming for cosiness rather than grandeur, and to achieve this she placed a bulk order for tasteful, simple furniture almost entirely free of the gold leaf that her husband favoured for his decoration. A typical guest apartment is open to the public today, and the poshest thing about it is its view over the family's private garden. The sitting room contains a round walnut table, four small armchairs covered in luminous blue-and-white flowered material that matches the wallpaper, a plain desk and a padded sofa. It was designed to be 'in the English fashion' – Chesterfield-style padding had just been invented and was very much in vogue, as was the English country-house look.

The bedroom featured twin beds that could be pushed together if required and a tall mirror fitted with candlesticks to ensure that the guests would be impeccably turned out when they left their rooms for one of the many parties for which they would receive an invitation card. It was also essential that they be on time, so a clock stood on every bedroom mantelpiece. Lateness would be punished with a small fine.

All in all, it looks less like a palace apartment and more like a suite that you might find in a chic country hotel today (assuming you could do without a widescreen TV), except perhaps for the *cabinet de toilette*, which testified to the lack of plumbing. On the marble-topped *table de toilette* stood a jug and bowl. Beside these, there was a china bidet on a wooden stand and a portable commode, and in one corner a low, round metal bathtub like the ones depicted by Degas in his nude bathing scenes.

The sanitary arrangements were similar in the more luxurious suites on a lower floor, where young Bertie would have stayed, but this wouldn't have bothered him, because his recent travels had got him used to desert camps and army bunks.

The most convenient thing about the carefully organized set-up at the Fontainebleau *séries* was that all the rooms were numbered, as in a hotel, and that the names of the occupants were displayed on each door, on a card handwritten by the Empress. Eugénie took it upon herself to allocate rooms, putting people who might be well suited close to each other. It was an arrangement perfectly conducive to making assignations and flitting from door to door.

So now, instead of having to sneak women into his rooms as he had at army camp and (probably) Windsor, Bertie would be able to issue an invitation and have a lady knocking at his door. Or he could be invited for a tête-à-tête *chez elle*. And, as one of Bertie's French biographers Philippe Jullian notes, his moral guardians would not intervene – Bertie was, after all, a personal guest of the Emperor of France, so supervision was not necessary, *n'est-ce pas?* Although what Jullian does not mention is that Bertie's moral guardian, General Bruce, was suffering from a fever that he had contracted in the Jordanian marshes during their tour of the Orient, so his guard was down and his young charge was freer than usual to enjoy himself.

Either way, to Bertie, it must have felt like leaving Saudi Arabia and arriving in Bangkok – or Paris.

II

In the opinion of Philippe Jullian, the key thing about Napoléon III's France was that it wasn't England.

Chez Victoria and Albert, hypocrisy ruled. The English upper classes engaged in adultery and homosexuality, and young men relieved their sexual frustrations with prostitutes, but if any whiff of scandal seeped out into the London smog, the guilty parties could be ruined, and often had to flee into exile – in France.

As Jullian puts it, in London, 'Vice – one can't speak of pleasures – was easy and brutal, with none of the gaiety of our Second Empire.' He describes London's 'sixteen-year-old prostitutes dressed in ragged lace', and evokes a world 'behind the superb façades of Regent Street and the Strand, a hidden hell of mean streets, courtyards and stables, home to child traffickers and schools for thieves'.

Even Dickens, he asserts, shied away from revealing the true horrors that went on there.

Rich Londoners were forced either to descend into this hell or hide behind tightly drawn Mayfair curtains if they wanted to indulge their sexual appetites. Their Parisian counterparts, on the other hand, could express themselves freely.

Bertie himself had already been on incognito outings to a few of London's more salubrious music halls and gin palaces with his army pals and Nellie Clifden, but now, in 1862, as he arrived at Napoléon III's summer residence in Fontainebleau, he was to get a first taste of real sexual freedom. Jullian describes the situation suggestively: 'In this amiable court, the Prince [Bertie] could breathe, and his entourage did not intervene . . . The women whom he had kissed as a small boy were prepared to give their all to the young man.'

Perhaps more importantly, Bertie would be able to discuss sex with his true father figure, Napoléon, without being ordered to keep his urges to himself until he was married. To Napoléon, unlike Albert, extra-marital or pre-marital sex was deliciously naughty rather than shamefully secret. Jullian says that 'one could speak freely about everything' with the Emperor, who 'always preferred to charm rather than intimidate'. He was the very opposite of Bertie's biological father.

Arriving at Fontainebleau, Bertie would probably have felt more relaxed than he had for a very long time. Most French writers talking about Napoléon's country houses stress how at ease they felt there. As we saw in Chapter 1,

both the Emperor and Empress combined a love of offi-
cialdom with a real gift for hospitality – something for
which Bertie himself would later become famous (infamous, even).

By 1862, Napoléon and Eugénie had found their feet
in French society and ensured that even the most snobbish die-hard royalists were desperate to belong to the
new imperial in-crowd. Napoléon was surrounded by a
staff of high-ranking army officers and aristocrats with
grandiose titles like Grand Maître du Palais, Grand
Maître des Cérémonies, and Grand Veneur (Master of
the Royal Hunt). Eugénie, although a cheated wife and
a foreigner, had overcome all the prejudices against her,
and reigned over her own highly regimented court, which
featured a Grande Maîtresse of her household as well as
a Dame d'Honneur (Chief Lady-in-waiting), her twelve
dames du palais and two *lectrices* – 'reading ladies' to keep
her and her clique amused with news and the latest
novels.

Alongside the small, slightly stooping Napoléon,
Eugénie was the epitome of Parisian elegance – not beautiful in the classic sense, but graceful, stylish and (to
contemporary eyes) very sexy. When Bertie met Eugénie
again in June 1862, she was at the height of her glory.
She had given Napoléon the long-awaited male heir, and
now conducted herself like a born empress. She had
become famous for her trademark way of greeting the
crowds that parted in her presence – she would nod her
head slightly to her right and left, according a mute smile
to the fortunate onlookers.

A poem written in 1861 gives an idea of how strong the Eugénie idolatry had become. The poet Edouard d'Escola published an ode to the Empress's beauty that oozes as much syrup as a *crème caramel*. Here is a typical verse:

Elle enchante par sa présence,
Riche, pauvre, faible et puissant,
Et vole aux deux bouts de la France
Pour la bénir toute en passant.

This could be translated as something like:

By her presence, she enchants
The richest and the poorest classes,
And flies all over France
Blessing all as she passes.

Admittedly, d'Escola was an obsequious patriot who also wrote a poem about Waterloo that was prefaced with a wonderful example of French denial – 'Defeats are only victories to which fortune has refused to give wings.' But everyone at court testified to Eugénie's regal presence amongst them. And now Bertie was instantly elevated to a position of equality, by her side, to bathe in her reflected glory. Aged only twenty, he was being parachuted in at the pinnacle of French society.

For a young man in need of entertainment, Bertie's arrival couldn't have been better timed. Despite all the rank and ceremony at Napoléon's court in Paris, the summer residences at Fontainebleau and Saint-Cloud and the winter residence, Compiègne, were run so that the guests would feel free.

While in attendance the guests were invited to share the imperial couple's daily life. Not in the way that Louis XIV made his courtiers watch him eating, dressing and even giving his morning performance on the commode,* but at a series of amusing dinners, dances, riding parties, games evenings and shows.

Eugénie had fitted out her private sitting rooms as a cross between a Buddhist temple and an English gentleman's club. Amidst Chinese vases, oriental woodwork and dragon statues, and presided over by Franz Xaver Winterhalter's group portrait of the Empress and her glamorous *dames du palais*, armchairs and sofas were set out around the room in convivial huddles. There were also card tables big and small, a baize-covered forerunner of a pinball table, and a piano with a wind-up music-box mechanism in case a proficient player couldn't be found. In summer, regular rounds of sorbets would be served, and *thé anglais* came punctually at five. Conversation, cards and constant refreshment – it was Bertie's ideal environment.

The plays put on in Napoléon's new theatre were sometimes classical, but the taste of the time was more for light entertainment, and the Emperor was fond of inviting out the starlets of the Paris stage, many of whom were better

---

* For more details of Louis XIV's absurdly ordered daily routine, see *1,000 Years of Annoying the French*.

known for their physical attributes and loose morals than their skill at memorizing Molière. This, as we will see in a later chapter, was the kind of French literary experience that Bertie enjoyed most.

In his memoirs, *Souvenirs du Second Empire*, the Comte de Maugny, who served in Napoléon III's Ministry of Foreign Affairs, writes that the fun and games out at the country châteaux also included such very French activities as a dictation, with participants having to write out a complicated text while making as few errors as possible. Maugny records one such occasion at Compiègne when, despite the presence of the famous literary critic Charles-Augustin Saint-Beuve and the writer Prosper Mérimée, the contest was won by the Austrian Ambassador Richard von Metternich. It is highly doubtful that Bertie, who at twenty still had problems elevating his English sentences above schoolboy level, would have felt tempted to join in. Besides, there were plenty of more rewarding pastimes on offer.

Napoléon, like Bertie, preferred repartee to spelling tests, and spent much of his time chatting up the wittiest, most beautiful women. 'He [Napoléon] would go and sit beside each of them in turn,' Maugny says, 'and, while talking to her, would hail any passing lady that came within range of his voice or gaze.'

At dinner, Napoléon would sit between his two favourite ladies amongst that week's crop, while Eugénie was always seated opposite him and between the two most important men. Bertie, during his first solo visit to Fontainebleau as a young man, would certainly have been one of them. The other guests sat where they wanted, or could find a seat. In an unusually modern spirit of equality, ladies who had not been selected by the Emperor or a prestigious male guest could choose which man to sit next to, and he would be her beau for the evening – and sometimes for the night as well.

The men were, according to the Comte de Maugny, guaranteed to find female admirers who 'made it their profession to go mad for them'. At the country residences, a female courtier's role was clear.

According to Philippe Jullian, during Bertie's visit to Fontainebleau in 1862, the Prince 'formed long-term friendships' with some very glamorous ladies. There was, for example, Mélanie de Bussière, one of Eugénie's closest friends. Mélanie, or the Comtesse Edmond de Pourtalès to give her her full married title, was in her mid-twenties and a striking, chestnut-haired beauty. She was the mother of two boys, and young married ladies who had done their dynastic duty were prime targets for adultery. As if this weren't enough, Mélanie was also renowned as a witty conversationalist. In short, Bertie's dream girl.

Others he met during this visit included Anna Murat, a granddaughter of Napoléon Bonaparte's sister Caroline, and Léonora, the wife of the banker Baron Alphonse de Rothschild, who was also a glamorous young mother.

Bertie would probably have renewed his acquaintance with Princess Mathilde, Napoléon III's cousin and former fiancée. She had a personal suite at Fontainebleau – appropriately enough in the former apartment of Madame de Maintenon, mistress and then secretly married wife of

Louis XIV. Mathilde was still living with her lover in Paris and holding literary salons for the likes of Gustave Flaubert (author of the adultery novel *Madame Bovary* which had been published in 1857). A sexy, scandalous divorcée, Mathilde would have been a no-holds-barred guide for a young English prince seeking to understand the ins and outs (no pun intended) of Napoléon's court.

Whether Bertie immediately invited himself into the guest suites of any of these noble *Françaises* is not clear. But he was the second most highly ranked member of the Fontainebleau house party that summer, and would have had his pick of the available ladies.

The atmosphere of sexual availability reigning at Napoléon III's court is vividly described in the kiss-and-tell memoirs of a certain Marquise Irène de Taisey-Chantenoy, who was one of the Emperor's many discarded lovers. Understandably, her stories drip with vitriol. Attempting to lambast Napoléon and Eugénie, the Marquise refers to 'this futile court, so seductive on the surface . . . that thinks of nothing but pleasures and enjoyments'.*

Coming from an old French aristocratic family, Irène de Taisey-Chantenoy felt superior to Eugénie, 'a Spaniard married because of her auburn hair'. Even so, the Marquise (who was also married) was desperate to get noticed at court, and was delighted when one day Napoléon deigned to speak to her, using a chat-up line that sounds horribly cheesy.

---

* In French: 'plaisirs et jouissances'. They are almost synonymous, but the second word is derived from the verb *jouir*, one of the meanings of which is to have an orgasm.

'Aren't you Madame . . . er?' he asks her. 'I'm sure we've met before. Where was it?' He goes on to tell Irène that she is 'séduisante', to which she adds, 'He wasn't the first to notice that.'

Once her youthful beauty has been officially recognized by Napoléon's roving eye, Irène's place at court is assured. She becomes a member of Eugénie's band of *caillettes*, a name which was supposedly a diminutive of *canaille*, or rabble, but could also come from a slang word of the time for prostitute – *caille* or quail. They were all rich ladies ('so that Eugénie could be sure we wouldn't ask her for money,' Irène notes), but were given risqué nicknames like Salopette (literally a small slut, it also means a pair of overalls) and Cochonette (from *cochon*, a pig, which is also an adjective meaning sex-mad).

These *dames du palais* spent their time discussing what Irène sarcastically calls 'insignificant things of great importance', like the fact that Napoléon had not drunk his coffee that morning, as well as exchanging all the latest salacious gossip about Parisian high society. She tells, for example, the story of a ballerina who went to see the Deputy Minister for Fine Arts to apply for promotion to the front row of the troupe. The Deputy has his way with her in his office and sends her in to see the Minister. However, when the Minister takes his turn at lifting the dancer's skirts, he sees that a memo from his Deputy's desk has got stuck to her backside. An old hand at the game of giving and receiving favours, the Minister simply files the sheet of paper in his in-tray and gets down to business. The ballerina, meanwhile, earns her promotion.

This sounds like the type of story that the newly experienced Bertie would have loved to hear – and exactly the kind of gossip that would have had his recently departed father reaching for earplugs and the Bible.

Irène also reveals the extent of the freedom enjoyed by married upper-class *Parisiennes* at the time. In an attempt to find out how call girls operate, she and a friend rent a private room at the notorious Café Anglais (more of which in Chapter 6) and pretend to be Belgian ladies on the prowl. However, their plans go awry when two prostitutes turn up and sense that things are not what they seem. The evening ends with Irène's friend getting roaring drunk and Irène herself being propositioned by a baron.

The Empress Eugénie also famously made a foray into the lower echelons of society, though more out of a desire to imitate Marie-Antoinette, who had romantic visions of being a shepherdess. Irène tells the story gleefully. While in summer residence at Fontainebleau, Eugénie and a friend dress up as farm girls and go to a peasants' dance. The ladies are invited on to the floor by a pair of stonemasons, who quickly make their amorous intentions rustically clear. At this point, Eugénie's disguised bodyguards intervene and a fight breaks out, only for the two masons to be unmasked as courtiers – they had got wind of Eugénie's plans and come to play a practical joke on her. Irène says that Eugénie was furious. Being fondled by two smelly yokels would have made the perfect anecdote back at court, and now the story was ruined, and she was the butt of the joke.

Given that the ruse involved Eugénie, it sounds likely that Napoléon himself had sent the impostors along. It was definitely the kind of joke he adored.

The most elaborate scheme of his that Irène describes is a visit to court by the King of the non-existent state of Oude and his entourage, who are in fact some of Napoléon's friends dressed up as Orientals. Napoléon announces that he is unable to attend the reception, and asks Eugénie to receive the head of state in his place. Flattered, she welcomes the veiled visitors in all her finery, telling them in slow, easy-to-understand French to go back to their people and inform them of the Emperor's great affection for their country. Then a laughing Napoléon bursts in, the veils are lifted, and Eugénie understandably erupts in a 'violent fit of nerves'.

Napoléon may well have been an inspiration for Bertie's own taste for practical joking at his house parties, though Bertie's humorous japes were often less subtle – one frequently repeated favourite was pouring brandy over his friend Christopher Sykes's head, to which the poor victim could only reply 'as your Royal Highness pleases'. Another involved serving mince pies that turned out to be filled with mustard.

Irène's most detailed descriptions are reserved for Napoléon's sexual mores. He 'will accept no obstacles or deprivations in his pleasures', she says. 'All the master's whims must be obeyed.' She recounts how Eugénie once walked in on her husband and an actress famous for 'showing her legs in a small theatre and the rest everywhere else'. The girl is invited to the Tuileries Palace, where

Eugénie catches Napoléon fondling the aforementioned body, and informs him that: 'Tickling a pretty girl's legs is not amongst the duties of a head of state.'

Even though the long-suffering Empress obviously had a talent for quotable putdowns, Irène is scornful, saying that by disapproving of her husband's waywardness Eugénie 'reveals the most bourgeois sentiments'. At Napoléon's court, as it would later be amongst Bertie's own set, upper-class spouses were not meant to object openly to their partner's adultery.

Irène quotes one cuckolded man who was forced to hide his embarrassment with some quick thinking. At one of Napoléon and Eugénie's Parisian parties, he is seen rushing around the palace looking for his wife, and a courtier asks him if he's jealous.

'Oh no,' he replies, 'one's wife always comes back, but tonight she's wearing 538,000 francs' worth of diamonds around her neck.'

Irène's crowning moment, and her downfall, comes when she gets her turn in bed with Napoléon. They are out at the Château de Compiègne, the imperial winter residence north of Paris, where Napoléon has installed a carousel so that he can watch the women swirling around with their 'flying skirts and exposed calves'.

In the gardens, after much manoeuvring, Irène catches Napoléon's eye and he takes her for a walk, complimenting her on her beauty and elegance, and eventually kissing her. (After which, she complains that she had to wipe her lips clean of a 'smelly grease that stung me' – Napoléon's moustache oil.) He helps her up into a seat on the carousel and watches her as she careers around exposing her calves. They part with a whispered 'à ce soir', and Irène's husband (who is present during the whole public courtship) is dispatched to Paris on a spurious errand.

A servant informs her that she is to spend the night in 'la chambre bleue', the bedroom next to Napoléon's. She goes there, slips into bed and awaits his visit. As she lies nervously in the dark, she thinks that if she changed her mind and fled the room, 'even my own husband would have regarded me as a stupid flirt, a deranged idiot'. Napoléon eventually stumbles in through a concealed door and, as Irène describes it, 'my destiny was fulfilled'.

She admits that she imagined herself becoming a long-term royal mistress, like Henri IV's Diane de Poitiers or Louis XIV's Madame de Maintenon, and that she is devastated when Napoléon doesn't come to her room on the second night. Worse, he then takes another woman for the same walk in the gardens, and helps her on to the same seat on the carousel. Irène realizes that she has been used as a quick imperial fix. So she sneaks to the carousel, partially unbolts the seat, and is delighted when the following day, the new favourite (who has lasted longer than a one-night stand) is thrown off the carousel flat on her face. Everyone, including Napoléon, laughs, and it is the end of the new affair, because, as Irène comments in a typically French flash of courtly wit, 'One recovers from an illness, but dies of ridicule.'

This tragi-comedy ends with Irène leaving Compiègne in a huff, but having the final word. A few months later, she bumps into Napoléon, who actually recognizes her and enquires whether she will be returning to court. Definitely not, she tells him.

'Even if I ask you to?' Napoléon says.

'*Especially* if you ask me to,' she replies. Touché.

III

All in all, Bertie's short stay at Fontainebleau in June 1862 would have been an unbelievably liberating experience. He had only just arrived in manhood, and already the loveliest, wittiest women in Europe were his for the taking.

This explains why, as soon as he became independent of his mother, Bertie would imitate almost everything about Napoléon and Eugénie's lifestyle – the easy switching from pomp to informality (as long as rank was respected, of course); the mix of people at court – not just stuffy dignitaries but achievers from very different walks of life (though Bertie himself would not be quite as keen as Napoléon on the literary set); and, of course, the virtual obligation for women to indulge in adultery at any house party, especially with the alpha male.

It is no exaggeration to say that on leaving Fontainebleau, Bertie was ready to mutate into a young Napoléon III, a process he would quickly begin to fine-tune by revisiting France as often as possible and by using the French model when he set up his own household.

When Bertie arrived home after his oriental voyage and its French finale, it was hardly surprising that Victoria found him looking 'bright and healthy'. Even better, her sinful son was now, she noted with satisfaction, willing 'to do whatever his Mother and Father wished' – Bertie was obviously feeling very pleased with himself, and was behaving so diplomatically that he even impressed the late Albert from beyond the grave.

What Bertie's parents, both dead and alive, wanted most of all was a wedding. A few months earlier, he hadn't been keen, but after his week in Fontainebleau, marriage must have held few fears for the twenty-year-old Prince. He had seen for himself, and no doubt been assured in a fatherly pep talk from Napoléon, that marriage was no barrier to fun and games.

On the contrary, to a man in Bertie's position, a wedding certificate would be a passport to unfettered philandering.

4

AN ANGLO-DANISH WEDDING
AND A FRENCH MARRIAGE

~

'A solemn holy act *not* to be classed with amusements.'
Queen Victoria's idea of a good wedding reception

I

In marriage as in everything else, Bertie was to find it almost impossible to please Victoria, who, like all interfering mothers worth their salt, sent out a barrage of contradictory messages concerning her son's wedding. The only consistent thing about the Queen was that everything she did was motivated by her own self-interest.

On the one hand, she campaigned in Bertie's favour with his future in-laws. She wrote to Princess Alexandra's mother referring to Bertie's 'fall' as 'this *(one) sad mistake*', and claiming that '*wicked wretches* had led our poor innocent Boy into a scrape'. In all her writings, Victoria was very fond of underlining words (usually represented in a printed text, including this one, as italics), but for her letter to Bertie's intended mother-in-law she resorted to capital letters to insist that she would look to Bertie's future wife 'as being HIS SALVATION'. Victoria even went so far as to assure the Danes that Bertie was 'very domestic and longed to be at home', which was either a white lie or a spectacular piece of denial.

Privately, though, Victoria was set firmly against Alexandra – she wanted a German daughter-in-law, not a Dane. Bertie's elder sister Vicky had married the heir to the Prussian crown, sealing for the foreseeable future (or so Victoria thought) England's friendship with the Germans. Ideally, Bertie would add a second link to this Anglo-Prussian family chain. The Danes, on the contrary, were in direct conflict with Prussia over the possession of the tiny border states of Schleswig and Holstein, which at the time were like two irritating grains of sand in the salami sandwich of northern European politics.

In Alexandra's favour, she was part German – her mother was from Hesse-Kassel, a small duchy that had provided Britain with soldiers (at a price) during the American War of Independence. But this pedigree didn't satisfy Victoria, mainly because the court of Hesse-Kassel was notorious for being too dissolute, too frivolous – too French. Exactly like Bertie, in fact.

Politically, then, Alexandra was a disaster. But even Prussia's English princess, Vicky, was all for the marriage because she astutely felt that the only hope of forcing Bertie to become anything like a stable husband was to find him a beautiful wife, and the eligible German girls she had met were all a bit too Kaiser-like. Alexandra was not as stunning as some of the French ladies Bertie had encountered, but she had natural poise and a delicate beauty that might, Vicky suggested, keep him interested.

Victoria's moral mentor, Uncle Leopold, King of the Belgians, was also in favour of Alexandra, but for a much more masculine reason. He thought her a good choice as a wife because, he wrote to Victoria, 'there is something frank and cheerful in Alex's character, which will greatly assist her to take things without being too much over-powered or alarmed'. His meaning was clear: Bertie was always going to be a womanizer, and Alexandra seemed to have what it took to survive the humiliation. In this, Leopold was something of an expert – he had an official mistress who was thirty-five years his junior, and who had borne him two illegitimate sons.

As it happened, Alexandra's mother was not at all re-assured by Victoria's lobbying. Princess Christian of Denmark had heard about the tempestuous relationship between Victoria and Bertie, and was terrified that the bad feeling between them would ruin Alexandra's chances of a happy marriage.

With so many conflicting opinions surrounding the Anglo-Danish match, it was left to seventeen-year-old Alexandra herself to sort things out. First there was a short introduction to Victoria in Belgium in September 1862, at which the Queen decided that Alexandra seemed 'dignified' and 'distinguished', even if her parents were not.

Then in November, Victoria summoned Alexandra to a meeting in England to be inspected more closely, without the support of her mother this time, and with her father banished to a nearby hotel. Petrified as she was at the prospect of a solo audience with the gorgon mother-in-law, Alexandra had the good sense to present herself to the mourning Victoria in a plain black dress, without any jewellery, and to put up with hours of lectures about Albert. She was a model of sobriety, piety and healthy melancholy.

The ruse worked. Victoria wrote to Vicky, saying, 'How beloved Albert would have loved her.' From beyond the grave, Papa had given his approval. 'She is so good, so simple, unaffected,' Victoria went on, unwittingly spelling out that poor Alexandra was the complete opposite of the French beauties that Bertie was so fond of.

He, meanwhile, was trying his best to reassure his mother that he would do his marital duty. After Alexandra had accepted his proposal, which was little more than a formality, Bertie wrote a letter to Victoria in his confusing style – half German, half Yoda from *Star Wars* – promising that: 'Love and cherish her you may be sure I will to the end of my life.'

Luckily, Alexandra was quite smitten with her jovial, impeccably mannered English Prince. She told Vicky: 'You perhaps think that I like marrying your Brother for his position but if he was a cowboy I should love him the same and would marry no-one else.' It should be noted that, at the time, a cowboy was not someone who rode the prairies in search of buffalo, whisky and good-time girls – he was simply the cattle equivalent of a shepherd boy.

Victoria, though, was terrified that Bertie might have

something of the wandering ranch-hand about him, and insisted that, even though the young couple were engaged, they should never be left alone together unless someone was sitting outside the room next to an open door. There would be no pre-marital rodeo-riding on Victoria's watch.

While arrangements were finalized, Bertie was exiled to the royal yacht *Osborne* (the renamed *Victoria and Albert*) for a short cruise in the Med. It was a stormy November, and almost everyone on board was seasick. One of the steamer's paddle wheels was damaged, and it was forced to moor in the Bay of Naples, where Bertie held a low-key twenty-first birthday party. This coming-of-age in exile looks very much like a deliberate ploy on Victoria's part, a punishment for Bertie's premature assertion of his adulthood with Nellie Clifden.

However, Victoria seems to have let her political and emotional manoeuvrings distract her, because she made a grave mistake in planning her son's short Mediterranean exile. On the way home, Bertie had to make an overnight stop in Paris to change trains.

Since poor General Bruce had died of fever just two weeks after the Orient tour, Bertie now had a new moral guardian – an aged veteran of the Napoleonic Wars called General Sir William Knollys. Nominally he was Bertie's 'comptroller and treasurer', the idea being that preventing the Prince of Wales's financial excesses would also limit his moral overindulgences. But Knollys was more lenient than Bruce, and would become loyal to the Prince rather than the Queen, so Bertie was able to escape from his base at the British Embassy and visit Eugénie, who was in Paris.

Eugénie was, as usual, surrounded by her charm school, and Bertie was introduced to yet another young married beauty, the dusky Anne-Alexandrine-Jeanne-Marguerite Seillière de Sagan, who immediately set about confiding in him that her husband was cheating on her (*quelle surprise*). For the moment, Bertie could only console the unhappily married French lady verbally, but it was a heavy hint that he filed away for later use. When he eventually acted on it, it would lead to a paternity scandal.

II

Bertie's wedding, like his engagement, was a mixture of youthful geniality and maternal gloom. The date, chosen by Victoria, was 10 March 1863, during Lent, the season of self-denial. When the Archbishop of Canterbury complained about the inappropriate timing, he was rebuked by the Queen, who reminded him that marriage was 'a solemn holy act *not* to be classed with amusements'. In short, Bertie was lucky he wasn't getting married on Good Friday – crucifixion day.

The British public, though, had no such negative thoughts. They were wholeheartedly in favour of a royal wedding, whatever the date. Just as in 1981, when Prince Charles married his own carefully selected virgin bride, the nation erupted in a frenzy of capitalistic monarchism. Streets were decorated with flags and bunting, and shop windows were suddenly overflowing with souvenirs. There were photos, marriage medals, even commemorative Princess Alexandra hair curlers. New celebratory songs were written, and the sheet music was published so that every household with a piano (and in those days there were many) could bash out a patriotic tune in their front room.

One of these songs was called 'Oh Take Her But Be Faithful Still', which, judging by the way the royal marriage would turn out, was one tune that Bertie didn't get to hear.

The official celebrations were set to begin three days before the wedding, when Bertie was to escort Alexandra through London after her arrival in England on the royal yacht. As soon as the route of the procession was announced, strategic windows and balconies were put up for rent at exorbitant prices. An American biographer, Stanley Weintraub, quotes one of the many small ads that appeared in *The Times*, which was offering a viewpoint for the procession with what must surely have been a deliberate spelling mistake and double entendre:

> Royal Procession: First floor, with two large widows, to be let, in the best part of Cockspur Street, with entrance accessible behind.

If Bertie saw the ad – and it became famous – he would probably have laughed. And asked to meet the two widows.

The procession attracted immense crowds – the biggest ever seen in London, it was said – but *The Times* reported that the royal carriages were 'old and shabby, and the horses very poor, with no trappings, not even rosettes'. Victoria had put her usual damper on the celebrations. Even so, for four long hours the crowd cheered a tumultuous welcome to Alexandra, who was looking beautiful and composed in an open carriage despite the cold March wind and her first exposure to public hysteria.

Almost as soon as the happy young couple arrived in Windsor, where the wedding itself was to take place, Victoria took them to Albert's brand-new mausoleum, finished just the day before. The Queen led Bertie and Alexandra into the shrine and joined their hands before the late Prince Consort's tomb. 'He gives you his blessing,' Victoria declared. Alexandra would have been forgiven for thinking she was marrying into the Dracula family.

Victoria insisted on holding the wedding ceremony in St George's Chapel at Windsor, which until then had been better known as a venue for royal funerals.* Within its walls were the tombs of Kings Edward IV, Henry VI, Henry VIII, Charles I, Georges III and IV and William IV, and its East Choir was being rebuilt as a chapel in honour of Bertie's father. A place of unbridled joy it was not.

Victoria had taken care to fill the church with her own guests, so that there was hardly any room for Alexandra's family. Even the King of Denmark had not been invited. Victoria herself was not amongst the congregation, either, and remained almost completely hidden from view throughout the ceremony. She watched proceedings from on high in Catherine of Aragon's Closet. This sounds like a wardrobe but is in fact a private recess on a balcony above the altar, built so that Catherine could observe the ceremonies of the Order of the Garter that were held in

---

* Edward VII himself would later be interred in the church where he was married.

St George's. (After she was estranged from Henry VIII, titillations in Catherine's life must have been few and far between.)

So, up in her closet, in a black dress with a white veil, wearing a miniature of Albert in a brooch, Victoria gazed down like an avenging angel. The first piece of music to be played, chosen by Victoria of course, was an oratorio written by her husband, and she was seen to sigh and raise her face to heaven as it was sung. It was a relief that she hadn't asked for Alexandra and Bertie to be brought to the altar in coffins.

The guests and the bridal couple did their best to jolly up the occasion – many of the men sported brightly coloured uniforms; the women were resplendent in their jewels and silks. Alexandra arrived (twenty minutes late) in a white-and-silver satin dress embroidered with orange blossoms that hung in clusters like mistletoe, as if to remind everyone that she was expecting a kiss on this funereal day. Bertie was looking elegant, if a little plump, in a general's uniform with the velvet cloak of the Order of the Garter wrapped around his shoulders. In a photograph taken just after the ceremony, the cloak's bulbously tasselled cord hangs down over his crotch like an historic fertility symbol.

When it came to the vows, Bertie showed himself up. He had to have Alexandra's six first names (Alexandra Caroline Marie Charlotte Louise Julia) read out in groups – he was apparently incapable of reciting them all from memory.

There were moments of lightness, though – Bertie's nephew, the four-year-old Wilhelm, future Kaiser of

Germany, who was wearing Highland dress, pulled the large gemstone from the handle of his dirk and had to be restrained from throwing it across the aisle.

Many members of the congregation were also distracted by the ample cleavage of the 65-year-old Duchess of Cambridge, a great-granddaughter of George II and now Princess of that frivolous court of Hesse-Kassel. And when the Archbishop's sermon droned on for what the orchestra considered too long, the musicians began loudly tuning their instruments.

After the ceremony, at the wedding lunch (which the Queen did not attend), the future Kaiser misbehaved again, crawling under the table to bite the exposed leg of his uncle Prince Arthur, who was wearing the uniform of a Scottish soldier – tunic and kilt. It was, of course, not Wilhelm's last attack on the British military.

During the lunch, the happy couple were called away from the celebrations to pose for a family photo that must have confirmed in the bride's mind that she had just married into some kind of ghost-worshipping sect. There are four characters in the picture. To the left is the white-veiled Alexandra, the only person gazing frankly into the camera. To the rear is Bertie, pouting morosely and looking away. In front of him, sitting rigidly at right angles to the camera, is Victoria, who is swathed in a voluminous black habit that makes her look like a cross between a nun and a hearse. She is ignoring the young couple, and staring up at a life-size head-and-shoulders bust of Albert on a plinth. If the photographer actually did say 'cheese', no one heard him.

That afternoon, Bertie and Alexandra were driven off to their honeymoon in a carriage, hailed by the crowds and the nation's bells. They were on their way to the railway station, where they were to catch a train to Southampton, then the royal yacht to the Isle of Wight, where they were to spend a week at Osborne – a house now transformed into yet another shrine to Albert.

Victoria, having got what she called a 'sad and dismal ceremony' out of the way, snuck back to the mausoleum to commune with her dead husband.

Not exactly an auspicious start to a marriage.

III

Princess Alexandra had one good reason to be thankful for Victoria's interference, however – for a while it drew Bertie closer to her. When in November 1863, the Schleswig-Holstein problem flared up into a short, unequal war between little Denmark and mighty Prussia, Bertie supported his wife in opposition to his mother.

'Oh! If Bertie's wife was only a good German and not a Dane!' Victoria moaned, while Bertie defended Alexandra and began to nurture the feeling (which became stronger throughout his life) that the Prussians were nothing more than bullies – yet another view that he would share with the French.

Victoria also united the young couple by pestering them about every aspect of their social life. She objected to late dinners and parties on moral grounds, and also did her best to discourage Alexandra from horse-riding, one of the

Princess's favourite hobbies, on the grounds that it would hinder childbearing. The Queen even gave orders that parties and receptions should be organized to avoid Alexandra's periods.

It seems strange that Victoria was so impatient to see an heir to the throne, because she expressed serious doubts about both Alexandra's and Bertie's suitability as breeding stock.

'Are you aware that Alix [as Alexandra came to be called by her family] has the smallest head ever seen?' she wrote to her daughter Vicky. 'I dread . . . – with his [Bertie's] small empty brain – very much for future children.'

It was largely Victoria's own fault if Bertie's brain stayed empty, because she still refused to let him have anything to do with matters of state. She didn't trust him to read cabinet papers, because she was afraid he would disagree with her or prove too indiscreet – and in both cases, her fears were entirely justified.

She didn't want Bertie to represent her at public functions, either, despite his success at doing so in America as a much younger man. She wrote to her Home Secretary, referring to herself in the third person as she usually did when communicating with politicians, that:

Her Majesty thinks it would be most undesirable to constitute the Heir to the Crown a general representative of Herself, and particularly to bring Him forward too frequently before the people. This would necessarily place the Prince of Wales in a position of competing as it were, for popularity with the Queen.

What else was there for 21-year-old Bertie and his 18-year-old wife to do than ignore Victoria's disapproval and enjoy themselves?

Shortly before their wedding, Bertie had take possession of the two houses that would be the main venues for his English partying for the rest of his life. Marlborough House in Pall Mall, built by Christopher Wren in 1710, belonged to the crown, and £60,000* of government money was spent on modernizing it as Bertie's London home. To this, the Prince added £100,000 of his own money (mainly income from the Duchy of Cornwall – land still owned by the Prince of Wales today), which he lavished on furniture and carriages for Marlborough, as well as jewellery for Alexandra and himself.

Like all other aspects of Bertie's private life, Marlborough House was modelled on what he had seen in France. It was redecorated in a French style, with plenty of gilding on the woodwork, and remodelled to provide a ballroom and a series of large reception rooms like those in which Napoléon and Eugénie held their Parisian parties. The décor included tapestries from the Gobelins factory in Paris given to Bertie by Napoléon, and paintings by Franz Xaver Winterhalter, the German artist who had painted the French imperial couple and the beauties at their court. Winterhalter now painted portraits of Bertie and Alexandra, making the Prince look a bit like a chubby

---

* To give an idea of how much this represented, the average wage of a household cook would have been about £35 a year, that of an experienced bank clerk about £150 a year.

boy Hussar and Alexandra a vamp with an alarmingly low-cut dress.

In deliberate defiance of his mother's wishes, Bertie fitted out a smoking room at Marlborough. Typically, though, he was terrified that Victoria would find out, so when she came to inspect the new home, the smoking den was camouflaged with a chalked message on the door saying 'Lavatory. Under Repair'. It was the only way to make sure that Victoria would not poke her nose in where it was not wanted.

The young couple's other playground was Sandringham in Norfolk, a country house comfortably far away from Bertie's mother. This he bought out of his own money for £220,000 (though its 7,000 acres of farms yielded a healthy £6,000 a year in rents, so it was a sound investment as well as a hideaway). Aptly, Bertie bought the house from an owner who spent most of his time away from home whooping it up in Paris, and had recently moved abroad permanently after shocking the Norfolk gentry by marrying his mistress.

Like Marlborough, Sandringham received a Napoléon III-style makeover. Bertie had seen how the Emperor was redesigning Paris, and he now built new roads on the Sandringham estate, laid out a pleasure garden for outdoor amusements, and founded schools and a hospital for his tenants. In the house, Bertie built himself a games annexe that included a billiard room and a skittles alley. Clearly needing to make up for a lost childhood, he would also hold tricycle races in the ballroom and toboggan down the main stairs on a silver tray.

The sense of fun extended to the choice of décor – alongside the predictable country-house paintings of rural landscapes and livestock was a real stuffed baboon that greeted visitors at the front door, its paws outstretched to receive their calling cards.

Alexandra was happy at Sandringham – flat Norfolk, she said, reminded her of Denmark, and on the country estate she was able to keep a vast pack of dogs of different breeds. She also enjoyed ice-skating on the ponds and – at first, anyway – joined in with the atmosphere of playfulness. On one occasion, when Mrs Gladstone (the mother of the boy who had informed on Bertie for kissing a German girl) was invited to Sandringham, Alexandra came to tuck her up in bed like a child.

The couple organized house parties that were as relaxed, if not quite as morally lax, as Napoléon and Eugénie's get-togethers. The indoor amusements at Sandringham usually took place away from the bedrooms, and consisted of raucous meals, long card games and music evenings, during which unlucky guests were sometimes subjected to the violin-playing of Bertie's younger brother Alfred, which Victoria's private secretary Henry Ponsonby once described as 'an appalling din'. Getting Alfred to perform sounds like one of Bertie's practical jokes.

But the aspect of Bertie's social life that was most obviously inspired by Napoléon III was the mix of people that he entertained, both in London and the country. In the face of the intense snobbery of France's hereditary aristocrats, the *parvenu* Napoléon had been obliged to invent a new social model for his court. By necessity, it was as much a meritocracy as it was an aristocracy. Bertie now began to play host not only to lords and ladies, but also to achievers from many different walks of life – his only requirement was that they were witty when describing their achievements.

The following is a description of Napoléon's guest lists at Fontainebleau written by a Belgian diplomat, Baron Beyens. It almost exactly matches Bertie's own taste in company: 'Official personages – civil and military, men of state and foreign diplomats, aristocrats from every country, artists, scientists, men and women of letters, as well as a selection of private individuals well known only because of their social situation.' The Baron went on: 'Sharing with them the pleasures of luxury and tasteful entertainment – was it not proof of a social mood free of pride and haughtiness, a simplicity of tone completely unlike the coldness of those sovereigns whose outdated sense of etiquette cuts them off from mere mortals?' He could have been describing Bertie's own mother.

These days, we would probably disagree with the Baron about Bertie's lack of haughtiness, and some of the entertainment as definitely less than tasteful (pouring brandy over defenceless social inferiors' heads, for example). But compared to Victoria, Bertie really was democratizing his social circle, and because of this he received plenty of 'advice' from snobs who wanted him to be haughtier.

Earl Spencer* warned the Prince of Wales that he

---

* This was the 5th Earl Spencer, a friend of the moralist William Gladstone. The current Earl, brother of the late Princess Diana, is the 9th.

should not attend a ball given by Lionel and Charlotte de Rothschild because 'they . . . hold their position from wealth and perhaps the accidental beauty of the first daughter they brought out'. But Bertie ignored this kind of thinly disguised English anti-Semitism. He had first met the Rothschilds in Paris, and always enjoyed being invited to the family's houses in England, where, according to French biographer Philippe Jullian, 'he could find the abundant luxury of the Second Empire, with its refined cuisine and international atmosphere'. No English snob was going to talk Bertie out of his French pleasures.

Another innovation imported by Bertie from France, Jullian claims, was a new tolerance towards women of less than spotless reputation. The Prince's London dinners were apparently the first occasions on which English upper-class ladies regularly agreed to share a table with actresses.

Duty obliged the Prince to invite some pompous guests who didn't quite fit in, but they were usually swallowed up in the crowd. And besides, European heads of state quickly came to realize that it was necessary to send two sorts of diplomats to London – crusty old ambassadors to please the Queen, and young, fun-loving aides who would get on with the heir to her throne.

Victoria knew what was going on, and watched Bertie's growing independence with a mixture of fear and disgust. She was sure that when she died, England would know 'nothing but misery' and that King Bertie would 'spend his life in one whirl of amusements'.

Her only consolation was that the young couple were at least providing her with plenty of descendants. Bertie and Alexandra's first son was born just less than ten months after their wedding, and was diplomatically named Albert Victor in accordance with grandmother's wishes. Only eighteen months later, a second son was born, the future King George V. In the space of seven years, Alexandra was to bear six children in all, though the last of them, Alexander, lived only twenty-four hours.

This fertility took its toll on the Princess. Quite simply, she couldn't provide babies while keeping up with Bertie's desire for a social life that resembled a perpetual motion machine. Alexandra tried her best – her second son was born at Marlborough House at midnight, after she and Bertie had attended an orchestral concert in town, on an evening when she was also scheduled to host a late supper party. Quite a *soirée* for a heavily pregnant woman.

Coupled with her frequent absences from the social calendar because of childbirth and lying-in, in early 1867 Alexandra suffered a serious attack of rheumatic fever that left her with a permanent limp. At only twenty-two, her wild dancing days were over. It was also becoming obvious that she suffered from a hereditary condition that causes progressive deafness – otosclerosis, abnormal bone growth in the inner ear. The problem was aggravated by pregnancy, so Alexandra was doomed to become less and less able to follow the lively banter that was the very *raison d'être* of Bertie's social gatherings (the ones at which his wife was present, anyway). Even more than physical beauty, it was wit that attracted Bertie to women, and Alexandra was growing into a silent wallflower, what Oscar Wilde would later compare to dining opposite a lily stuck in a wine glass. Not much of a conversation partner for a chatty young prince.

At the beginning, Bertie's sister Vicky had expressed a touching faith in the healing power of marriage over her errant brother: 'As he is too weak to keep from sin for virtue's sake, he will only keep out of it from other motives, and surely a wife will be the strongest?'

This was apparently the case for many Victorian men, even the upper classes who are so often depicted chasing chambermaids and making fools of themselves with actresses. In the mid-nineteenth century it was quite common for rich Englishmen to sow their wild oats with prostitutes and servants (and, more frequently than was admitted, with male friends, too) throughout their twenties and well into their thirties, finally marrying at a relatively late age and settling down to baby-making and approximate monogamy.

However, Bertie had been forced into marrying young, and now, as Alexandra spent more and more time with her children and her dogs, he looked elsewhere for amusement. Not that he waited until Alexandra was deaf and limping. In 1864, when he had been married less than two years, Victoria apparently knew that Bertie was still living the bachelor life: 'I often think her [Alexandra's] lot is not a happy one,' Victoria wrote. 'She is very fond of Bertie, though not blind.' This was presumably not a joke about Alexandra's deafness.

Prince Albert had married Victoria when he was twenty and never strayed from the path of saintliness, but Bertie seems to have adopted an entirely different attitude to marital respectability. He quickly turned Alexandra into what one of his biographers, Gordon Brook-Shepherd, describes as 'the most courteously but most implacably deceived royal lady of her time'. Crucially, though, he was forgetting the Empress Eugénie.

Bertie's attitude to marriage, like his attitude to so many other things in life, was Napoleonic. He once wrote to a friend, Sir Edward Filmer, referring to himself in French as an 'homme marié' who was perfectly justified in going off 'on a tack by himself'.* At the time, it was almost expected of a chic Parisian husband that he would live a life of barely concealed adultery. As we have seen, the Emperor's court was organized to make illicit couplings with single ladies or other men's wives almost unavoidable.

Of course, there was no gender equality in this arrangement, and the wives of the alpha males were required to be beyond reproach. The Empress Eugénie was known to be a model of virtue, and Bertie no doubt assumed his own wife would be the same. But being married to a model of virtue only made adultery easier.

When rumours of his frequent nocturnal outings to

---

* Bertie might well have been writing the letter out of guilt at having been seen 'spooning with Lady Filmer' (Sir Edward's wife, Mary) at Ascot Races in June 1867. In the nineteenth century, this verb meant behaving flirtatiously rather than lying down and snuggling up before or after sex.

London theatres, gentlemen's clubs (which were basically smoking and drinking dens with comfortable armchairs) and racy parties began to circulate, while poor Alexandra was left to fret about when her husband would get home, one of Bertie's friends, John Wodehouse, became seriously worried about the Prince's lifestyle. 'He is ruining his health as fast as he can – eats enormously . . . smokes incessantly, drinks continually "nips" of brandy; he has only to add, as I fear he will, gambling and whoring to become the rival of the "first gentleman in Europe".'

This 'gentleman' was, of course, a *monsieur* – Napoléon III.

5

SEX AND THE CITY OF LIGHT

~

'All he asked of the Parisians was that they should introduce
him to *Parisiennes*.'

Philippe Jullian, in his biography Edouard VII

I

It seems to have been Victoria herself who set Bertie off
on the next stage of his French voyage of sexual discovery.

In the autumn of 1864, when Bertie and Alexandra were
in Stockholm as part of a Scandinavian trip, Victoria fired
off a letter berating her son for staying at King Charles
XV of Sweden's castle. She was worried that Bertie would
set a precedent and that from now on, any minor royal
visiting England on holiday would expect free B & B at
Windsor. She wrote:

I was much surprised and annoyed at your accepting an

95

invitation at Stockholm in the Palace after it had been agreed upon and settled . . . that your visit should be a perfectly private one, and that you should live at the Legation [the British Embassy] or in an Hotel, the King being no relation of yours or Alix's.

Before leaving for Scandinavia, Bertie had made one of his frequent requests to squeeze in a quick stopover in France, but now Victoria seized the chance to frustrate him:

I am rather doubtful about your visit to Paris. If it does take place it must be on the *complete understanding* that it is in real incognito, which your other visits have not been, and that you stop at an Hotel, and do not lodge with the Emperor and Empress and do not accept an invitation to Compiègne and Fontainebleau, which *all* the Ministers strongly object to, as much as I do. The style of going on there being quite unfit for a young respectable Prince and Princess, like yourselves. Of course, you might accept a day's shooting at Compiègne and visit and drive with the Emperor and Empress, but nothing more.

In the end, Victoria went the whole hog and insisted that Bertie return home from Scandinavia via relatives in Germany and Belgium, but the seeds of a mighty oak were sown. *Merci* for you excellent idea, Mama, Bertie might well have said. Even without the excuse of a change of train when returning from an official visit abroad, it was perfectly possible – as Victoria herself had suggested, *n'est-ce pas?* – to slip across the Channel as a private citizen, check into a hotel using his old alias of Baron Renfrew, and enjoy Paris incognito. And if his mother objected to the 'style of going on' at the imperial palaces, there was a whole city to explore.

In any case, despite his mother's ability to dictate his travel plans, Bertie must have felt much freer now. He had done his dynastic duty, and even if Victoria reminded him constantly that a morally dissolute prince would make a bad king, his own kingship must have looked a long way off. His mother was not yet fifty, and she led such a sheltered life that there was little chance of her succumbing to fever and exhaustion as his father had done. If anything, she seemed to have been made ageless by widowhood, pickled in mourning.

And if Victoria alternated between refusing to let Bertie take part in anything political and shouting down his opinions about Denmark and Prussia, why shouldn't he amuse himself in a neutral country – France?

According to most sources, Bertie's first chance to go on a full-length French jaunt as a bachelor came in the spring of 1867, when he was invited by Napoléon III to attend that year's Exposition Universelle.

Bertie went to Paris with his brother Alfred, Duke of Edinburgh, who was two-and-a-half years younger and even more weak-willed than Bertie himself. Alfred, 'Affie' to his family, had a violent crush on Alexandra, and it is quite conceivable that Bertie might have taken him to France to show him that there were enough available women out there for him to stop pestering the Princess.

It wasn't a state visit, but Bertie and Affie appeared on

the VIPs' podium at the Exposition and attended a variety of official functions with other royals. Their sister Vicky's husband, Friedrich of Prussia, was there, as were Prince Oscar of Sweden, Prince Umberto of Italy and the Sultan of Turkey, amongst others. And in between functions and tours of the Expo grounds, the brothers used their spare time to explore the city itself. In fact, Bertie's trip to Paris was much like an archetypal husband's conference junket: Those endless dinners and parties will be *such* a bore, darling, and I'll miss you terribly, but it's all part of my job.

Parties there certainly were. Bertie and Affie weren't invited to all the imperial receptions because some of them were reserved for heads of state and crowned sovereigns. But they were the honorary hosts of a ball given at the British Embassy for 1,100 guests that was attended by Napoléon and Eugénie. Bertie opened the dancing with the Empress and, as one London journalist reported, 'was extremely talkative and gallant, and made himself so charming that one would almost think he was striving to win the hearts of all the ladies present'. The observant correspondent went on to write that:

> After dinner, there was a *cotillon* [a sort of square dance], and the Prince danced with the celebrated beauty the Marquise Georgina de Gallifet,* whom he had met in the

* This lady in her mid-thirties was one of Eugénie's *dames du palais*. She was bisexual, and famous for her string of male and female lovers. No wonder Bertie was so engrossed in conversation with her. Incidentally, she was also the wife of one of Bertie's closest French friends, Gaston de Gallifet.

garden and engaged to dance with him after a long conversation. The *cotillon* lasted nearly two hours, during which time the Prince talked incessantly with the Marquise, and it was observed that he could hardly resist the charms of the renowned Parisian beauty.

The tone for Bertie's trip was set.

Affie was less successful. The same journalist observed that 'he was very shy compared to his brother; and while the Prince of Wales made many a lady blush with the fire of his glance, the Duke of Edinburgh, if a lady only looked at him rather intently, instantly reddened with confusion.' Affie bowed out of the dancing and was later seen in the dining room, 'making a hearty meal of half a roast fowl and some sherry'. Still, it was early days, and the young Duke had come to Paris to learn.

Sadly, Napoléon was less available as a mentor than he had been on Bertie's previous visits because he was starting to suffer from serious health problems. In 1864, he had had an embarrassing heart attack while visiting his mistress, a young 'actress' called Marguerite Bellanger. The Emperor was also plagued by painful attacks of gout, acute haemorrhoids and agonizing bladder stones. He was in a temporary period of remission when Bertie arrived in Paris for the Expo, but even so Bertie found Napoléon a much-diminished man, and wrote to his mother that he looked 'ill and worn'.

If Victoria was relieved to hear this, she was mistaken, because Bertie was to prove himself more than capable of going it alone.

II

The Exposition wasn't all about partying, though. On his mother's advice, Bertie refused an invitation to spend his Sunday at the races in Chantilly, north of Paris – although he was seen 'accidentally' catching a glimpse of a race from a balcony while breakfasting at the Château de Chantilly. And he seems to have taken the official reason for his visit seriously, spending a lot of time touring the huge exhibition space on the site where the Eiffel Tower would be built a few decades later.

Since Bertie's first outing to a French Expo in 1855, technology had moved on, and there were plenty of innovations to see. Exhibits at the 1867 show included industrially produced false teeth, fishnet-making machines, refrigerators, tumble dryers, mechanized bread makers and deep-sea diving suits that were demonstrated in a 'human aquarium'.

In a detailed account of all the royal visits to Paris for the 1867 exhibition called *Les Souverains à Paris* the writer Adrien Marx praised Bertie's excellent attendance record – he was 'one of the princes seen most frequently at the Champs de Mars', and was observed letting himself be ushered patiently around all the stands and pavilions by exhibition guides.

The correspondent for an Australian* newspaper, the

---

* Australia has a free website of digitized newspapers dating back to 1803. In the nineteenth century, most of the international content was reprinted from English papers or written by on-the-spot correspondents. It's at http://trove.nla.gov.au and it's a wonderful resource.

Melbourne Argus, was a lot more sceptical, but expressed similar admiration: 'Both the Prince of Wales and the Duke of Edinburgh have done the exhibition pretty thoroughly, and if they take away with them, after their rapid pedestrian feats, any definite idea besides that of huge boredom, they are clever fellows.' The reporter was not surprised to catch Bertie taking time out from admiring machines and national costumes to puff a quiet cigar on the roof of the Chinese pavilion.

And it wasn't only the sheer number of exhibits that Bertie found tiring – apparently he was turning into one of the Expo's biggest attractions himself. Other visiting royals were not recognized by the French public, the Australian said, and he saw the King of Belgium wandering around the show being completely ignored, whereas Bertie was often mobbed: 'The other day, when the Princes were dining at the Russian restaurant, the windows and doors were perfectly lined with foreign ladies, flattening their noses with praiseworthy diligence, so as to note every mouthful that was eaten.'

And a lot was certainly eaten. Both the Australian reporter and Adrien Marx reveal the menu* for a private lunch given at the Expo, which consisted of:

The website invites readers to correct digitized text – some of the scanning is haphazard.

* A long menu like this did not imply that everyone ate everything. At larger functions, people would often be served from the bowl nearest to them, or if they were important enough, they would instruct the servants to give them a helping of their favourite dishes.

Hors d'œuvre and shrimps
Turbot *sauce hollandaise*
Fillet of beef Madeira with stuffed tomatoes
Lamb cutlet with peas
Sautéed chicken
Roast duckling
Salads
Asparagus
Soup
Strawberries, cherries, apricots.
Wines: Haut Sauternes, Saint-Julien.

Despite the hours that Bertie put in at the Expo, he was, of course, less fascinated by innovations in false-teeth design than by the huge changes that his favourite city had undergone since his earlier visit. By 1867, Napoléon III's plans for renovating his capital were well on the way to completion, and it must have looked to Bertie as if the new Paris had been specifically conceived for philandering.

This wasn't (it would be nice to think) the initial purpose of the massive urban regeneration that went on under Napoléon III and continued after his demise. By the 1850s, Paris had become an overcrowded, filthy and unhealthy city. Picture the Marais or the Latin Quarter today, with their narrow, winding streets and leaning medieval buildings, and take away the street sweepers, rubbish collectors, running water, sewage pipes, lampposts and laws. And then add in crowds of hungry Parisians and rats.

Sitting in the centre of all this squalor was the royal palace, the Palais des Tuileries, with its costume balls, gala dinners and priceless art collection. What pleasure-loving emperor wants his playground to be hemmed in by sick, embittered poor people, the same Parisians who had hacked* the *aristos* – or anyone perceived to be *aristo* – to death only a few decades earlier?

Consequently, as soon as Napoléon came to power, he set about doing to Paris what the Great Fire of 1666 had done to London – giving it a thorough clean-out. He had admired England's urban parks and tree-lined avenues when he was exiled there at various times in the 1830s and 1840s during France's first post-Bonaparte period. To achieve a similar result in his own capital he set about expropriating city neighbourhoods and carving a new road system through them – the boulevards. The biggest of these were the propeller-like group of avenues radiating out of the place de l'Opéra; the southern loop of the boulevard Saint-Germain through the Latin Quarter; and the great north–south avenue between the Gare de l'Est and Montparnasse, which had meant flattening most of the buildings on the île de la Cité except for a small parcel around Notre-Dame (even Napoléon was wary of the wrath of more omnipotent powers than himself).

Lined with theatres, cafés and boutiques, the Opéra's *grands boulevards* became instantly fashionable. In his book *Souvenirs de la Vie de Plaisir sous le Second Empire*, a former Parisian playboy called Gaston Jollivet remembers that he

---

* See the chapter on the French Revolution in *1,000 Years of Annoying the French*. The *aristos* and 'traitors' who survived to be guillotined were the lucky ones.

rarely left this area except to venture westwards along the Champs-Élysées and into the new residential areas beyond the Arc de Triomphe. He confesses that he 'knew as little of other neighbourhoods as though they were in Central Africa'. These were also to be Bertie's main hunting grounds during Napoléon III's reign.

To implement his plans, Napoléon chose Georges-Eugène Haussmann, a Parisian politician so ruthless that he famously demolished his own birthplace during the renovations. Napoléon entrusted Haussmann with a mission to 'aerate, unify and beautify the city'. This demand for unity is what gives much of Paris its image today: the six- or seven-storey apartment buildings with their sloping zinc roofs, balconies on the fifth floor and startlingly similar façades with almost identical rows of windows. Under Haussmann, the architects had no choice but to conform.

Social unity was also the goal. The well-off and well-dressed had been deserting the city's festering streets in droves, and now Napoléon wanted them back. The new *haussmannien* buildings all had shop space on the ground floor, and roomy apartments above, with a whole floor of specially built *chambres de bonne* – maids' rooms – at the top. The more elegant of these buildings often had two floors of servants' quarters as well as an *escalier de service* – service staircase – so that the wealthy occupants didn't even have to see deliveries being made or buckets being carried about. In Napoléon's new Paris, even the middle classes were meant to feel as though they were living in a palace. None of his Parisians were going to be calling for his head on a pole.

There were also health reasons for the renovation – the

new underground sewers meant that the days of Paris's cholera epidemics were at last over. And the improvements went far beyond the expanding boundaries of the capital – in 1840, for example, eight years before Napoléon came to power, there had been 500 kilometres of railway in France. By the end of his reign in 1870, there were 17,000, including Paris's new Petite Ceinture (Small Belt), the predecessor of the Métro, which ferried cargo and commuters around the edge of town, relieving congestion in the centre. And, by no means coincidentally, the railway extensions also included lines out to Napoléon's country châteaux in Fontainebleau and Compiègne and the fashionable racecourse at Chantilly.

So Napoléon was a genuine reformer with a desire to modernize his country and rival the economic exploits of England. But he was also a shameless hedonist who seems to have decided that industrial progress and urban renovation should be harnessed to give his France a superior *art de vivre* – more elegant people, smoother travel, fresher food and more beautiful homes. It was a French version of *Vorsprung durch Technik*, all of it geared towards creating an atmosphere of permanent seduction.

It has often been said that Napoléon's boulevards were designed to bring air and light to the city or to allow troops to circulate easily and quell rebellions. But this is not the whole truth – they were also places where Parisians could amble and ogle.

In the daytime, the broad, clean pavements were crowded with ladies on innocent shopping trips, the ideal prey for men on the prowl. The Parisian *monsieur*-about-town Gaston

Jollivet recalled that when he spotted a good-looking woman walking along the boulevard, he would quickly step ahead of her and then turn around to ask: 'Are you following me, madame?' If she stopped to talk, he could invite her to a café or offer to buy her a handkerchief or a pair of gloves from one of the newly opened *boutiques*. If she didn't take the bait, another would soon pass by.

Similarly, the new theatres and cafés were perfect places to entertain recently made acquaintances, or to meet up with lovers and ladies of the night, and there was now plenty of parking space where carriages could wait outside to whisk couples discreetly away.

The brothels didn't need to be hidden down dark medieval alleys any more, but if they were, the wider streets criss-crossing the city made it easier to reach them. A cab could take a group of roistering men within a few streets of the amoral slums, and they were much less likely to get their clothes and wallets confiscated before they'd had their fun. Napoléon was creating his 'City of Light',* but there were still plenty of shadows where lecherous men could satisfy their darker appetites.

On the fringes of the city, the new parks with their wide tree-lined alleys – the Bois de Boulogne and the Bois de Vincennes – were places where posh Parisians in open carriages could doff their hats to each other, or, like

* Paris's nickname, la Ville-Lumière, is said to have several origins, including its reputation for philosophical and scientific enlightenment in the seventeenth and eighteenth centuries, as well as Haussmann's new street lighting and the clearance of densely built medieval neighbourhoods.

Madame Bovary in Gustave Flaubert's 1857 novel of the same name, opt for a closed vehicle and indulge in some mobile lovemaking. Gaston Jollivet used to enjoy driving around the artificial lake in the Bois de Boulogne, watching people 'in a dizzying variety of carriages, big and small, seeing who was with whom, who was alone, who dared to show themselves with their lover, and – even more shocking – who ventured out with their own spouse'.

The memoirist Comte de Maugny summed up Napoléon III's new Paris well: 'Never was there more elegance,' he wrote in his *Souvenirs du Second Empire*, 'more desire to amuse oneself, more dazzling parties and more beautiful people.' For the young Bertie arriving in 1867, it was a city of endless opportunities.

The workers who had to create all this elegance by slaving for long hours on dangerous, heavily polluting machines might not have shared Bertie's enthusiasm, especially if they had been thrown out of their old apartment buildings because Haussmann decided to turn their neighbourhood into a park or a boulevard. But two sets of people were all in favour of the changes in Parisian society engineered by Napoléon III: first, there were the emerging *bourgeois* inhabitants of the *haussmannien* neighbourhoods, who were opening new shops and working in the burgeoning service industries; and then there was a new upper echelon, the *haute bourgeoisie*. Napoléon had instigated a very English system of financing his public works with private funds, thereby helping bankers, builders and industrialists to make immense fortunes. And thanks to his enforced lack of snobbery, these *nouveaux riches* could now rise to the very top of *la bonne société* instead of being looked down upon by the aristocrats. They could buy or build themselves a château or *hôtel particulier* (a mansion within Paris) and hold glittering receptions that would attract the *crème de la crème* of the city – including visiting royalty like Bertie.

During Napoléon III's Second Empire, Paris was awash with chic people, either aristocratic or able to act the part, with money and plenty of time to spend it. And the great thing for Bertie was that he was instantly a member of this club, with automatic privileges of rank. He was a popular member, too, because he was not only a prince but also a jovial, friendly young man who loved nothing more than joining in the fun and splashing cash and champagne about. Even better for Bertie, this generation of fun-lovers with whom he got on so well was interested in only one thing: sex.

III

This, at least, was the opinion of the novelist Émile Zola, a chronicler of his times who wrote a series of thematic novels that give a stark (if sometimes over-detailed) picture of France in the mid- and late-nineteenth century. Zola covered, for example, the worlds of art (*L'Oeuvre*), food (*Le Ventre de Paris*), crime (*La Bête Humaine*), mining (*Germinal*) and even shopping – his book *Au Bonheur des Dames* is set in one of Paris's new department stores.

Zola's novel about sex is *Nana*. This is a pet name derived from Anna, probably a reference to a notorious

actress/prostitute of the times called Anna Deslions, nick-
named the 'lioness of the boulevards'. She was famous
because of her affair with Napoléon III, her raven hair,
and what one French commentator discreetly called
'certain talents'. But the title of the novel is more than a
name-check. In modern French *une nana* is a general slang
term for a girl, but in Zola's day it meant a prostitute.*
The novel is as generic as that – it is the life of a typical
Parisian sex worker, albeit a high-class one who associates
with the moneyed members of Napoléon III's new *haute
bourgeoisie*. And in the fictional Nana's case, she even gets
to meet the real Bertie.

Zola's opinion of Napoléon's Paris was brutally direct.
He wrote in his preface to *Nana* that the novel described
'a whole society chasing ass. A pack of dogs behind a bitch
who is not in heat and laughs at the dogs following her.'†
The story was, he said, a 'poem of male desire, the great
lever that sets the world in motion'.

When talking about the sexual goings-on in mid-nineteenth
century Paris, it is important not to over-romanticize what

---

* The word *fille*, meaning girl or daughter, was also commonly used
to mean a prostitute. If you said, for example, that you had seen 'une
fille dans la rue' – a girl in the street – and wanted make it clear that
you weren't referring to a hooker, it was necessary to specify 'une
jeune fille', a young girl. Though how this should make things clearer
isn't completely obvious.

† In French: 'Toute une société se ruant sur le cul. Une meute derrière
une chienne, qui n'est pas en chaleur et qui se moque des chiens qui
la suivent.' *Cul* is a crude word for the backside and, like ass, a general
word for sex. *Se moquer* means both to mock something and not to
give a damn about it.

was essentially sex tourism, and pretty sordid behind its glamorous façade. But at the time it must have seemed to young Bertie that this was just the way Paris swung. The city was awash with registered, legal prostitutes, as well as an incalculable number of *insoumises* – a word that describes someone who refuses to bow to authority, as if the women were fighting for their right to prostitute themselves.

In her *Confessions*, Napoléon III's mistress Marguerite Bellanger said that during the Second Empire, the *insoumises* 'clogged the boulevards, the Champs-Élysées and the Bois de Boulogne. They filled the theatres, not only in the boxes but also on stage, where they paid to be exhibited. It was one big shop counter, a market for human flesh of varying freshness.'

And these unregistered, unofficial hookers were often much richer than we might think. A beautiful, ambitious woman could earn herself a fortune in a matter of months as wealthy men outbid each other for their favours. The real women who, like Nana, aroused and took merciless advantage of Parisians' desires, were collectively known as the *cocottes*. They usually came from poor backgrounds out in the provinces and, like Marguerite Bellanger, exploited their charms to climb up the socio-economic ladder – making sure to expose a well-turned calf at every rung. The most beautiful of them got themselves noticed as singers, dancers or actresses, using their on-stage performances to attract lovers of increasing wealth and prestige – Marguerite Bellanger started with an army lieutenant and ended up with Napoléon himself.

In his memoirs, Gaston Jollivet describes the typical *cocotte*'s complicated love life. She would, he says, have a principal lover, who would be known to the maids as 'Monsieur', and would probably be paying for the *cocotte*'s accommodation. Then there would be one passionate love affair – with a young, reckless nobleman, for example, who would be known as the *amant de cœur* (lover of the heart). The *cocotte* always made it brutally clear, though, that this *amant* would take second place whenever Monsieur wanted to exercise his rights. There would also be constant one-night stands and quickies, with suitors competing to put on shows of outlandish generosity in order to attract the lady's attention.

A letter written by one of the famous *cocottes*, Augustine Brohant, shows us how the system worked. She tells her lover: 'Dear friend, I was very touched by your intentions yesterday, and I am enchanted by your gift today. It is hard to express my gratitude for your kind attention to my self-respect. I don't love you more, but I love you better.' At least she was honest.

According to another anecdote, a notorious *cocotte* was with some men at a café when one of them sent a waiter out to buy a metre of silk so that he could write a poem on it for her. The next day, the woman probably had the verses washed off so that the costly material could be made into a blouse – for a *cocotte*, life was a battle for survival, a constant struggle to maintain a lavish lifestyle and justify her high prices.

The *cocottes*' servants would also be taking their cut. A good maid would earn generous tips from men wanting to know when her mistress would be home, for example, or for passing a message to the *cocotte*. The maid would also negotiate hefty commissions from the tradesmen supplying food for the frequent parties and all the clothes required to keep the *cocotte* looking fashionable and desirable. A clever maid could retire on her earnings from a *cocotte*'s career without having to sleep with all the men.

The most skilful of the *cocottes*, like the fictional Nana, were known as the *grandes horizontales* and would demand such high prices for their services and so many 'gifts' of money, jewellery and real estate that they would often drive their suitors to bankruptcy. Marguerite Bellanger tells us that: 'To cover us with gold – and I don't want to set myself above the flock because I was one of the better-paid sheep – sons would steal from fathers or take out ruinous debts, and cashiers would empty their cashboxes.' She used her status as the imperial bedfellow to attract countless other lovers, and earned herself a château, a lifelong pension and a comfortable future for her illegitimate son. She was such a well-known *cocotte* that she is name-checked in Zola's story as a public personage of the time.

Nana first appeared as a serial in the magazine *Le Voltaire* starting in 1879, and was published as a complete story in 1880, but the plot begins in April 1867, and the characters are based on real people, including Bertie and some of the actresses he consorted with in Paris that year. The character of the heroine is said to be in large part a portrait of the most notorious *cocotte* of them all, Hortense Schneider, whose long list of royal lovers earned her the title 'le Passage des Princes'. It was a highly descriptive nickname: the real Passage des Princes was one of the tunnel-like shopping arcades that were being built along the new boulevards.

And if a French person says they are 'de passage', it means they are just passing through. Hortense was clearly quite an energetic lady.*

A police report of the time began its file on Hortense: 'She arrived in Paris with a pair of clogs and a dress made of canvas. The women Martin and Desfontaines launched her and introduced her to her first lovers.' It was a typical start to a *cocotte*'s career. In Zola's novel, we get to see exactly how hard a lower-class girl worked to elevate herself socially, and how enormous the rewards were. Nana, like all the *cocottes*, has a full diary of sexual partners – the official gentleman friend who has provided her with a chic apartment, as well as the numerous pretenders to his throne and frequent spur-of-the-moment clients. Zola shows her spending the night with a shop-owner who gets up early to be home at eight o'clock. A young nobleman is watching out for him to leave, and slides into the warm bed with Nana, where he stays until ten o'clock, when he in turn has to leave on business. Another time, an old lady who acts as Nana's procurer brings a message – does she want to make twenty *louis*† at three o'clock this afternoon? *Oui*, Nana says, just give her the man's address and she'll be

---

* In fairness to Hortense, it is said that her 'Passage des Princes' nickname was coined by a jealous rival, another singer called Léa Silly.

† A *louis* was a name commonly given to the *napoléon*, a twenty-franc gold coin. To give an idea of the value of a *louis*, one of the workers laying paving stones on Napoléon's boulevards might be earning about 4 francs a day, a fifth of a *louis*, so sex with Nana would have cost him about a hundred days' wages. Not that she would have entertained anyone with dirt under their fingernails.

there. Meanwhile Nana spends most evenings appearing in a risqué play, and often brings home one or more of the men who flock backstage to proposition her. Her dream in life, she confides, is to be able to spend one night, just one night, alone in bed. Though of course she will make time for an English prince.

Zola takes cruel pleasure in satirizing the twisted morality of the times. Although Nana entertains a horde of married clients, she is shocked when she finds out that one of them is a *cocu* – meaning that his wife has a lover. Nana can't believe it: 'It's too dirty!' she says. 'They've always disgusted me, those *cocus*.' Her hypocrisy is meant to be ironic, but at the same time it was almost certainly a view shared sincerely by all of her lovers.

The most vivid sections of the novel are Zola's descriptions of the raw sexuality surrounding Nana's performances, including the one witnessed by Bertie. Her stage skills don't extend much beyond hamming a few clichéd lines and squawking a song, but appearing naked in a see-through costume is something that she does rather well, and the sight of her body drives men wild. Zola describes the scene in front of the theatre before a performance where there is 'a growing clamour, a buzz of voices calling for Nana, demanding Nana, in one of those bestial moods of brutal sensuality that grip a crowd'.

Inside, the theatre-goers are a typical Second Empire mix, Zola says: 'All of Paris was there, the Paris of literature, finance and pleasure, lots of journalists, a few writers, financiers, more *filles* [prostitutes] than honest women; a singularly mixed crowd made up of all sorts, all of them

Victoria and Albert in 1854, apparently traumatised at the idea of visiting Napoléon III the following year.

Bertie as a teenager, enduring his tyrannical education. Note the books on the table, resolutely closed.

Over: Empress Eugénie of France (fourth from left) and her 'dames du palais'. Bertie met these glamorous ladies in 1855.

Emperor Napoléon III of France, shameless hedonist and Bertie's male role model. The teenaged Prince told him: 'You have a very beautiful country. I would like to be your son.'

Bertie in 1865, presumably trying to convince his mother that he was studious.

By his early 20s, France had turned the shy, repressed youth into a true Parisian playboy.

Above: Unlike his own father, Bertie was an affectionate parent. His only failing – not to prepare Prince George (top left, in a dress) for the throne.

Opposite: Queen Alexandra, 'the most courteously but most implacably deceived royal lady of her time'.

Over: Bertie aged about 28, the most fashionable man in Paris, friend and lover of aristocrats, actresses and famous prostitutes.

tarnished by vice.' And appearing amongst them very soon will be Bertie.

Nana comes on stage and releases a musk of pure sexuality. She can't sing or dance, but it doesn't matter. When she realizes that she's about to miss a high note, she simply covers it up with a wiggle of the hips and a thrust of her cleavage, earning herself a storm of applause. Watching Nana's character in the play, Venus, seduce Mars, 'the audience was possessed, and every man was her slave. She made them go into a rut, like a crazed animal, and it spread throughout the theatre. Her every movement breathed desire into them, her little finger was mistress of their flesh.'

The news of Nana's sexual powers inevitably reaches Bertie's ears, and she learns that he has booked the best seat in the house – in those days, there were boxes on each side of the stage so that the richest customers could sit mere inches above the actresses, who would be looking them almost directly in the eyes as they performed. And Bertie is not the only dignitary expected – the manager is hoping for the Shah of Persia and maybe even the German Chancellor, Otto von Bismarck. But it is the Englishman who arouses the highest expectations.

Zola always did extensive research for his novels, and in the case of *Nana*, some of this consisted of talking to people who had been to see Hortense Schneider at the theatre and who had witnessed Bertie in action there. So when the 'Prince of Scotland' (a disguise as thin as Nana's costume) finally arrives to see one of the actress's performances, we can be sure that it is a pretty faithful portrait of the real Bertie as he was perceived by the Parisians.

The most remarkable thing about Bertie's appearance in the novel is how comfortably he adopts his role as top dog in the Parisian pack of sexual predators. He comes to see Nana's show three times in a single week, and on the third night, he and a couple of French aristocrats, including the Comte de Muffat, a previously moralistic man who is now under Nana's spell, are shown into her dressing room unannounced. She is half-naked and hides behind a screen, though not before the visitors have been treated to a tantalizing glimpse of her charms. The theatre manager tells her to come out: 'It's His Highness,' he says, 'don't be so childish. *Mon dieu*, these men know very well how a woman is put together. They won't eat you.'

'Don't be so sure,' Bertie quips in fluent French, and everyone breaks out in forced laughter as the manager congratulates him on his 'perfectly Parisian wit'.

So Nana emerges from hiding, her breasts barely covered by a low-cut corset. She is only eighteen, but knows how to toy with the men and apologizes for her undressed state, 'her arms naked, her shoulders naked, her nipples exposed, in the adorable blond fleshiness of youth'.

Bertie manages another gallant riposte: 'I'm the one who should apologize, madam. I couldn't resist the temptation to come and compliment you.'

More young men arrive with champagne (and this is only the interval – Nana has to go back on stage in a few minutes) so that the dressing room is soon crammed with people toasting the semi-naked young performer. Zola comments that: 'No one found this strange mix of people laughable – this real prince, heir to a throne, who was drinking Champagne with a ham actress, at ease in this . . . charade of royalty, amongst dressers and whores, stage hands and procurers of women.'

Bertie teases the lovelorn Comte de Muffat with an Anglo–French jibe: 'You don't pay enough attention to your pretty women. We'll steal them all.' And the purpose of his visit to the theatre, and to Paris itself, was just that.

Bertie stays to enjoy the view as Nana's dresser helps her into her flimsy, see-through tunic, and Zola notes that: 'With half-closed eyes, his [Bertie's] connoisseur's gaze followed the swollen contours of her chest.' Bertie asks to watch the rest of the show from the wings, and there, as Nana waits to go on, a fur coat protecting her against the draught, he pounces. Ushering her to one side, 'the Prince spoke to Nana, still coveting her with his half-closed eyes' and 'without looking at him, she smiled and nodded her agreement'. The deal has been done. She slips off her fur coat and walks on stage, practically naked.

After the show, Nana's admirers follow her out of the theatre and crowd excitedly around the stage door, and then one of them, the frustrated Comte, suddenly notices that she has disappeared. 'His Highness had calmly taken her into his carriage.' The other men are annoyed, but they're not really jealous of Bertie. This was the natural order of things. Nana was there to be shared, and she went to the highest payer or the highest man in the social hier-archy, in this case the English Prince. Even compared to these sophisticated Parisians, Bertie made winning the game of seduction look effortless.

IV

Zola might have painted an accurate picture of Bertie (or of people's memories of him, anyway), but he was slightly unfair to the real Hortense Schneider. For a start, she was in her mid-thirties when she met Bertie, whereas Nana is still in her teens. Hortense was also a much better singer than Nana, a soprano who became the face and voice (not to mention the curvaceous figure) of German-born Jacques Offenbach's operettas in Paris. In describing the amateurish acting performances, Zola seems to have been more inspired by a *cocotte* called Méry Laurent, who, like Nana, was eighteen in 1867, and who made her name as Venus in Offenbach's hit opera *La Belle Hélène*, during which she appeared naked in a golden shell, a plump version of Botticelli's painting of the same subject.

Hortense Schneider, on the other hand, was a professional performer. A journalist who heard her sing wrote that she had a voice that Auber (a fashionable composer) 'went to listen to whenever he felt the need to give his ears a delightful washing out'. It sounds like a French medical treatment but was definitely intended as a compliment.

In 1867, Hortense was starring in *La Grande-Duchesse de Gérolstein*, a satire by Offenbach of a minor German duchy where the head of state, the Grand Duchess, has a fetish for men in uniform and falls for a common soldier called Fritz. She appoints him head of her army, outranking its previous leader, the aptly named Général Boum. The show, with its apparent anti-Prussian message, was the hit of the season, and on 15 May 1867, Bertie came to see it

118

at the Théâtre des Variétés on the boulevard Montmartre. Like everyone else in Paris, he seems to have fallen instantly under Hortense's spell.

In describing the voluptuous Nana, Zola certainly wasn't exaggerating the real Hortense's effect on men. The Parisian journalist who quoted the above compliment about her voice also said that she possessed 'the flesh of a Rubens, a winning smile and flirtatious eyes, a combination which would have driven an archbishop to damnation'.

A young cabaret singer, Paulus, remembered Hortense as:

. . . the triumphant figure of the Second Empire. Her court was as popular as that at the Tuileries [Napoléon and Eugénie's Parisian palace], but more amusing. Any sovereign visiting Paris rushed to her side as soon as they had paid their official respects, to beg the beautiful star for a smile . . . and the rest. And her heart was as open to visitors as her house.

Amongst Hortense's admirers and supposed lovers were Napoléon III, Tsar Alexander II of Russia, Prince Ludwig of Bavaria, King Luís I of Portugal, Emperor Franz Joseph of Austria and Bertie. If she had been a spy or a diplomat, Hortense Schneider could have ended war in Europe for the whole of the nineteenth century.

In short, in 1867 Hortense was the unrivalled female star of the Paris stage, and having her as a notch on his bedpost was a major coup for Bertie – a more modern equivalent would be a young English prince going to

Hollywood and squiring Scarlett Johannson or (if we want to get really modern) Brad Pitt.

During his visit to the 1867 Exposition Universelle, Bertie seems to have done exactly what the journalist Paulus described – he followed up his *bonjour* to the imperial couple with a lusty *bonsoir* to Hortense – and apparently he kept up the relationship for some time. Bertie's biographer Christopher Hibbert calls Hortense the Prince's 'favourite companion' of 1868, even though at the same time she was carrying on a long-term affair with the Viceroy of Egypt, Isma'il the Magnificent (a name of his own choosing, no doubt), whom she had met when he came to Paris for the Exposition, and whom she visited in Egypt the following year. Like the fictional Nana, Hortense Schneider was a lady who managed her love affairs with the skill of a theatrical agent, which explains how she was able to quit public life in her forties and live out a long retirement on her earnings, theatrical and otherwise.

V

In 1867, Bertie also found time to enjoy the company of another notorious *Parisienne*, Giulia Beneni Barucci, the self-styled 'number-one whore in Paris'. Known as La Barucci, this sultry Italian who spoke unashamedly bad French was one of the best-known of the top-tier courtesans, the *grandes horizontales*, and by the age of thirty she had earned enough selling her services to buy herself a mansion on the Champs-Élysées. She was living just across the road from one of her colleagues, La Païva, who had started her career sleeping with English lords in London in the 1840s, and now held chic society *soirées*, one of which Bertie apparently attended during his trip to the Exposition.

Today, when we look at photographs of these women, we might be forgiven for considering them dowdy and unattractive, with their lank, pre-shampoo hair parted grimly in the middle and their dresses that hid their lower body behind a firewall of billowing cloth. There is a photo of La Barucci in which she doesn't even have uncovered shoulders, and seems to be dressed for a funeral. But tastes were very different in the mid-nineteenth century, and the men were, if anything, even less alluring, with their comb-down haircuts, straggly beards and cigar breath.

A contemporary of La Barucci's gives a description that explains why Bertie was so keen to meet her. She had, the playboy Comte de Maugny wrote:

> . . . large dark eyes, penetrating and hard but languorous at the same time; wide nostrils that quivered like those of a thoroughbred race horse; a lascivious mouth, protuberant breasts, a long, vibrant throat, a curvaceous body that was statuesque from head to foot, with a sweeping waistline; and she was taller than average, possessing the grace of a queen . . .

You can almost hear Maugny throwing down his pen and leaping on the woman.

There is a famous anecdote about Bertie's first meeting with La Barucci in 1867. He and his brother Affie were introduced to her by a French duke, Agénor Gramont, a favourite of Napoléon III and an infamous philanderer who, incredible as it may sound, had previously been France's Ambassador to the Vatican.

Apparently, Gramont summoned La Barucci to meet the visiting English princes, and was annoyed when she turned up forty-five minutes late (although Bertie himself was probably used to waiting for ladies, given his wife's notorious lack of punctuality). To excuse herself, as soon as she arrived La Barucci hoisted up her dress to show everyone that she hadn't wasted those forty-five minutes choosing underwear. Beneath her layers of crinoline, she was completely naked.

Strangely, Gramont seems to have thought that the meeting didn't go well, although Bertie himself must have been delighted with her no-nonsense approach. When the French duke reprimanded La Barucci, she famously replied: 'But you told me to behave properly with His Highness. I showed him the best I have, and it was free.' It was the kind of story that would have echoed around Paris's theatre corridors and cafés, enhancing the *Italienne*'s reputation and, of course, attracting even more high-paying customers. As for Bertie, he was already on her list.

Foolishly though, he let things go beyond the realms of the saucy anecdote and left behind written proof of his dalliances with the Italian prostitute. After La Barucci died of tuberculosis in 1871, her impoverished brother threatened to sell Bertie's intimate letters at auction in Paris or make sure they were sent to London to cause a scandal there. Bertie dispatched a negotiator to France, and considered having the brother arrested, but finally paid 6,000 francs (five or six years' wages for a Parisian worker) for twenty letters, most of which he had thoughtlessly signed 'A.E.'. Still a relatively new player of the game of adultery, Bertie had apparently not realized that what happened in Paris had to stay in Paris.

In his defence, this was Bertie's first full excursion into the swampy moral territory of Parisian adultery. It was not surprising that he stumbled into a few patches of quicksand. Many Frenchmen, like Nana's helpless lovers, were no more cautious, and often got themselves entrapped in the depths of the *demi-monde*, the 'half-world' that was Paris's soft but treacherous underbelly.

And apart from his bad habit of signing letters to prostitutes, Bertie seems to have learnt well from his first full Parisian experience. According to French writers of the time, during his several visits in the late 1860s, he became a semi-permanent fixture about the place, building up a catalogue of regular haunts, many of which were fashionable simply because he went there.

In old age, a Frenchman called James de Chambrier looked back on Napoléon III's Paris and called Bertie 'ce Parisien de Londres' (this Parisian from London). 'We saw him passing by,' Chambrier recalls in his book, *La Cour et la Société du Second Empire*, 'lively and cheerful . . . everyone in Paris knew his handshake, his frank eyes, his handsome smile . . . Skilful with words, the pen* and cards, he created solid friendships with people of all backgrounds.' Bertie's

---

* Chambrier was probably talking about flirtatious messages and thank-you notes rather than essays on French society.

greatest quality in Parisians' eyes was, according to Chambrier, that he was 'completely free of austerity, and not at all fond of his mother's puritanism'. Which was lucky, given the kind of Parisian places that Bertie frequented in those last heady years of Napoléon III's empire.

6

PAINTING THE TOWN *ROUGE*

❧

'As long as Parisians are having fun, the government can sleep soundly.'

William Reymond, French theatre critic

I

When Bertie came to Paris in the spring of 1867, he and his brother stayed at the British Embassy, but on other occasions he would behave much like any wealthy tourist. Accompanied by just an equerry or one of his roistering London friends like old Etonian Charles Wynn-Carrington, he would take up residency at his favourite hotel, the Bristol* on the place Vendôme, and ask for the

---

* Now called the Hôtel de Vendôme, and not to be confused with the current hotel Le Bristol just down the road from the French presidential palace in the rue du Faubourg Saint-Honoré.

guest list in case he knew anyone else staying there. Especially if she was female.

This done, the Prince would then check the *Courrier des Théâtres* – the listings magazine – and choose the play, opera or musical he wanted to see that evening. Naturally, he had no problem getting tickets, even for the biggest box-office hit, unlike Parisians today who have to book months ahead for any popular show.

The theatre was *the* place to go in Napoléon III's Paris. The city's new architecture, with its chic apartment buildings replacing the old tumbledown medieval houses, attracted hordes of middle-class migrants into town, and all of them wanted entertainment.

Whole new city squares were constructed around theatres – Châtelet, for example, with its face-to-face Théâtre Lyrique and Théâtre Impérial, both completed in 1862; the now-defunct Théâtre de la Gaîté, built in the same year just north of Châtelet; and, grandest of all, Napoléon's new opera house, the Opéra Garnier, with staircases worthy of a château and a *grand foyer* that looks more like a palace ballroom.

The design of the new Opéra, which dominates the whole area of the city as much today as it ever did, was so over the top that the Empress Eugénie herself got confused when she saw the plans.

'What is this style?' she asked. 'It's not Greek, it's not Louis XV, it's not Louis XVI.'

'It's Napoléon III,' the young architect Charles Garnier replied.

Napoléon was delighted. 'Don't worry,' he reportedly whispered to Garnier, 'she doesn't know what she's talking about.' The most important thing was that the building should stand out, and that it certainly did, with its huge letters 'N' for Napoléon sculpted along the façade.

More than a dozen theatres sprang up along the boulevards, most of them sumptuously decorated. The foyers and corridors, with their frescoes, sculptures and immense mirrors, were as much performance spaces as the stage itself. The theatres were places where Parisians went both to see plays and to be seen at play.

Bertie was a frequent visitor to the city's new venues, though according to an Irish journalist of the time, Justin McCarthy, he had very strict ideas about the kind of things that should and should not happen on a stage: he had no taste for 'high art' and preferred 'little theatres where vivacious blondes display their unconcealed attractions'. Poetic dialogue did not seem to be top of Bertie's list of priorities.

The most fashionable form of theatre of the day was vaudeville. We think of this as a nineteenth-century invention, but it had been a popular genre in France for centuries before it came into its own in Napoléon III's Paris. Originally the name vaudeville described light-hearted, often satirical songs, like those written by a fifteenth-century Norman poet, Olivier Basselin, who came from the Vaux-de-Vire – the Vire valleys. By Napoléon III's time, these had evolved into musical comedies featuring catchy new songs and farcical plots based on misunderstandings and barely credible coincidences. The French playwright Etienne Jouy, who wrote the libretto for Rossini's opera *William Tell*, scorned vaudeville as 'looking hard for puns and usually making too much of them' – though this would have been perfect entertainment for a conversationalist with a short attention span like Bertie.

Along with the only slightly more highbrow *opéras comiques*, vaudeville plays were quite simply a good night out, with songs that you might still be whistling as you strolled or drove away along the boulevard after the show. And we shouldn't forget that half of the enjoyment for Bertie was the idea that he might sleep with the star of the play or an attractive audience member. As one French observer put it, Bertie 'understood what theatre was about'. If he didn't like a show, he could simply walk around inside the building 'without being distracted by what was on stage'.

Bertie wasn't alone in this – fashionable Parisian males didn't consider the *raison d'être* of the theatre to be the plays and operas advertised on the posters outside. Gaston Jollivet tells us that 'in the late afternoon, men would drift towards the opera house in the rue Le Peletier, where the dancers were coming out of rehearsals'. And later, at the performance, 'many men would miss the second act if they had met up with a lover'. It needed a very special performance on stage to hold a man's attention.

We have already seen Bertie in action with Hortense Schneider at the Théâtre des Variétés, and he made similar appearances at a host of other Parisian theatres. One of his favourites was the Théâtre du Gymnase on the boulevard de Bonne Nouvelle, which, fortunately for Bertie, had made a U-turn in its choice of repertoire to fit in with the moral climate of Napoléon III's régime. Previously known for its edifying dramas, it switched over to more populist plays featuring what one commentator called 'compromising situations, turpitude and calculated effrontery'. Exactly Bertie's type of show. And it was a small theatre, with boxes where spectators could sit on a level with the stage. Bertie didn't even need to go backstage – the actresses could step directly on to his lap.

Another of his evening haunts was the Théâtre du Vaudeville, which relocated in the 1860s, moving a kilometre or so from the place de La Bourse to a brand-new building on the boulevard des Capucines at Opéra.* The Vaudeville troupe was famous for having put on the first stage version of Alexandre Dumas the younger's novel *La Dame aux Camélias*, the highly topical tale of a rich *cocotte* who falls in love with a young bourgeois man and gives up her amoral lifestyle (and all her generous clients) for him. It's a sincere love story, but just to underline to middle-class audiences that a tainted woman can never change her spots, the former *cocotte* heroine, Marguerite, has tuberculosis and wastes away, coughing increasingly large blood-spots into her lace handkerchiefs.

In the mid-1860s, the story would have been given extra poignancy because, coincidentally, Marguerite was the name of Napoléon III's official mistress, a practising *cocotte*. In any case, *La Dame aux Camélias* was a huge hit when it opened in 1852, and is said to be the first play in Paris ever to have a run of more than a hundred performances. Bertie almost certainly saw a version of the show, especially because later in the century, the role of Marguerite was

---

* This building still exists and is now a rather elegant multi-screen cinema.

played by one of his mistresses, Sarah Bernhardt (of whom much more later).

The goings-on in Paris's theatres are vividly described by the retired but unashamed playboy the Comte de Maugny in his memoirs, *Souvenirs du Second Empire*. He looks back fondly on riotous evenings in the late 1860s spent watching the Italian opera troupe Les Italiens who performed regularly at the Odéon theatre, where Bertie was known to go. Maugny tells us that the Odéon had large, convivial dressing rooms where you could sit and chat (meaning, of course, arrange dates with the performers), and that sometimes the female singers would swoop out into the front row to choose a willing suitor.

When a cast was particularly good-looking, Maugny says that the front rows would be booked by members of gentlemen's clubs who would bombard the stage with offers of supper after curtain-down. The ballet was one of their favourite targets. On one occasion, Maugny notes, fifty or so members of the Jockey Club (one of several Paris clubs that Bertie belonged to) 'occupied the front seven rows, and dominated the room, providing the dancers with their protectors'. Apparently young ballet dancers needed protection from predatory males by other predatory males.

The Jockey Club was so influential in the world of Parisian theatre that it was not the done thing for an opera director to stage a ballet scene in the first act – club members were notorious for arriving late at performances, and did not want to miss the sight of so many short skirts on stage. In Napoléon III's Paris, it was therefore de rigueur to bring out the full company of dancers in Act 2. It is even said that one opera failed because the director defied the Jockey Club and put his ballet in the first act, provoking a boycott by the playboy set. This all sounds very frivolous, but the attitude amongst the rich, aristocratic young men of Paris that the city belonged to them and should run to their timetable would have grave consequences when anarchy broke out at the end of Napoléon III's reign.

Sometimes the posh male members of the audience even invaded the stage. One of Bertie's French biographers, André Maurois, describes how, during performances of *Fédora*, a melodrama written for Sarah Bernhardt by Victorien Sardou, the actress would allow gentlemen admirers to take part in the action. 'At the end of one act, [she] wept by the deathbed of a murdered prince. Many Parisians enjoyed playing, for one night only, this silent, invisible role. And the Prince took his turn.' Anything, it seems, to liven up an over-serious play.

André Maurois tells another story that illustrates how Bertie would let nothing come between him and a night at the Opéra.

Once, in Paris, he was just about to leave for the theatre with a few friends when news arrived that a distant royal relative had died. His friends looked at each other, clearly disappointed that their evening was going to be spoilt.

One of them dared to ask, 'What shall we do?'

The Prince thought for a moment and came up with the answer: 'We'll put on black cufflinks and go to the play.'

II

Even the lightest opera or vaudeville play was heavyweight compared to the entertainment at other bastions of Paris's nightlife: the *café-concerts*. They had started out in the mid-1850s as places where classical actresses might come and declaim monologues from Racine or Corneille. But they quickly evolved a mixed, crowd-pleasing repertoire of what one French specialist has described as 'short comic items, vaudeville scenes, impressions, excerpts from operettas, as well as popular songs that could be naïve, suggestive, erotic or just plain anatomical'.

Famous venues like the Moulin Rouge and the Folies Bergère would come into their own later in the nineteenth century, after the painters and poets of Montmartre had made their hangouts in northern Paris more fashionable.* But in Napoléon III's Paris of the 1860s, the *café-concerts* in 'safer' areas around the Champs-Élysées, Opéra and the *grands boulevards* were already popular with satin-cloaked night owls like Bertie.

The Café des Ambassadeurs and its twin, the Alcazar d'Été, were smart night spots where risqué singers and flirtatious dancers would perform for the *bourgeois*. These two *café-concerts* were set in almost identical buildings, a cross between a hunting lodge and a Greek temple, in the gardens along the Champs-Élysées. The Ambassadeurs was one of Bertie's favourites, conveniently situated just around the corner from his hotel. Edgar Degas's painting

* See Chapter 11.

Le Café-Concert aux Ambassadeurs gives an idea of the atmosphere that Bertie must have enjoyed there. Amidst Greek columns and a leafy décor, four women in brightly coloured, low-cut dresses are on stage. One, in scarlet, leans out into the audience as she sings, her right hand provocatively on her jutting hip, her left pointing at someone in the crowd, perhaps to aim a risqué line at an admirer. Another performer, in pastel blue, sits and gazes demurely over her fan, possibly to make eye contact with a rich member of the audience who has made it clear that he would be interested in some *après*-action. Degas gives us a close-up on the audience, too – a man sporting a floppy moustache and a top hat is apparently accompanied by three women, at least two of whom seem more interested in him than the show – reminding him, no doubt, that he is spoken for. At least for tonight.

In the 1860s Bertie watched and 'got to know' a star of the Alcazar d'Été, a singer called Thérésa. And when Bertie 'got to know' a female Parisian artiste, it didn't usually mean that they met after the show to swap *boeuf bourguignon* recipes. Thérésa, whose real name was Emma Valladon, was famous for songs that combined bawdy lyrics with yodelling. These songs, known then as *tyroliennes*, were so fashionable that Thérésa was invited to perform for Napoléon III in person. It's easy to understand why the Emperor would enjoy lines like these:

Bastien talks of marriage, but marriage demands reflexion,
The same man every night in bed – a very strange
invention.

Though given the Emperor's interpretation of his own wedding vows, the Empress Eugénie might have found the song less amusing.

Thérésa's rise to fame was a fairly typical one. She was a simple country girl from Normandy who came to Paris to work in clothes sweatshops when she was only twelve, and was fired because she spent too much time singing in bars and taking bit parts in theatres. After doing the rounds of low-paying *café-concerts*, in 1863 she found her yodelling voice and suddenly had producers outbidding each other for her services. She even published her autobiography – *Mémoires de Thérèsa, Écrits par Elle-même* (*Thérésa's Mémoirs, Written by Herself*) – though unfortunately for us it came out in 1865, before Bertie's first outings to the *café-concert*. By the time he saw Thérésa in the late 1860s she had become even more successful and was earning 1,500 francs a month, probably about 500 times her wages as a teenage seamstress.

In her autobiography, which is well enough written to suggest that Thérésa might have had a little help with the grammar and spelling (unlike modern celebrities, of course), she tells a typical hard-luck story of battling her way to the top. She hints at other singers taking immoral short cuts to fame and fortune, but assures her dear readers that she preferred to struggle honestly to pay her rent. She even describes a scene in which a bailiff lets her off her debts in exchange for a song. Perhaps it's just modern cynicism that makes this sound like a blatant euphemism.

In any case, a make-up seller tells Thérésa that she is 'une idiote'. She should be more like 'petite L****' who 'in the last six months has gobbled up a baron and two viscounts, and now she's tucking into a duke!' Thérésa insists that she's going to make it on the strength of her singing alone, although if we are to believe the rumours, within a couple of years she would be carving herself choice morsels of French emperor and English prince.

Judging by her photos, Thérésa was not what you would describe as a beauty, even in those plumper times. Degas painted her on stage in a picture called *La Chanson du Chien*, and did nothing to romanticize her huge biceps and manly jaw. Neither, apparently, did Thérésa herself, because one of the reasons for her popularity was that she was giving her upper-crust audiences a caricature of the crude, low-class *Parisienne*, combining a powerful voice with lewd gestures and meaningful winks. One French journalist who saw Thérésa said that she had a 'marvellous frankness and an infectious good humour that was incomparable'. He also pointed out, defending the singer against accusations that she represented all that was bad about Napoléon III's Paris, that she had little choice: she was obliged to play to 'the bad taste of an unhealthy period when society was rotten from the top down'.

III

Before and after the theatre, chic Parisians including Bertie and his friends would crowd into the cafés along the boulevards. Under Napoléon III, going out to dinner and supper had become more fashionable than ever, and new venues were constantly springing up.

One innovation that had been brought about by the invention of the boulevard was the café terrace. There was now space in the street to set up tables, and plenty of reasons to people-watch. Men would loaf at strategic vantage points like the Café de la Paix on the corner of the place de l'Opéra and admire what one observer poetically called 'the little feet that went clop, clop, clop'. And he wasn't talking about Shetland ponies.

Strange as it may sound, another new invention of the new boulevard eateries was the menu. Only now did it become common practice for Parisian restaurants and cafés to print a list of dishes and let their customers come in off the street and choose. The old-fashioned restaurants, like the ones clustered around the Palais-Royal, had always insisted that clients pre-order dinner the previous day. Yet another reason for diners to migrate outside the old city centre and up to the boulevards, where chic new establishments like the Café Anglais and the Maison d'Or – two of Bertie's favourite hangouts – were soon doing a roaring trade.

The menus weren't as varied as they are today. In the 1860s, the Café Anglais would propose only a soup, one fish course, one roast meat, one vegetable and a chocolate mousse. But then people didn't really go there for the food – they were more interested in the other customers.

The Café Anglais, on a corner of the boulevard des Italiens, was already a legendary meeting-place when Bertie began going there. In 1866, it had earned a mention in Offenbach's operetta *La Vie Parisienne*. The librettists Meilhac and Halévy wrote that it was:

The place that mothers fear,
That terrible place where under-age sons
Spend the money earned by their fathers,
And fritter away the dowry of their sisters.

They describe:

Bursts of laughter, champagne-fuelled rows,
People fighting over here, dancing over there,
While the creaking piano plays popular songs
To accompany strange debauchery.

The debauchery, in which Bertie was apparently an enthusiastic participant, went on mainly in the upstairs rooms. Unlike Paris's boulevard cafés today, the Café Anglais occupied the whole of a five-storey building. Downstairs was the public room, the *salle commune*. This was the place for business lunches or where married ladies could be seen without being frowned upon. The upper floors were reached via a side entrance and a hidden staircase. Respectable *dames* would never go upstairs for fear of bumping into prostitutes or their husbands. Up there were the *cabinets privés* – private lounges – where illicit gatherings large and small would go on, served by discreet waiters.

Though not all the waiters could be trusted to keep a secret. At the Café Anglais, a well-placed bribe would ensure that a communicating door would stay slightly ajar, so that people in the *salle commune* could see who was coming in the back door.

The most famous of the Café Anglais's *cabinets* was 'le Grand Seize' (Big Number Sixteen). This was a sumptuous private room with plush red sofas and walls swathed in velvet, and Bertie was an *habitué* there. One of its most frequent female visitors was the notorious *cocotte* Anna Deslions.* And it was in this room, though apparently not in Bertie's presence, that one of his favourite *grandes horizontales* performed a stunt that turned her into a legend.

Cora Pearl was an Englishwoman whose real name was Emma Crouch and who was born in either 1835 or 1842 depending on which story you believe. The daughter of a cellist and composer, she had some real musical ability – maybe not as much as Hortense Schneider, but certainly enough to earn her a role in the 1867 production of Offenbach's operetta *Orphée aux Enfers*. Apart from a voluptuous figure and a beautiful face, her other great quality was a determination to get rich quick. She is said to have turned to prostitution after being raped, and had a reputation for taking lovers, asset-stripping them and then humiliating them.

A social commentator writing under the name of Zed painted a vivid picture of how Cora's mind worked:

> One day at her apartment we saw an unbelievable account book, divided into three columns. One contained the names of her clients, most of them public figures or friends of ours. In the second she had recorded the date of their . . .

---

* See Chapter 5.

stay. In the third was the sum donated by each pilgrim for the hospitality he had received. And the fatal register also contained, and may God forgive me, a column of remarks, not all of which were very flattering.

Even Bertie wasn't spared Cora's vengeful sense of humour. When he sent her a huge consignment of rare orchids, she showed her scorn for the gesture (no doubt because it cost him a lot but earned her nothing) by inviting some friends over, throwing the flowers on the floor and dancing a hornpipe on them.

Perhaps Bertie was being over-romantic. Most men knew all too well that the only way to earn Cora's (temporary) affection was to give her cash – one lover gained her favour by sending a box of *marrons glacés* (glazed chestnuts) individually wrapped in 1,000-franc notes.

Cora embraced the spirit of the times with brash displays of her burgeoning wealth. She bought a luxury apartment near the Champs-Élysées and fitted a pink marble bathtub with her initials inlaid in gold. And to maintain her lifestyle, she courted scandal. Partly thanks to her widely publicized affair with Napoléon III, she was the first *cocotte* to be called a *grande horizontale*. She also had another nickname – 'Plat du Jour', which translates nicely as 'dish of the day'; this she earned one night in the Grand Seize room at the Café Anglais.

A dinner party was being held there, and Cora bet the men present that they would not be able to slice up the next course to be served. They accepted the wager, and she left the room. A few minutes later, the waiters came in bearing an immense serving dish. Laid out on top, garnished with strategically placed sprigs of parsley, was a naked Cora Pearl. It is a dish of the day that Paris has never forgotten.*

During the 1867 Exposition Universelle, the immoral goings-on at the Café Anglais weren't confined to the upper floors. There were so many wealthy tourists in town that even the *salle commune* was invaded by professional *belles de nuit* touting for business. Much like the hostesses in a girlie bar, they would earn themselves food, drinks and tips, and hope to find a man to take home in exchange for little more than the day's rent at their boarding house. It wasn't all glamour in Napoléon's Paris.

Another of Bertie's favourite Parisian cafés during the late 1860s, and the city's most expensive, was the aptly named Maison d'Or, the House of Gold, which would later change its name to the almost identical Maison Dorée – the Gilded House – a recognition perhaps that its charms were superficial.

It occupied a large building on the boulevard des Italiens, almost across the street from the Café Anglais. According to the *Courrier Français*, a weekly magazine of the time, the Maison d'Or was a pioneer of its genre: 'This is the place that began the reign of the *café splendide*, where paintings, mirrors, gold and luxurious furnishings dazzle the eye. Everywhere there are medallions, pendants, light

---

* Though these days it probably only gets served to professional footballers.

fittings, sculpted panelling and ornate ceilings.' Its wine cellar was reputed to contain 80,000 bottles.

In the daytime the Maison d'Or was mainly frequented by financiers holding meetings and impressing clients, much like Paris's luxury hotels today. In the evening, though, the café lit its lamps and beckoned in the *jeunesse dorée* and older men with money to throw about. Bertie began as the former and grew into the latter, so it was only natural that he should become a regular.

The Maison d'Or also attracted famous writers: Alexandre Dumas *père*, creator of *The Three Musketeers*, established a newspaper in the building; one of Balzac's characters held a ruinously expensive dinner there; and the café features in Proust's *À la Recherche du Temps Perdu* – the main character Swann comes looking for his beloved Odette here, doesn't find her, and so falls even more deeply in love with her.*

The café attracted such a rich, fashionable and influential clientele that it became known as the 'heart, mind and stomach of the boulevard'. Though in calling it this, Parisians were neglecting the other body parts that were put to good use in the private rooms upstairs.

The layout of the Maison d'Or was much the same as the Café Anglais. The restaurant was divided into two sections, one with a large door opening out on to the boulevard and the other a separate area accessible only from the side street, the rue Laffitte. Here, in the private *cabinets*,

---

* This is the kind of foppishness which, in this author's humble opinion, makes Proust so impossible to take seriously.

married men could relive their bachelor days confident in the knowledge that Madame would never find out – unless she was in one of the other *cabinets* and bumped into hubby on the way out to the rue Laffitte.

Even without female company, rich men would meet here for illegal gambling, so discretion was the key. A typical anecdote of the times has two strangers arriving upstairs at the Maison d'Or late at night and trying to get into a *cabinet*. Their way is blocked by a man who asks them what they want.

'To play cards,' they tell him.

'Would you like to tell me your names?' the regular asks.

'Never!' they reply.

'Très bien, go in.'

The most prestigious of the *cabinets* at the Maison d'Or was number 6, though at one point it endangered its reputation for privacy. Customers began to complain because the waiters were refusing to close the curtains and allow the occupants the secrecy that they could get in the other *cabinets*. Only later was it revealed that a rich Englishman was living opposite, and was paying the staff to let him enjoy a spot of voyeurism.

Gaston Jollivet and his friends had a regular reservation at a Maison d'Or *cabinet*, and their favourite game was to invite *soupeuses sensationnelles* – sensational female supper guests. The man who invited the most scandalous lady didn't have to pay for his meal. Gaston tells the story of his proudest moment. One evening he is at the theatre, cruising the corridors in search of feminine company. He gets stuck behind a strange couple – a woman who is 'considerably padded' and her friend who is 'as thin as a pickled herring'. Then he recognizes the padded one's voice – it is the singer Thérésa, whom he'd seen at the Alcazar the previous night. He accosts the ladies and invites Thérésa – with her thin friend, of course – to supper after the show. She hesitates but he clinches the deal by accidentally dropping his hat and making her laugh.

After the show, he escorts Thérésa and her chaperone to the Maison d'Or. Making a triumphant entry into the *cabinet*, he orders the most expensive dishes on the menu, secure in the knowledge that his friends will foot the bill. Thérésa also tucks in so heartily that over dessert she has to unlace her corsets and let her ample form hang out.

Everything goes swimmingly, Gaston tells us, until one of his friends starts licking the food off Thérésa's fingers, and offers to take her home. He has a carriage waiting outside. Poor Gaston gets stood up. Definitely not the kind of humiliation that would have happened to Bertie.

IV

In many of these nocturnal activities, Bertie would not have been a lone operator.

His wife, of course, was almost never invited along, even for a respectable night out at a non-risqué play. In any case, poor deaf Alexandra would not have been able to hear theatre dialogue, so what was the point? Only once during Napoléon III's reign did Bertie take Alexandra to the Hôtel Bristol for a few days. This was in May 1869, when they were on their way home from a seven-month trip to Egypt,

Turkey and the Crimean battlefields (how Alexandra must have enjoyed limping around the Russian plains having the carnage described to her). She was pregnant when the royal couple arrived in Paris, and she expended all her energy at a ball given by Napoléon at the Château de Compiègne, so it is not hard to imagine Bertie advising the weary Princess to put her feet up at the Bristol while he nipped out alone.

He would often go out with an English brother in arms or French friends. His love of company and need for constant amusement meant that he was more than happy to join one of the roving, testosterone-fuelled gangs that Gaston Jollivet and the Comte de Maugny describe so well. Paris's élitist clubs were, of course, delighted to add an English prince to their membership, and Bertie was quickly voted into the Jockey Club, the Yacht Club de France, the Cercle des Champs-Élysées and the Union Artistique, all of them regular meeting places for rich men in search of boisterous fun.

Like their English equivalents, these were places where, so Maugny tells us, aristocrats mixed with 'nouveau-riche millionaires' for 'gambling, smoking and boasting'. The men would go out to a show and supper, and then, the champagne still bubbling in their veins, head back to the club – usually a chic house or apartment – in the small hours of the morning. There, Maugny says, 'until dawn, in this private company, men would have the most shocking conversations and perpetrate schoolboy jokes that would have caused a priest to burst his spleen'. Behind closed doors, the *top de la top* of French manhood would, for example, pretend to be donkeys and ride each other rodeo style until everyone was shaken off. All this, of course, after doing very similar things with actresses in the cafés' private rooms.

All in all, with Napoléon III as his role model and Paris's rowdiest males as his playmates, Bertie was sure of expert guidance when he first went prowling the streets of Paris, which must explain how he met all the naughtiest women so quickly. He did venture out on his own as well, though, to sample a slightly more refined type of gathering – the *salon*.

By the time Bertie first attended a *salon*, these exclusive get-togethers had been part of Parisian social life for centuries. They were parties where the rich and fashionable listened to sparkling conversation – and showed off their ability to get invited to *salons*.

The host (or more often the hostess) of a *salon* was only as fashionable and powerful as the calibre of his or her guests. Top of the pile was, naturally, the Empress Eugénie, who could call on anyone in the city to grace her Monday-night parties, the *Lundis de l'Impératrice*. Eugénie, presiding regally from her armchair, would surround herself with her beautiful *dames du palais* and lead a select group of a couple of dozen people in conversation, dinner and dancing.

Everything about these *soirées* was highly stylized. The male guests had to come dressed in a special black uniform, with below-the-knee knickerbockers and stockings, and play the gallant Frenchmen to the classiest women in Paris. Foreign royalty, including Bertie, would flock to the Tuileries at Eugénie's command, along with the most prestigious diplomats (especially those with charming wives) and anyone who was flavour of the week. The scientist Louis Pasteur, famous as the inventor of pasteurization,* was invited along to give the Empress and her friends a demonstration of one of his new microscopes. He apparently showed them the difference between human and frog's blood. It would be nice to think that Eugénie was witty enough to serve *cuisses de grenouille* for dinner that night.

Outside of the imperial court, the key to a successful *salon* was to have enough pulling power to attract a mixture of long-established aristocratic names and new, exciting celebrities, usually (this being France) writers, painters and philosophers. Back in the seventeenth and eighteenth centuries, the hostesses had usually been *grandes dames* themselves, but things had changed under Napoléon III, and now a *cocotte* could compete for space in the social calendar on an equal footing with a duchess.

The *salons* sound very grand, though the word only means living room, and the gatherings would often consist of little more than carefully placed armchairs and regularly served refreshments. It was up to the guests to enliven the décor by looking or sounding so wonderful that *le tout Paris* would hear about the hostess's fabulous party. Bertie's own high-society bashes in London could have been called *salons* if the level of intellectual conversation had risen beyond the number of grouse to be bagged in Norfolk or

---

* It is interesting to note that Pasteur initially invented his preservation technique not to save people from drinking bad milk, but to stop wine going bad. His were the priorities of a nineteenth-century Frenchman.

how funny it was to pour alcohol on someone's head. Paris's *salons* aimed much higher than that, even when the hostess was a prostitute.

Bertie is known to have attended the *salons* of respectable people like the Austrian Ambassador Richard von Metternich, who was popular in Paris not just because of the political importance of the Austrian empire in the Franco-Prussian power game, but also because he had married his stupendously beautiful niece Pauline. The couple had been in Paris since 1859 and Pauline hosted what was widely acknowledged to be the most glittering *salon* in Europe. In the late 1860s she had just turned thirty and was at the height of her beauty. A portrait of her by the society painter Franz Xaver Winterhalter shows a voluptuous, dark-haired young woman gazing out at the world and challenging it to live up to her expectations. It was not surprising that she became a 'close friend' of Napoléon. Whether this friendship came at a price isn't entirely clear, but given the fact that she was also a close friend of Eugénie's, and that the Emperor apparently kept up a nonstop seduction campaign for the whole time Pauline was in Paris, it might be safe to say that she didn't give in to his advances.

Pauline's beauty ran deep. She had a boundless enthusiasm for life that would have endeared her instantly to Bertie. She is credited with teaching Parisians how to ice-skate (Eugénie herself became a big fan of the sport) and for reassuring women that they could smoke cigars without losing their femininity – a subject very close to Bertie's heart.

Bertie also attended the *salons* organized by Mathilde, Napoléon's scandalous cousin, in her mansion in the rue de Courcelles, a chic area just beyond Opéra. These were highly select gatherings, but were one step down the ladder towards the *demi-monde*, the shadowy place where reputable and disreputable Paris met. The only drawback for Bertie was that Mathilde cultivated an image as a literary hostess, and invited arty types like Gustave Flaubert, the Russian novelist Ivan Turgenev and the Romantic poet Théophile Gautier. There is a painting by Sébastien Charles Giraud called *Le Salon de la Princesse Mathilde, Rue de Courcelles* which depicts a very chic but stilted-looking party in a luxurious sitting room. Amidst chandeliers, candlebras, gilted panelling and deep carpets, a group of people in evening dress are chatting. The men sport frock coats and white high collars, the women wear flowing off-the-shoulder dresses. But there are only eight of them, one apparently an aged matriarch in a lace cap. There is a piano, but it sits alone and unplayed. Not the fun and frolics that Bertie usually looked for while he was in Paris.

This probably explained why he was more often seen at the *salons* given by the *cocottes*, where the mood was ripe for flirting with fast women and there was less chance that some writer might start warbling on about the need for more realism in the modern novel. During at least one of his trips to Paris between 1867 and 1870, Bertie went to visit the *grande horizontale* La Païva at number 25, Champs-Élysées, a magnificent building that has survived to the modern day and now houses a restaurant on its ground floor. In the late nineteenth century, its courtyard and the avenue outside would have been crowded with the carriages of the rich and racy.

A painting called *Une Soirée chez la Païva* by Adolphe Monticelli looks much more fun for someone like Bertie than an evening with Mathilde. The décor is insanely kitsch, with walls that seem to be made of solid gold, and the guests are having a riotous time. There are only eleven of them, but eight are women and three are standing on the table. A devilish man in a white top hat has a girl under each arm and seems to be singing a bawdy song, if the shocked expressions on the faces of several of his listeners are anything to go by. Meanwhile in the foreground, a woman in a scarlet dress is knocking back a glass of champagne with an abandon that suggests that it's been a long, eventful night. Champagne, lewd songs, luxury and loose women. This was why an English prince came to Paris.

But whether the entertainment was refined or debauched, the Parisian *salon* was a perfect environment for Bertie, because he was such a skilful social animal. His French bodyguard Xavier Paoli, who saw him in action over many years, expressed this perfectly:

No matter what the milieu, be it a political salon or the theatre, at a club, the races or a restaurant, his curiosity was always alive. He was keen to listen to others' opinions and observe their attitudes. He didn't speak a great deal, but his talent for making others speak was admirable. His affable directness put you at ease, his loud joyous laugh made you trust him.

In short, Napoléon III's Paris had turned young Bertie into a French playboy seducer.

V

It was all too good to be true, and the end was very near, for Napoléon at least. As early as 1861, a literary critic called William Reymond had described the Second Empire's fatal flaw. In Paris's theatres, he said, costumes could be as revealing as you liked, but the text could contain no political allusions. The intention was to keep the French – or Parisians, anyway – in a permanent erotic daze because, as Reymond put it: 'As long as Parisians are having fun, the government can sleep soundly.' But beneath the veneer of luxury and sex, the less privileged parts of Napoléon's France were grumbling, and their grumbles would soon swell to a murderous roar.

Bertie himself experienced an early symptom of the coming disaster that shows how deeply the discontent had spread. In 1869, he tried to organize a party at the Château de Versailles, in the Trianon, the small palace that Eugénie had recently turned into a museum dedicated to its most famous former resident, Marie-Antoinette. Napoléon and Eugénie approved of Bertie's idea and offered to lend him their chefs and staff for the occasion, along with a set of imperial crockery so that the table would look sufficiently regal.

However, Bertie was co-organizing the party with two Parisian friends who had never been invited to a reception at the Tuileries or a house party at one of Napoléon's country residences. When these two men heard that they would be hosting a meal cooked by imperial chefs and served on plates decorated with a golden N, they called the whole thing off. Rich men refusing a chance to party? Bertie must have been shocked. France was clearly not as carefree as he had always thought.

The summer of 1869 was the last of the Second Empire. Out at Fontainebleau, there was the usual parade of rich, witty guests, but it was like Berlin at the end of the 1920s or New York just before AIDS – the frenzied, live-like-there's-no-tomorrow partying could not go on. The privileged people at Napoléon's court were, to put it crudely, fiddling with each other while Rome burnt.

In fact, ever since the Exposition of 1867, the Emperor's declining health had reflected the state of his country. People were beginning to see through his new clothes.

Napoléon may have overseen great strides in progress at home, but his foreign policy was a disaster. For example, he had backed the Confederate South in the American Civil War, which understandably annoyed the US government. This mistake caused a débâcle in Mexico, which Napoléon had tried to turn into a sort of French colony. Back in 1864, in a bid to ally himself with the Austrians (who were rivals of the dangerous Prussians) he had helped to install the Austrian Emperor's brother Maximilian as ruler of Mexico – Emperador Don Maximiliano I. When a revolution threatened to oust the Franco–Austrian régime in April 1867, the recently annoyed Americans stepped in on the side of the revolutionaries. Napoléon saw the way the pendulum was swinging and ordered French troops to sail home, leaving

Maximilian to defend himself. The inevitable happened, and as Maximilian crumpled in front of a firing squad, so did Napoléon's hopes of keeping a Franco-Austrian alliance alive.

At the same time, France's rivalry with Prussia caused what is probably the most exciting thing ever to happen in Luxembourg. To annoy the Prussians, in March 1867 Napoléon offered to buy the duchy of Luxembourg from its owner, the King of Holland. Luxembourg was a highly fortified buffer zone between France and its warlike German neighbours, so it would have been like acquiring a ready-made Maginot Line. Napoléon's cunning plan succeeded on two counts – first, his offer of five million guilders was accepted; and secondly, he annoyed Bismarck, Chancellor of Prussia, a lot. So much, in fact, that Bismarck ordered the King of Holland not to sell to the French. Given that, at the time, almost every European nation was connected to almost every other by contradictory treaties, the Dutch King invoked an agreement with Prussia whereby he had to submit the sale of Luxembourg to Bismarck, and suddenly the deal with France was off. When Napoléon did not rise to the bait and try to take Luxembourg by force, his humiliation was complete.

This was especially bad news for Napoléon, not because he was looking forward to enjoying the many charms of Luxembourg without having to show his passport, but because the French were fiercely nationalistic, and were furious with him for this public slap in the face. Even the pomp and ceremony surrounding the 1867 Exposition Universelle couldn't entirely distract his patriotic people.

*   *   *

Despite all his outward signs of self-confidence, Napoléon became increasingly aware that you couldn't prop up a régime with ballgowns and candelabras alone, and took some steps to appease his critics. In January 1870, he persuaded a moderate republican called Émile Ollivier to become *chef du gouvernement* (prime minister). Ollivier reduced press censorship and removed unpopular politicians like Haussmann, who was still merrily demolishing poor neighbourhoods and enriching property speculators. Ollivier was so willing to compromise his former politics that he even sent out the army to crush a strike in the metalworks at Le Creusot in central France, killing six workers.

In fact, throughout most of the Second Empire, republicanism and revolution were always in the air, even if they were usually smothered by the heady perfumes of Napoléon's courtiers.

Emile Zola captures this mood of political unrest and hurt nationalistic pride in his novel *Nana*. As the Second Empire heads for its downfall, the heroine Nana, both a symptom and a cause of the decadence, sets the tone. After her fling with Bertie, she has gone on to humiliate a whole series of men, ruining several, driving two to suicide and two more to crime. In May 1869 she goes to the races at Longchamp, the new racecourse in the west of Paris. Napoléon and Eugénie are attending, but all eyes are on Nana as she preens herself amidst her own court of male admirers, and the high-society women can barely hide their jealousy.

Bertie is up in the royal box, and Nana examines him

through binoculars. He's looking fatter, she thinks, and wider, than when she last saw him. She pours scorn on the whole gaggle of courtiers and imperial hangers-on.

'These people don't impress me any more,' she tells her friends. 'I know them too well. I've got no more respect for them. They're all dirty, from top to bottom.' Bertie, she now decides, is 'a prince, but a bastard all the same'. It seems that the Anglo-French friendship that has been alive ever since the Crimean War and Bertie's childhood visit to Paris is finally crumbling.

One of the races features a filly called Nana, an outsider that belongs to one of her lovers. The favourite in the race is an English horse, and Nana's friends can't bear the thought of it winning: '"A fine thing if the English one wins," shouted Philippe in an outburst of patriotic pain. His feeling of suffocating fear began to spread through the tightly packed crowd. Surely they weren't going to suffer yet another defeat?' But at the end of a breathtaking race, the French outsider wins and Nana hears the whole stadium chanting her name: 'Vive Nana! Vive la France! Down with England!'

If anything like this actually happened, poor Bertie must have felt that his dream world was crashing down around him – could this mean that his French lovers had fallen out of *amour* with him already? Could they really be so fickle?

In the case of Napoléon III, the answer was a loud 'oui'. He fell from power just as suddenly as more recent, and much more repressive, dictators like Romania's Nicolae Ceauşescu and Libya's Muammar Gaddafi.

It was yet another dispute between ruling European

families that finally put an end to his partying. When Spain's Queen Isabella abdicated in June 1870, the Spanish government offered the throne to a German, Leopold of Hohenzollern, a Catholic married to a Portuguese princess. Napoléon protested at the idea of being encircled by Germans, and Leopold stepped down, but the French Emperor went a step too far and demanded an official, written renunciation, saying that a refusal would be a *casus belli*. Bismarck refused, despite (or more likely because of) France's threats, and on 19 July 1870, when Napoléon would have preferred to be hosting a garden party at Fontainebleau, the French Emperor declared war. His personal view was that the conflict was doomed to failure, but his hand was forced because the French people and its politicians were howling for Prussian blood.

It soon became clear that France's officers had been spending too much time in dress uniform chatting up the ladies, and that its heavy industry had been concentrating too hard on producing trains and pleasure boats, and not enough on armaments. With his troops outnumbered two to one, commanded by inexperienced officers and outgunned by new Prussian artillery, Napoléon pulled on his fighting boots and trudged eastwards, declaring that he was resigned to 'death on the battlefield'.

On 1 September, after a few inconclusive skirmishes, he suffered a final defeat at Sedan, near Metz. When he tried to negotiate peace in person with Kaiser Wilhelm I,* who

* The grandfather of Kaiser Wilhelm II who would later lead Germany into World War One.

had after all been one of his guests of honour at the Exposition of 1867, Bismarck prevented the meeting and held out for total surrender. Napoléon was taken prisoner, along with 92,000 of his soldiers, and his régime was at an end. On 4 September, a French republic was proclaimed.

Probably the most relieved person in Europe was Queen Victoria. A year earlier she had written to Bertie while he was in Paris with Alexandra, complaining about its 'luxuriousness, extravagance and frivolity', and saying that it 'reminds me of the Aristocracy before the French Revolution'. A clairvoyant queen indeed.

Now, as France tumbled (or rose, depending on your point of view) towards republicanism, Victoria repeated her favourite theme in a letter to her eldest daughter Vicky (a sympathetic ear – Vicky was, after all, the Empress of Prussia), declaring that Bertie had been 'carried away by that horrid Paris . . . and that frivolous and immoral Court' that was characterized by an 'utter want of seriousness and principle in everything' and a 'rottenness which was sure to crumble and fall'.* What the Queen seems to have meant was that France was great fun when she and Albert were enjoying Napoléon and Eugénie's hospitality in 1855, but less harmless when she saw its effects on her son, the future King Bertie.

Bertie felt France's blow much more personally. When Napoléon was captured at Sedan and Eugénie had to flee a Parisian mob with the aid of her American dentist, Bertie

---

* Victoria was of German origin, so *Schadenfreude* came naturally to her.

wrote a remarkably insightful letter to his friend Charles Wynn-Carrington.

'I fear there will yet be a fearful carnage in Paris if peace is not made,' Bertie predicted, declaring that revolution would be the 'final and inevitable result. It is a sad business, and so unnecessary. France will not recover from this shock and humiliation for years to come.'

As well as sympathizing with his homeless French friends, Bertie was of course worried for himself. If France descended into violent revolution, there would be no more champagne parties. No longer would an English prince be able to stroll the boulevards puffing cigars and shaking hands with admiring passers-by. The theatres would put on operettas ridiculing everyone rich and royal instead of just poking fun at Prussian duchesses. And the *cocottes* would want to sleep with dashing revolutionaries instead of plump English toffs. *Quel désastre!*

But even Bertie could not have suspected how unpleasant France's 'sad business' was about to get.

7

IF YOU CAN'T BE WITH
THE ONE YOU LOVE . . .

~

'Your Highness should come and live here and make monarchy
more popular.'
'Oh no! You use up your kings too quickly.'
Conversation between Bertie and French actress Anna Judic

I

There is a frequently told story about Bertie getting caught red-gloved at adultery with an aristocratic English lady. A certain Sir Charles Mordaunt came home to his country mansion one summer's day to find his wife, Harriet, showing off her carriage-driving skills in the grounds by putting her two white ponies through their paces. Her one-man audience was the Prince of Wales, who was standing on the front step of the house as though he owned the place. They weren't actually doing anything illicit, but Harriet was clearly 'entertaining' Bertie one-to-one at home, and everyone knew what that meant. It was all very awkward, because husbands were usually dignified enough to keep out of the way when the Prince was on the prowl. Wanting to avoid any hint of confrontation, Bertie quickly took his leave and left the married couple to deal with the embarrassing situation. This Sir Charles did by undoing the harnesses of the two white ponies, which he had given to Harriet as a birthday present, leading them on to the front lawn and then shooting them dead before her eyes. The message was clear – in Victorian England, there were times when male pride was even more important than a neat front lawn.

The discomfort that Bertie felt on hearing this story would have been much the same as his anguish about the state of France in 1870 and 1871. His foreign mistress was being attacked by heavily armed Prussians, and he would have loved to step in and calm things down, but propriety meant that he had to stay away and let the violence take its course.

Unchecked by any serious international disapproval, the Prussians were free to give Bertie's sexual second home a severe pasting. And then, to make things worse, even before the Prussians had ceased hostilities, the French themselves descended into a period of terrifying self-abuse.

Paris's worst mugging of both the nineteenth and twentieth centuries began almost as soon as Napoléon III surrendered at Sedan on 1 September 1870. The Prussians charged westwards towards Paris, more or less unopposed by a badly prepared French army – a situation that would be exactly reproduced in 1914 and 1940.* By 19 September, France's capital was encircled and a four-month siege began.

Paris was easier to defend in 1870 than in 1940 because it was ringed with fortifications and guarded by more than a dozen forts, most of them the typical star-shaped French bastions that look from the air like red-brick tortoises. Unfortunately, though, when France went to war with Prussia most of the forts were unarmed, so in the late summer of 1870 cannons had to be dragged in from the (less important) provinces or hurriedly forged in makeshift arms factories that were set up within Paris, including one in the Louvre where there was, of course, a handy supply of bronze in the sculpture galleries.

Meanwhile, with most of France's troops having surrendered to the enemy, Paris rounded up regiments of untrained civilian troops who – this being a newly formed republic – were allowed to elect their own officers. Perhaps not the best way to nominate the men who would organize the city's defences.

Sexual equality was just beginning to seep into French culture, so a women's brigade was founded in Paris, the so-called Amazones de la Seine. Their uniform: black trousers with orange stripes, a black hooded jacket and a black cap with orange trim. It was all very egalitarian, but the official announcement (obviously written by men) specified that, as well as defending the city ramparts with 'light

---

* One of France's most endearing qualities is that it never seems to learn from history and keeps believing the impossible until it is much too late.

rifles', the women would be expected to 'give combatants . . . all the domestic and sisterly services they require, as long as they are compatible with military discipline'. The city thought it necessary to specify that the ladies weren't there to make guard duty more fun.

When the modernized, highly trained Prussian army heard about all this, their generals must have giggled into their pointy helmets. Even so, by the time the Germans had billeted themselves in the comfortable palace at Versailles and occupied a ring of villages around Paris, the city had about 400,000 officially enrolled defenders, three-quarters of them untrained.

Almost immediately, Bertie would have heard disturbing news – on 13 October, the Château de Saint-Cloud, where he and his parents had been so majestically entertained by Napoléon and Eugénie in 1855, was demolished by artillery fire. Not Prussian fire, but French. The château stood on high ground overlooking the Seine and was being used as an observation post by the enemy, so the unsentimental Parisians, for whom the building (which still contained most of its priceless furnishings) was little more than a reminder of Napoléon's frivolity, bombarded it. Within hours, it was a smouldering ruin. It must have felt to Bertie, and even more to the fleeing Eugénie, like a very strong hint that their flamboyant Parisian lifestyle was a thing of the past.*

*   *   *

* Is it going too far to say that unlike the French generals of July 1940, those of October 1870 proved that they were willing to destroy Parisian buildings rather than put up with occupation?

For the whole of the following autumn and bitingly harsh winter, no one in Paris enjoyed the lifestyle that had made the city famous for the previous two decades of Napoleonic rule. Those that could went into exile south and west of the Prussian lines, while the people who stayed behind sank slowly into illness and starvation. Of course, as in many sieges, the illness and starvation were doled out along class lines. If you had money or influential friends, you could find food and firewood. But almost everyone in Paris had family members amongst the troops who kept up a constant aggressive attempt to dislodge the occupiers, and all lived in terror of the artillery shells that were used by the Prussians as negotiating tactics. The city became a massive army base, with militiamen camping in the parks and training on the boulevards, prostitutes disappearing off the streets to sew uniforms in workshops, and cafés closing at ten o'clock. The playboys had to go out on guard duty or stay at home.

For almost half a year, the invaders brought in fresh troops, weapons and supplies to tighten their stranglehold, letting the Parisians stew in their own juices. At first, the inhabitants carried on eating almost normally thanks to the many small farms within the ring of fortifications, but soon supplies were running low and new sources of protein were needed. Anything with four legs became a potential meal. Amongst the thousands of mules and horses pulling carts and carriages around the city, only those needed for the war effort were safe from slaughter. Pets were eaten, and a report from November 1870 speaks of a butcher on the boulevard de Rochechouart, in the poor north of the city, starting to sell dogs, cats, rats and even sparrows on a stick. Outside the Hôtel de Ville a rat market opened. Clients would choose the rodent from a crowded cage, it would be strangled to death by a (presumably well-fed) bulldog, and dinner was served. Meanwhile, the only winged creature off the menu was pigeon. Carrier pigeons were so vital to communications with the outside world that it was made a capital offence to kill one – that bird on your plate might well have been a highly trained messenger carrying news of Prussian troop movements.* For the same reason, in the occupied zone, the Prussians imposed the death penalty on anyone keeping pigeons – it was the nineteenth-century equivalent of the Nazi ban on owning radio equipment.

To help Parisians adapt to their new cuisine, a newspaper, *Le Quotidien des Nouvelles*, published recipes. Amongst the most appetizing (or least inedible) were dog cutlets with peas, dog liver skewers, fillet of cat's back with mayonnaise, roast dog dressed with baby rats, rat salami and, for dessert, plum pudding with the cream replaced by a horse marrow *jus. Bon appétit* indeed.

Meanwhile, as stocks of flour dwindled away, bread gradually became more strictly rationed and less breadlike. By the end of the siege much of it was little more than mashed straw.

On the other hand, if you had money and an inquisitive palate you could eat pretty well throughout the siege. At

---

* Just as other wars have inspired leaps in technology, the need to send messages out of Paris by pigeon in 1870 led to the invention of the microfilm by the French photographer René Dagron.

the end of October 1870, the zoo at the Jardin des Plantes began sacrificing its exhibits. Some of these were sources of conventional meat – deer, ducks, swans and buffaloes. And the yaks, zebras and antelopes can't have tasted much different from horse or beef, especially in the hands of French chefs, though even they would have had more trouble with the elephant trunks that went on sale for forty francs per pound (at a time when the wage of a soldier was 1.50 per day, and a rat cost two francs).

Many of these exotic animals were sold as 'fantasy meat' at the Boucherie Anglaise (English butcher's) on the boulevard Haussmann, near Bertie's favourite haunts. And given his taste for slaughtering exotic beasts, he would probably have loved to sneak into Paris to attend the dinner served on Christmas Day 1870 at the Café Voisin, just an *apéritif* stroll away from his usual hotel. Amongst the delicacies on offer that night were elephant consommé, camel 'roasted English-style', kangaroo in its own juices, haunch of wolf and antelope pâté with truffles. All this washed down with excellent wines including a Mouton Rothschild 1846. And Bertie would certainly have brought along whisky and cigars to round off the evening.

That he would have liked to go to Paris and lend moral support to France is not idle fantasy. Bertie had paid a quick visit in the summer of 1870 as war loomed, though this might well have been to get a last taste of Napoleonic luxury in case it all came tumbling down. And one of the things he did while there was persuade the *grande horizontale* Cora Pearl to come to London, which she did, just in time.

Indeed, throughout the whole of the Franco-Prussian war, Bertie fought a lone battle against his pro-German family back in England. While his sister Vicky lobbied the Queen in favour of her father-in-law's cause, and Victoria carried on with her moral crusade about the need for puritan Prussia to beat the frivolity out of France,* Bertie was urging the Austrians (who had fought against Prussia in 1866 over Schleswig-Holstein) to join forces with the French. At least that was the report sent to Bismarck by Count Albrecht von Bernstorff, the Prussian Ambassador to London, who said that Bertie had loudly and publicly expressed his certainty that Austria 'was going to join with the French, and his hope that we [the Prussians] would do badly'.

Victoria was forced to write to Vicky defending Bertie and denying the story, though we can assume that she was less defensive towards her undiplomatic son in person.

In addition to this, one of Bertie's French playboy friends, Gaston de Gallifet, was a military man and had been captured by the Prussians after leading a cavalry charge at Sedan. Bertie tried to plead for his liberation, but the Prussian Ambassador in London refused to forward his letter.

Bertie made things even worse by offering Empress Eugénie exile in England without consulting either his

* Victoria was seen nodding her approval when listening to a sermon given at Balmoral by her favourite preacher Dr Norman Macleod, who declared that France was 'reaping the reward of wickedness, vanity and sensuality'. In Victorian English eyes, the Prussian siege was a holy war.

mother or the British government. In a well-written letter in French containing only one minor grammatical error,* Bertie offered Eugénie the use of 'our country house at Chiswick', a vast neo-classical villa that he was renting from the Duke of Devonshire. It was a thoughtful offer – the house had strong French connections and had previously welcomed another French exile, Voltaire, as well as the philosopher Jean-Jacques Rousseau and the first American Ambassador to France, Thomas Jefferson.

The exiled Eugénie refused Bertie's hospitality because she had already arranged to rent a house in Chislehurst in Kent, but such thoughtfulness towards a deposed French ruler was not a wise diplomatic move, and Parliament accused Bertie of meddling in international affairs. He was forced to grovel to Victoria, assuring her that it was impossible for him to be pro-French – he had so many German relatives that, he told her, 'It is not likely that I should go against them.' Not likely, perhaps, but only too credible.

In an effort to prove his neutrality, Bertie declared that he was willing to act as a negotiator between the warring parties. He wrote to his mother telling her that: 'I cannot bear sitting here and doing nothing whilst all this bloodshed is going on. How I wish you could send me with letters to

* For French grammar fans, Bertie wrote to Eugénie that he and Alexandra would be happy if she would accept their offer: 'nous serions heureux si vous l'accepteriez'. However, 'accepteriez' is a conditional, and here he should have used the imperfect, 'acceptiez'. It was lucky that Eugénie was of Spanish origin, otherwise she might have refused the offer on grammatical grounds.

the Emperor [Napoléon] and King of Prussia . . . I would gladly go any distance.' Especially to Paris, he could have added. And he might well have been a good candidate for the job – after all, he had friends in one camp, family in the other – but his offer was dismissed out of hand by his mother, who didn't think that he was 'personally fitted for such a very difficult task', and even more brutally by Prime Minister Gladstone who thought the idea was 'royal twaddle'.

If Bertie's plan had been to go to Paris and feast on zoo animals, however, it would have been a risky meal. The Prussians were shooting anyone (or anything) trying to break through their lines in either direction – even unarmed Parisians who strayed too far while scavenging for food. No one could get in, and hot-air balloons were the only way of getting anyone out. On almost every day of the siege, a balloon took off carrying people and mail, though the passengers could never be sure where they were going to land. Some fell almost immediately to be captured by Prussian troops, one balloon drifted all the way to Norway, another crashed into the sea off Plymouth, and on one humiliating occasion, a vital cargo came down in Bavaria. This balloon was carrying divers and their diving suits (which had been one of the innovations at the 1867 Exposition). The plan was for the divers to sneak supplies back into Paris along the bed of the River Seine, but in the event the lead-booted suits ended up as war trophies in Prussia, in a smaller version of the Exposition.

Paris was well and truly cut off from both practical and moral support. In a way it was even harder on the inhabitants of what are now the suburbs of the city, because not only were they occupied by Prussians, they were regularly bombarded by Parisians. The Impressionist painter Camille Pissarro had a house in Louveciennes, a small town on the Seine just west of Paris, and he was forced to flee to London, leaving hundreds of paintings behind him. When he returned a year later, his home had survived but had been partially requisitioned as a Prussian latrine. Some of his canvases had been cut up for use as (rather stiff) toilet paper, while others had served as tablecloths for butchering animals. Even the artist's neighbours had helped themselves, and local women were wearing what would now be priceless paintings as laundry aprons.*

All through the coldest winter in living memory, Paris fought on until the Prussians finally lost patience and began a murderous three-week-long artillery barrage in January 1871. Day and night they fired randomly into the city, hitting houses, schools, hospitals and churches. Weapons technology was still primitive in modern terms, so the damage was light compared to the bombardments that would completely flatten other French towns and cities during the two World Wars, but enough shells landed in the Latin Quarter, the Luxembourg gardens, Montparnasse

---

* It should be pointed out that, at this point, in France the Impressionists were thought of as deranged hippies who couldn't paint. The next time Germans occupied the area, they would crate up Impressionist masterpieces and send them to Goering to add to his private collection.

and on the Invalides (home to Napoléon Bonaparte's tomb) to convince the Parisians that further resistance was useless.

An armistice was negotiated, which allowed the Prussians to occupy Paris itself. Only partially, however – the occupiers were to take over a small area of the city on either side of the Champs-Élysées. And very briefly – they left again after two days. The Prussians' main motive for carrying out this perfunctory occupation seemed to be that it gave them the chance to hold a self-congratulatory cavalry parade through the Arc de Triomphe and down the Champs-Élysées.

The Parisians snubbed them – windows were shuttered, businesses closed, and a cordon of the city's makeshift soldiers made sure the occupiers did not leave their sector. When a group of unarmed Prussians went to the Louvre it caused a public uproar, and a proposed visit by the victorious generals to the Invalides was cancelled. As a result, the unloved invaders left almost as soon as they arrived, and France's Minister of the Interior, Ernest Picard, praised the population. In the enemy's presence, he said, 'The behaviour of Parisians was beyond any praise. Everywhere, public buildings, factories and shops were spontaneously closed.' How different it would be in 1940, when many of the cafés, cabarets and brothels of Paris would welcome these Prussians' great-grandsons with open arms.

II

If Francophiles like Bertie were hoping for a return to normal service in Paris, they were to be very disappointed.

Even before the Prussians had withdrawn all their troops, France held parliamentary elections and voted in a large majority of royalist *députés* (MPs). It was a typically French contradiction – the new Third Republic was being led by men who wanted to put a king back on the throne.

The President was Adolphe Thiers, a 73-year-old statesman who had married the eldest daughter of his mistress, thereby joining a rich banking family and earning himself a sumptuous Paris mansion. Thiers had been King Louis-Philippe's Minister of the Interior, so it was a case of back to the future, and the Parisians (who believed that they had just endured a siege to defend their republican revolution) refused to accept the situation, disdaining the new government as a 'rural parliament'. The MPs took the hint and relocated to Versailles, which only made things worse – a so-called republican parliament electing to sit at the traditional home of royal power? The Parisian working classes knew (or were reminded by left-wing politicians) that the previous three revolutions – in 1789, 1830 and 1848 – had all ended in an empire or a monarchy, and this time they were determined that things would be different. In March 1871 the city elected a 'Communal Council'* and decided to govern itself. La Commune had begun.

---

* One of the men elected to a special artists' committee on the council (this was a French council, so it had to have artists) was the Impressionist Edouard Manet, who had no desire to have his name on a list of revolutionaries, and went into exile until the troubles had died down. Another painter, Gustave Courbet, was a willing member of the council, and was later imprisoned for it.

Unfortunately, the city was still completely surrounded by hostile forces. The Prussians, who opposed the idea of a French republic, immediately freed 60,000 prisoners and handed over their artillery to Thiers. Suddenly he and his royalists had a large, well-armed army.

Hostilities between France's government and its capital city began on 17 March 1871 when Thiers sent in soldiers to grab Paris's cannons from the hilltop of Montmartre. The mission failed, mainly because the troops began fraternizing with Parisians who were objecting on the grounds that their taxes had paid for the manufacture of the guns during the Prussian siege, so they didn't see why they should give them up. The generals leading the mission were taken prisoner and shot. It was a declaration of civil war.

For the next two months, there was a second siege of Paris, as government forces and Communards relived all the horrors of the previous winter. The difference this time was that about half the city's population got out of town and left the workers to defend themselves.

The well-off residents of the new boulevards wanted no part of a populist uprising. The civil servants fled, deciding that they would be better off siding with the people out in Versailles who paid their salaries. Other middle-class professionals such as lawyers, teachers and the owners of the city's many small factories also deserted the town. Paris was left to its manual workers, small shopkeepers, left-wing politicians and all the anti-royalists amongst the men and women who had taken up arms against the Prussians. They began to rip up the cobblestones from Napoléon's boulevards and block the streets with barricades. Photos of the time show men and women posing beside cannons that point along the streets where today's Parisians go on carefree shopping expeditions. On many of the photos, the uniforms are clean and the cuboid cobblestones neatly stacked. But they were not to stay that way for very long.

The Parisians who fled the city during the Commune were probably wise to do so, because by all accounts, a frenzy of class paranoia seized the city, and anyone suspected of anti-Communard activities was condemned to death by a revolutionary court. The painter Auguste Renoir, famous for his pictures of plump ladies and sunny landscapes, was almost a victim of this casual life-and-death justice. He had initially left Paris before returning in May 1871, and was happily painting a riverside scene when some Commune soldiers arrested him on suspicion of drawing a map for the enemy. Renoir only avoided a firing squad thanks to the last-minute intervention of another Communard, whose life the Impressionist had previously saved by lending the man a smock and a paintbrush when he was being pursued by a squad of Thiers's troops, so that he could pretend to be a harmless artist.

The Communards did much more than execute perceived traitors, though. Realizing that they might not have very long in power, the members of the revolutionary council quickly responded to their new independence by voting in modern-sounding reforms like equal pay for women, free and secular education for all, and a totally free press.

One of the new newspapers was called *Le Vengeur* (*The Avenger*) and this spirit of retribution was expressed in deeds as well as words – we might think that political demonstrations in today's Paris get out of hand, but in the spring of 1871 Communards attacked and burnt down the Ministry of Finance, part of the Palais-Royal, the Hôtel de Ville, which contained all the city's archives including its birth certificates, and the imperial library in the Louvre (the Louvre itself was only just saved from destruction by an art-loving Communard).

They also wreaked more personal revenge. The house of Eugénie's writer friend Prosper Mérimée was destroyed, as was Adolphe Thiers's *hôtel particulier* (city mansion).* The premises of the Jockey Club near the Opéra were trashed as a gesture against the idle rich who – as we saw in the previous chapter – had been acting for the last twenty years as though the city belonged to them.

The worst piece of class vengeance, though, which would have hurt Bertie even more than the destruction of the Château de Saint-Cloud, was the burning down of the Tuileries, the palace where Napoléon and Eugénie had held their most sumptuous receptions, and where Bertie had first encountered the beauty and loose morals of chic Parisian womanhood. Over two days, Communards systematically packed the palace with wagons of explosives and cans of oil, tar and turpentine. They then moved

---

* Thiers later got the government to pay for his house to be entirely rebuilt, and it can be seen today on the place Saint-Georges, just south of Pigalle.

through the building soaking floors, furniture and curtains with oil, and on 23 May the imperial bonfire was set alight. It quickly exploded, blowing off large sections of the roof, and blazed for three days, leaving a shell filled only with embers, blackened stone, melted bronze and shards of marble from statues that had shattered in the heat. The frivolity of Napoléon III's Second Empire was officially in ashes.

The deposed Emperor himself had been freed by the Prussians in March, and joined Eugénie in England. He was planning his comeback when he got the news that his former neighbours had torched his palace and almost all his possessions. It was not exactly a sign that he would be welcomed home.

In the event, Napoléon would never return, and he must have felt safer in England when he heard about the bloodshed that was being inflicted by Frenchman on Frenchman (and -woman). The demolition of the Tuileries had been a last desperate show of defiance carried out when the anti-Commune troops finally broke into Paris. Let in by a traitor at the porte de Saint-Cloud in the far west of the city on 21 May, 70,000 government infantrymen were fighting their way north, storming barricades, taking few if any prisoners and summarily executing anyone with traces (or suspected traces) of gunpowder on their hands. Some 500 Communard prisoners were shot in Montmartre, the Luxembourg Gardens and in the chic Parc Monceau, one of Bertie's promenading haunts. In reprisal around fifty hostages were shot by the Communards, including ten priests and the Archbishop of Paris.

One by one the barricades fell as the government soldiers fought their way into the poor northeastern *quartiers*, and resistance ended on 28 May in the Père-Lachaise cemetery, where, after an all-night last stand amongst the gravestones, the last 147 Communard fighters – male and female – were lined up and shot.

Still the slaughter wasn't over. As columns of prisoners were marched out of the city, Bertie's friend Gallifet embarked on a personal terror campaign, pulling captives out of the ranks and having them executed. Some of his victims were wounded and moving too slowly, others he just didn't like the look of. On one Sunday in Passy, a southwestern suburb, he told a consignment of prisoners that 'all those with grey hair should come forward', and 111 men did so. 'You', he yelled at them, 'are more guilty than the others. You also took part in the 1848 revolution.' He had them all shot. One French historian estimates that Gallifet was personally responsible for 3,000 deaths. When working-class Parisians put a stop to Bertie's aristocratic friends' champagne-fuelled soirées, vengeance could be swift, extreme and brutal.

Some sources estimate that 30,000 Communards were killed, while others put it as 'low' as 6,000 (the French always have two figures for any controversial event – the official and anti-establishment estimates). Thousands more were transported to prison camps in the colonies to catch tropical diseases and die in chains. The British often bemoan the cruel disparity between the working classes and the rich in Victorian England, but in France the class war was a massacre.

A decade later, in commemoration of this enormous self-inflicted French suffering, the construction of a cathedral was begun – the Sacré-Coeur in Montmartre. What few people realize, though, is that the church was originally conceived by the clergy as an apology to heaven for 'the crimes of the Communards'. In short, when tourists today take smiling photos of themselves outside the Sacré-Coeur, they are in a way celebrating the massacres of 1871.

III

While Paris was seeing its paving stones ripped up and its people shot, Bertie was still in action. Having failed to get himself appointed as a peacemaker, he did the rounds of the French exiles in London, undertaking a personal opinion poll about the future of his favourite travel destination – and taking the opportunity to enjoy some French fun on home soil.

He became close to the Comte de Paris, a claimant to the French throne vacated by Louis-Philippe in 1848, and therefore a rival to both Napoléon III and the republicans. The Comte de Paris was the grandson of King Louis-Philippe, a man of about Bertie's age who had been an exile in England for a dozen years, and who was planning his return to Paris now that the political landscape was a heap of rubble and there was a chance of installing a real monarchy rather than a Napoleonic empire.

Despite his friendship with Napoléon and Eugénie,

Bertie was for obvious reasons a royalist at heart, as were many of his Parisian friends. And in 1871 the Comte had a real chance of stepping in to take power, because, unlike Louis-Philippe, he was a man of action. In the early 1860s, he had got bored in exile and gone to fight in the American Civil War – not, as we might imagine of a French conservative, on the Confederate side, but with the anti-slavery Union. He had even seen action in battle, at Gaines's Mill in June 1862, although it is surely a coincidence that the presence of a French aristocrat in the Union army led to one of its only defeats of the whole war.

The Comte was not at all Bertie's usual choice of friend – he was renowned as a thinker, and his contemporaries found him prudish and cold, which probably explains why he would never become ruler of France. His wife (and cousin), the half-Spanish Marie-Isabelle, was more Bertie's type, and might have reminded him of a younger Eugénie. She was a keen smoker, fond not only of cigars (she often used to steal Bertie's) but also of a pipe, and it is said that Bertie 'liked' her a lot – though whether he went so far as to sleep with a French queen-in-waiting is doubtful.

Even after a republic was well and truly installed in Paris, Bertie felt so close to these French pretenders' cause that he tried to unite the British and French royal families. In 1891, his son Prince Eddy decided (albeit briefly) that he was in love with Hélène, the Comte de Paris's daughter, and Bertie attempted to convince Queen Victoria that a marriage was possible, despite the fact that the French family was staunchly and politically Catholic. The government refused, though, and Eddy remained a promiscuous bachelor until his untimely death from flu in 1892.

Meanwhile, back in 1871, Bertie also kept up his relationships with friends from Napoléon's court and held gatherings for them at Marlborough House, his London home. The star amongst these was the half-American Blanche, Duchess of Caracciolo, a scandalous woman who had openly cuckolded her husband with one of Napoléon III's equerries. She was another heavy smoker – always a trait that endeared Bertie to women – and was in the habit of paying a slightly perverse public homage to Alexandra. Although she was almost certainly having an affair with Bertie, Blanche would dress like Alexandra, in high collars and tight-bodiced dresses, which his mistresses often did to confirm their status as royal bedfellows. It was heavily rumoured that Blanche's daughter, born in 1871, was Bertie's child – the girl was christened Alberta in his honour and he would later set mother and daughter up in a house in Dieppe that he liked to visit on short yachting expeditions. One of Bertie's biographers, Jane Ridley, says that Alberta could not have been Bertie's child because Blanche's husband registered himself as the father, but that seems slightly naïve – a man of the period, especially a nobleman, would not refuse to acknowledge paternity of his wife's offspring unless he was determined to ridicule himself and disgrace his family name. Legitimate bastards were on every branch of the noblest family trees.

So in late 1870 and early 1871, Bertie was a loyal friend to French exiles of different persuasions, even if it was partly because the female members of the families were amusing. But this public closeness to royalist and imperialist sympathizers from across the Channel was not winning him any friends at home. Emboldened by the swift fall of Napoléon III and the uprising in Paris, British republicans were speaking out – and shocking new revelations about Bertie's private life would only add fuel to the bonfire that they hoped to light under Victoria's throne.

8

SAVAGED BY THE PRESS

~

'Even the staunchest supporters of monarchy shake their heads and express anxiety as to whether the Queen's successor will have the tact and talent to keep royalty on its legs and out of the gutter.'
Reynolds's Newspaper, *February 1870, after Bertie appeared in court in a divorce case*

I

There had long been republican rumblings in England (the French usually forget, when boasting about their own revolution of 1789, that Britain decapitated a king 150 years earlier), and in 1871 the decibel count rose considerably. The widowed Victoria was playing at Greta Garbo – and with her slightly Germanic accent, it would have been a good imitation – while Bertie was doing his best to provoke howls of outrage, and not only because of his attitude to France.

The outrage wasn't all Bertie's own fault. In the spring, while Paris was undertaking its campaign of self-destruction, he and Alexandra suffered their own loss. Their sixth child, Alexander John, was born prematurely and survived only twenty-four hours. At the small private funeral, Bertie wept. Despite his constant extra-marital adventures, he was a genuinely affectionate father – unlike his own. This pregnancy had caused Alexandra a lot of suffering, physical as well as emotional, and doctors told the young couple that another could be life-threatening. From now on, even though they were only in their mid-twenties, it was suggested that they stop sleeping together.

Not that they had been tearing off each other's royal pyjamas very often. Bertie's sexual attentions were, as we have seen, often distracted, and all Alexandra's contemporaries agree that she was not a vixen in the bedroom. She was attractive – in some of her photos, she looks chillingly like Princess Diana. She was also eternally youthful – her face hardly gained a wrinkle until she was well into middle age. And she laughed infectiously, even during official ceremonies. But she wasn't, so everyone agreed, seductive. It was for this reason that although Bertie was very fond of Alexandra, sex had always belonged to his extra-marital life – like his gambling and smoking – rather than being an integral part of a loving marriage. This was also why he had been captivated by Frenchwomen, who were the opposite of Alexandra – if she was a cute, playful kitten, then the sophisticated *Parisiennes* were witty, shameless tigresses.

Even so, this apparently final medical verdict must have

hit Bertie hard. These days, we would immediately think of contraception, but in 1871, there was no sure means of avoiding pregnancy other than abstention. In England, only *coitus interruptus* was used by married couples. Rubber condoms had been available since the 1850s but the early models were as thick as kitchen gloves and used mainly when men had sex with prostitutes. This, after all, was one reason why men like Bertie chose married mistresses. Any accident could be attributed to the husband (although Bertie was to regret this policy, as we shall see very soon).

High-class French *cocottes* often got pregnant because their main method of trying to prevent this professional problem was the bidet. They didn't use condoms. Disease was therefore a real concern – if Napoléon Bonaparte made prostitution legal in France in the first place, it was so that the women would be under medical surveillance. Which was another reason, incidentally, why Paris was such a popular destination for playboy tourists – the prospect of safer sex.

Although Alexandra was relatively naïve about sexual matters, she was aware of her husband's affairs and must have known about the danger of catching syphilis from him. Wayward Bertie had been lucky to have such a tolerant, sexually available wife. But now his luck had run out, on doctors' orders.

Of course Bertie had never been one to sit around moping about abstinence, and this was no exception. Unfortunately for him, though, lack of contraception took its toll almost immediately. One of his mistresses, Susan Vane-Tempest, was a close friend of the family – she had been a bridesmaid at Bertie's sister Vicky's wedding – and had been in the Prince's little black book for several years when, in September 1871, she told him that she was pregnant. She was young – thirty-two – but a widow, which meant that unless Victorian society believed in immaculate conception amongst the upper classes, only a lover could be to blame.

Bertie dealt with the matter clinically, by setting up an appointment with a doctor who was known to perform abortions. But Susan's pregnancy was too far advanced and the doctor refused. Bertie therefore decided that his embarrassing mistress would have to be exiled. Not to France, where he sent Blanche de Caracciolo (so that he could visit her again discreetly) but to the more prosaic Ramsgate, where Susan settled, accompanied by a maid who was also pregnant (*quelle coïncidence*). Susan sent Bertie heart-rending letters, begging for just one face-to-face farewell, but he ignored them all, and their baby, if it was born (there are suspicions that the doctor finally performed an abortion despite the dangers), has been erased from history. Perhaps the maid declared it as hers without knowing its true royal origins. Perhaps it died in infancy, as so often happened. In any case, the whole affair revealed a ruthlessness in Bertie that can only be explained by his terror that the truth would come out. In 1871 his (and the British monarchy's) reputation was on a knife-edge.

A year earlier, Bertie had been cited in a divorce case. This scandalous event had been provoked by Sir Charles Mordaunt (the man who shot ponies on his lawn) after his wife confessed that her new baby wasn't his. She had done this in a panic because she was terrified that the infant was showing symptoms of syphilis. Breaking the high-society rule whereby marital problems were dealt with by discreet separation, gritted teeth or executing pets, Sir Charles had sued for divorce on the grounds of infidelity, creating a paper-chase of names with his accusations. Issued with a summons, Bertie had actually been forced to go to court to deny, Clinton-style, that he had had sex with this woman. The judge believed him but the press, predictably, reported all the lurid details.

Then, around the same time as Susan Vane-Tempest went into exile, Bertie had to deal with the Barucci letters* – the notes he had sent to the Parisian *cocotte*. The fact that he was willing to make a huge blackmail payment showed how keen he was to keep his sullied name out of the papers.

Bertie was also under fire from the press for wild spending on more pleasurable luxuries. Deprived of France, he had indulged that summer in some heavy gambling at a German spa, Bad Homburg (so much for his sympathies in the Franco-Prussian conflict), and it was rumoured that he had suffered heavy losses. *Reynolds's Newspaper*, a scandal-hungry English weekly founded by an anti-privilege campaigner called, predictably, Reynolds, pilloried Bertie for throwing away gold 'that he obtained from the toil and sweat of the British working man, without himself producing the value of a half-penny'. Headlines about 'royals throwing away our money while we starve' are strong

* See Chapter 5.

arguments for republicanism at any time, and the nine-teenth century was no exception.

Calls for a French-style republic in Britain were being led by the radical Liberal activist Joseph Chamberlain (father of the future Prime Minister Neville, who would sign the infamous agreement with Hitler in 1938) and the Liberal MP Charles Dilke, whose favourite speech around this period was a call for an end to what he called the 'political corruption that hangs about the monarchy'. These battling young politicians and their party were determined to reform conservative England, and royal-bashing was an effective campaign tool, especially when Bertie was the target.

As rumours of his adultery and German gambling were repeated and embroidered upon, Bertie got himself into even more trouble by inviting a boxer to Sandringham. Today, when we live in a celebritocracy, this might not sound very shocking, but in 1871 prize-fighting was illegal in England. Even so, the word was that the Prince of Wales and his society friends were frequent spectators at bloody, bare-knuckle bouts, and were betting small fortunes on the outcome. So by inviting a boxer, a soldier called Charley Buller, on a rural retreat, Bertie was confirming the rumours and proving – to republican eyes, at least – that he thought he was above the law of the land.

Perhaps it was because France, his comfort blanket since his teenage years, had been taken away. Perhaps it was the news that Alexandra was also going to be unavailable, and the loss of their baby. Either way, Bertie had been walking a tightrope across the Niagara of public opinion, and in the autumn of 1871 he was wobbling dangerously.

II

Plumbing is like the soundtrack of a film – if things are running smoothly, you hardly notice it's there. When it gets too noticeable, however, things become unbearable. This was exactly what happened in November 1871 when Bertie, Alexandra and twenty-odd friends went to Scarborough in Yorkshire to help control that county's exploding grouse population. In between doing their bit to redress the balance of nature, the guests were constantly twitching their nostrils at the fetid smells seeping out of the pipes at Londesborough Lodge,* the home of the Lord of the same name where they were all staying. The house's fragile plumbing had apparently failed to cope with the number of visitors, and there must have been overflows of dirty water into clean, because almost as soon as the shooting party left the house, some of its members began to shiver and feel sick. Bertie developed a fever and a pink rash and took to his bed, where he was soon singing, throwing pillows at his doctors and raving so scandalously that women had to be rushed from the room.

When one of the other Scarborough guests, Lord Chesterfield, died of typhoid, a chill passed over Bertie's

---

* Interestingly, Londesborough Lodge was repeatedly put on the market between 2009 and 2013 by its owners, Scarborough Borough Council, and failed to find a buyer despite being hyped as a house in which Edward VII had stayed.

whole family – it was almost ten years to the day since Prince Albert had gone the same way. For the first time ever, Victoria came to Sandringham, and Bertie's country house was turned into a giant nineteenth-century sick room, with all the horrors that that entailed. Windows were sealed to keep out the cold, the air became stale, and the entire royal family – the Queen, the Waleses and various princes and princesses – were almost wiped out by a gas leak that was only discovered thanks to the persistence of Bertie's uncle George, the Duke of Cambridge, who complained so repeatedly about an ominous smell that the gas company was called in to investigate.

On 13 December, the day before the anniversary of Prince Albert's death, it looked as though Bertie would die, thereby following in his father's footsteps for the first and last time in his life. A coughing fit almost cut off his breathing entirely and carried him away. Things looked so bad that the doctors, obeying nineteenth-century logic, asked Alexandra to leave Bertie's bedside for fear that her presence would 'excite' him. She was forced to creep back in on hands and knees to be near her dying husband.

Finally, though, Albert's ghost seems to have decided that it didn't want to be reunited with its lost son just yet, because the next day Bertie began to rally. He asked to see his mother and greeted her not with a thrown pillow but with a polite 'so kind of you to come'. His fever was down and the coughing was, like Scarborough's grouse popula-tion, under control. If Victoria whispered a prayer of thanks, we can guess whose name she evoked.

Before this near-death experience, the press had been

extremely cruel to Bertie. The worst example was another article in *Reynolds's Newspaper*, which had greeted the death of the royal baby John with morbid glee: 'We have much satisfaction in announcing that the newly born child of the Prince and Princess of Wales died shortly after its birth, thus relieving the working men of England from having to support hereafter another addition to the long roll of state beggars they at present maintain.' Politics at its most personal.

By association the reclusive Queen was also tainted, mainly for not managing her son more strictly. In her biography of Bertie, Jane Ridley quotes a damning attack on Victoria by the previously loyal *Economist*: 'The Queen has done almost as much injury to the popularity of the monarchy by her long retirement from public life as the most unworthy of her predecessors did by his profligacy and frivolity.' This last jibe was at the previous Prince of Wales, later King George IV, who was remembered by Victorians as an infamous moral degenerate. The inference was clear – Bertie was sliding down the same amoral slope. The monarchy was under attack on all fronts.

Bertie's illness changed all that. While he was at death's door, the doctors' pessimistic bulletins kept newspaper readers on the edge of their seats for fresh news, especially after the Associated Press agency issued a false report of his demise. The real prospect of Bertie's death erased the past and swung public opinion back on his and the monarchy's side. Papers called for public prayer, and when it was apparently answered, there was huge relief. Cannily, Prime Minister Gladstone suggested that Bertie stage a procession through London and a thanksgiving service at St Paul's. Victoria objected (of course) but was overruled, and on 27 February 1872 the streets of London were thronged with cheering crowds who were so enthusiastic that one poor baby was suffocated in the crush and a tree collapsed under the weight of the people who had climbed up to get a better view. The Queen had changed her mind and came out to wave from an open carriage, while Bertie, frail but happy, raised his hat to his new fans.

He was, everyone noticed, looking very bald, and chubby-faced – at the age of only thirty, any youthful slimness that he had hung on to was gone forever. And when he walked up the aisle of the cathedral on Victoria's arm, he limped. Rather like Alexandra, in fact. But the sight of his suffering, his evident closeness to his wife and family, and his pious determination to give thanks to heaven for his salvation, thawed public hearts. Calls for a London Commune were effectively at an end.

Even better news for Bertie was that France was also getting back on its feet after its recent troubles.

Time for a little visit, perhaps?

III

Bertie's convalescence had brought him closer to Alexandra, who enjoyed having her husband at home for once. She gave him wifely rubdowns to ease his aches and pains, one thing led to another, and for a while she was afraid that she was pregnant again – Bertie clearly wasn't the kind to abstain from sex on doctor's orders.

For some time after he was off the danger list, he suffered from painful swelling in his left leg, as well as the occasional bout of fever. But soon he was feeling strong enough to go to France again – albeit with his wife. The idea was to spend the spring cruising on the Mediterranean, which, as always, was an excuse for a stopover in Paris on the way there and back. As his train pulled into the city, Bertie must have felt a mixture of nostalgia and fear. His beloved mistress had taken a beating. Would she have lost all her charms? Would she remember him? Or even recognize him after his rapid bout of ageing?

Bertie's first impressions of post-Commune Paris can be gauged from an account given by Robert Lytton, the Secretary of the British Embassy, who arrived there in 1872 to find that the city was suddenly full of 'petits bourgeois', that the 'cupids of the Second Empire have disappeared' and that Paris had become 'dowdy and almost respectable . . . like a battered and tired dandy in reduced circumstances' – which could have described Bertie himself.

Having little energy to go out on the town, Bertie took the opportunity to do some politicking, no doubt wanting to see whether the Third Republic would welcome the occasional visit from an English royal. He must have been reassured that the President was still Adolphe Thiers, the man who had suppressed the Commune, and who was seen by royalists as a convenient stopgap until a king returned to reign over France.

However, Bertie didn't want to wait until the next French monarch emerged. Much better to go along to the Palais de l'Élysée, just a couple of doors down from the British Embassy, and declare his enduring empathy with France, whoever was leading it. His meeting with Thiers had to be secret – Bertie was still under orders not to show any public support for France – and it apparently went well, despite the fact that according to one English observer, the President's wife sat there all the while looking like a 'dragon watching over the new republic'.

Bertie also hooked up with his old friends at the Jockey Club, and although he wasn't yet fit enough to join any of their escapades, he was pleased to see that their premises had been refurbished, and to hear their reassurances that the good life was just around the corner. After all, whatever change came would come peacefully, seeing that all the revolutionary troublemakers had been either shot or sent to the tropics.

In short, Bertie's personal espionage mission would have been a complete success if he hadn't bumped into the Thiers family again in Trouville on the Normandy coast shortly afterwards, and been spotted fraternizing with *les Français* by a German agent. The spy informed Bismarck, who complained to Victoria, and Bertie was in trouble *yet again* for his political indiscretions.

Things got even worse for Bertie when poor Napoléon III was killed by an English doctor.* It wasn't quite as straightforward as strangulation by stethoscope, but it

---

* For a more detailed account of the demise of Napoléon III, see *1,000 Years of Annoying the French*. By the way, no doubt in a spirit of political fairness, the British also put paid to King Louis-Philippe.

might as well have been for all the problems it caused Bertie.

Napoléon and Eugénie had been living happily in a mansion called Camden Place in Chislehurst, a few miles southeast of London, plotting the Emperor's return to power in France (at the time, almost every Frenchman in England was plotting his own return to power in France). Napoléon wanted to follow the example of his uncle who had come back from his Italian exile on Elba in 1815 to a rapturous welcome from his people. But his health had not been improved by his imprisonment in Prussia, or by his time in Chislehurst, which was no Italian island, and his old stomach pains were getting stronger than ever. Diagnosed with bladder stones, he was operated on by a British expert on the condition, a certain Henry Thompson, but died on the operating table on 9 January 1873 of complications that Thompson and his anaesthetist quickly attributed to kidney failure.

Bertie was determined to go to the funeral, but his mother and Gladstone forbade it, even though they had been willing in the past to visit the imperial couple discreetly at Chislehurst. The difference between private visits and public occasions was one that Bertie still had to master, except where most of his mistresses were concerned.

He was a faithful friend, though, and Napoléon had been his mentor in the aspect of his life that was most important to him, so he defiantly went to the lying-in-state of the coffin, and spent some time commiserating with Eugénie, who now knew that she would definitely not be returning to France as an empress. Bertie also invited some of

Napoléon's exiled friends and supporters to Sandringham to reminisce about the good old days and, all in all, did just about everything that a Prince of Wales could do to embarrass a British government that was trying to stay on good diplomatic terms with republican France, short of putting on a wig and going to a fancy-dress party as Marie-Antoinette.

Gladstone tiredly declared that gaffe-master Bertie had a 'good nature and sympathy' but suffered from a 'total want of political judgement, either inherited or acquired'. The answer, Gladstone belatedly suggested, was an education in political matters – Bertie needed to 'adopt the habit of reading'. Victoria had no illusions about her eldest son, though, and replied that Bertie had 'never been fond of reading . . . From his earliest years it was impossible to get him to do so. Newspapers and, very rarely, a novel, are all he ever reads.' Which was unfair. As we've seen, Bertie absolutely devoured the Parisian theatre listings.

As any hope of useful employment faded thanks to his political incompetence, Bertie occupied himself as best he could in England. He began affairs with a married Canadian woman called Mrs Sloane-Stanley, and a teenaged Irish beauty, Patsy Cornwallis-West, who was only sixteen when she began sleeping with him. She was hurriedly married off as soon as her family heard about her precarious situation. Marriage, though, only made it easier for Bertie to continue the affair and he remained close to Patsy long enough to help her daughter marry into the English aristocracy, which in turn only increased rumours that at least one of her three children was of royal descent.

His health was improving rapidly, and he also began 'seeing' a French *cocotte*. She was in fact a Liverpudlian called Catherine Walters who had set up shop in Paris in the 1860s, and had returned to England when the Commune spoilt her business. Catherine was nicknamed Skittles, either because of her ability to bowl men over or because of her figure. There is a photo of her on horseback, sporting a jacket so tight that she could have worn a dog collar as a belt.* The slenderness of her waist only emphasizes the curvaceousness of the portions of her that are perched upon the saddle.

Taking up with a former Parisian prostitute must have reminded Bertie fondly of his recent past and given him yearnings to get back to the city, because in 1874 he started campaigning for another cross-Channel expedition. He had been invited to France by an eminently respectable man, the Duc de La Rochefoucauld-Bisaccia (the respectability of a Frenchman was often judged by the impossibility of fitting his whole name on the front of an envelope) who until very recently had been France's Ambassador in London. The fact that Rochefoucauld had been recalled to Paris (in other words, fired) because of his outspoken royalist declarations did nothing in Bertie's eyes to make him less respectable, even though it would have been clear

---

* Prime Minister Gladstone is said to have taken Skittles's measurements with his hands. Learning that he was fond of visiting prostitutes and trying to 'convert' them, she invited him to her house, where he complimented her on her figure and gripped her waist to stress his point. She thought the visit was hilarious, and told Bertie all about it.

to anyone with more political sense that the Duc was a very hot *pomme de terre*.

Bertie was emboldened by the fact that the moralist Gladstone had lost a general election and been replaced by the worldlier Benjamin Disraeli, so that it looked as if his mother had been deprived of an ally in her war against her son's French indiscretions. And when Victoria appealed to Disraeli to forbid the trip to Paris, Bertie's optimism was confirmed – the new Prime Minister's letter of disapproval said only that he was unsure 'whether a visit to France at all is, at this moment, desirable', which was a little like putting a chocolate cake on the table and telling a child that it might not be a good idea to take a slice. Disraeli also showed that he was either a weak psychologist or that he had one eye on Bertie's future succession to the throne, because he told the Prince of Wales that only he could decide whether it was advisable to go to France: 'No living man is more competent to form a correct judgement . . . than Your Royal Highness.'

That decided it – the cake was to be consumed at once.

What was more, Bertie wanted to eat it undisturbed by his wife. He decided to use the old stopover excuse, and announced that he intended to spend some time in Paris on his way back from attending the confirmation of his nephew, the future Kaiser Wilhelm II, in Germany.

Everyone knew what this implied, and some serious disapproval was expressed. Bertie's comptroller and treasurer, Sir William Knollys, wrote a letter to Victoria decrying Paris as 'the most dangerous place in Europe, and it would be well if it were never revisited. In fact, remaining on the

Continent, whenever it involves a separation of the Prince and Princess of Wales – cannot be otherwise than most undesirable.'

But if Bertie knew about the letter, he took as much notice of Knollys as if he had been a grouse begging for mercy on the moors. Paris? Without the wife? He was off.

IV

After a short stay in Baden to lose some money, which provoked another flurry of reports at home about his excessive gambling, Bertie was in Paris in October, obliging London to reassure the world via *The Times* that this was not a state visit, and that Bertie was neither expressing anti-German sympathies nor trying to put a king on the French throne.

It might have been simpler to say, 'Honest, he's only going there for the sex.' Though to be fair to Bertie, that wouldn't have been entirely true. At Disraeli's insistence, he paid a visit to the new President of France, Patrice de Mac Mahon, a marshal who had seen action in the Crimea, where he was credited with winning the siege of Sebastopol. He had also fought alongside Napoléon III at the Battle of Sedan, where he had been wounded and taken prisoner, before being released by the Prussians so that he could lead the 'Versaillais' army that massacred the Communards. The new President was a staunch royalist, even more anti-republican than Adolphe Thiers.

Mac Mahon's family, who claimed descendance from Irish kings, owned a superb château in Burgundy, and he took Bertie shooting, a bonding exercise during which their royalist sympathies no doubt gelled. According to Bertie's biographer André Maurois, when the two men sat down at dinner, the centrepiece on the table was a vase of ferns, which Bertie interpreted as a sign of French rebirth. He may not have been sympathetic to wild animals, but where plants were concerned he was obviously quite the poet.

Bertie also took up the invitation of the former Ambassador to London, the Duc de La Rochefoucauld-Bisaccia, to stay at the glorious Château d'Esclimont, some seventy kilometres southwest of Paris. It is the epitome of a Renaissance château with its conical peaked towers, moat and wooded hunting grounds – the perfect place to forget that the Commune ever happened. Here, the Duc had assembled a veritable mob of monarchists to greet Bertie and make his return to the French good life a memorable one.

Most memorable of all was Hélène Standish, the glamorous 27-year-old wife of Henry Standish, who was a French aristocrat despite his name – his father was an Englishman who had moved to France and married into blue French blood. Hélène Standish was of noble birth herself, and was by all accounts both classy and sexy – exactly the kind of woman who attracted Bertie to France. Like others who sensed that he occasionally needed some subliminal excuse for his adulterous adventures, Hélène often dressed like Alexandra, in a high collar and tight bodice, and even possessed a startlingly similar face. Bertie had met her in London the previous year and now made sure that he wouldn't waste his golden opportunity to pursue their acquaintance.

Back in Paris, Bertie was seen entering Hélène's house (or rather, her husband's house) on the chic avenue d'Iéna, near the Arc de Triomphe, where he apparently spent 'many hours'. We know this because he was being followed by the Parisian police who, unlike many of their royalist politicians, were anxious to protect their new republic, and didn't want the English Prince plotting to bring it down.

The police were right to have their suspicions, because a coup d'état was a real possibility. Bertie's royalist friends in Paris had started organizing banquets in their *hôtels particuliers* in the old medieval neighbourhoods, away from the flashy boulevards, as if to demonstrate to the city that theirs was a longer-lasting aristocracy than the fake one created by the *nouveau-riche* Napoléon III.

Bertie attended some of these parties before travelling north of Paris to Chantilly, to see more evidence of the growing royalist resurgency. He paid a visit *chez* his old friend Henri d'Orléans, Duc d'Aumale, the third surviving son of former King Louis-Philippe. Bertie had met Henri while he was living in Twickenham following his father's abdication, and been instantly impressed. Bertie told a friend that he loved talking to Henri because he represented 'the flower of exquisite French politeness. Every time I speak to him I feel as though I am receiving a lesson in French history. His knowledge is so vast and his memories are so precise.' Henri had returned to France as soon as the Commune was over, and was now a general with a whole army under his command. The preparations for a new royalist page in France's history book couldn't have been clearer.

Henri's country seat, the Château de Chantilly, had escaped being requisitioned by both Napoléon III and the new French republic because it was a complete ruin. Now Henri was back on his home turf and having the château completely rebuilt, transforming it into the veritable palace that it is today. The intention was clear – this was to be a home fit for a king.

In Henri's vast personal forest, Bertie rode to hounds, ostensibly to hunt stags, but he was probably more interested in pursuing one of the other riders, the scandalous Anne-Alexandrine-Jeanne-Marguerite Seillière de Sagan, famous for ball gowns that, according to one witness, 'left the company in no possibility of doubting the symmetry of her limbs and general shapeliness of her person'. She was the flirt who had confided to Bertie at their first meeting in 1867 that she was unhappily married* – and at the Chantilly hunt, he took the hint. They became lovers, and their affair was even formalized by inspiring an obscene French pun. It was said of them that 'Sagan est son gant' – 'Sagan is his glove'.

Bertie followed Madame de Sagan as far as her own home at Mello, just north of Chantilly, where she too had had the builders in. Work had recently finished on a new Renaissance-style château, replacing a castle dating back to Louis XV that Madame had considered too plain. The interior was renowned to be one of the most lavishly

* See Chapter 4.

furnished and decorated in the country. Anne-Alexandrine-Jeanne-Marguerite was a financier's daughter who knew how to spend money.

Perhaps inspired by the château's name, Bertie was obviously feeling mellow, because while there he excused himself from the other guests and retired with his hostess into her boudoir for some privacy. But he was too complacent and left his clothes where they could be seen by Madame de Sagan's son. The jealous teenager picked them up and threw them into a fountain. When his mother found out, she was so furious that she sent him away to a religious boarding school. In her house, children should neither be seen nor heard, especially when she was with one of her lovers.

In this sophisticated set, jealousy was confined to young-sters, and also present at that Mello house party was Hélène Standish, Bertie's other notable conquest on this trip. So he was sleeping with the mistress of the house in the presence of a second mistress.

Apparently only one woman refused Bertie's attentions on this trip, but in a playful, almost Alexandra-like way that must have made him chuckle. After spending an evening practising his French subjunctives into the ear of a certain Marquise d'Harcourt, the lady finally acquiesced to his advances and told him that she would put a rose outside her bedroom door so that he would be sure to find her. But when Bertie let himself in later that night, he found the bed occupied by the ugliest kitchen maid in the house. The Marquise's little joke. The question is: Was Bertie bothered? As the French proverb goes, 'In the dark, all cats are grey.' And in the autumn of 1874 he was a man on a mission: with Napoléon III out of the game, he had to prove to himself that he could don his mentor's mantle and become Paris's alpha male.

The omens were excellent. Bertie had overcome typhoid, just as Paris had survived the violence that had destroyed the Tuileries. He had come to France despite the opposition of his Teuton mother, just as Paris had shrugged off the memory of its Prussian occupiers. Now his charms were working again, and Frenchwomen were as desirable and available as ever. Paris was his oyster – no, his oyster buffet, to be consumed at will.

So what if one marquise wasn't interested? *Bof*, the kitchen maid was warm, willing and no doubt in complete awe of her royal visitor . . .

It was official – Bertie, and Paris, were back.

9

THE FRENCH TRY
TO BE ENGLISH

~

'The cut of his coat, the shape of his hat, even the colour of his gloves, were like laws.'

James de Chambrier, French writer, on Bertie's clothes

I

Even in his new format – rounder and balder – Bertie was still a popular sight around Paris. The locals were, overall, glad to see him return. As one of his French biographers, Philippe Jullian, expresses it, his attitude during the difficult period they had just lived through 'proved the Prince's loyalty to France'. Though Jullian was lucid about the reason for this fidelity: 'To people of a superficial nature, the strongest ties are those of pleasure. And he showed that he was not ungrateful to us for having amused him.'

Bertie was a very recognizable sight, even in the days

before the omnipresence of photographs. Having little to occupy him other than his personal habits, he was maniacal about his clothes. Wherever he went, he was always careful to dress exactly *comme il faut*. Parisians kept an eye out for him not only to see what mischief he might be getting up to, and with whom, but also for hints as to how they themselves should be dressing. It seems incredible, but at that time Paris looked to a plump Londoner for fashion tips.

But Bertie was more than a simple fashion victim. He had enough money to make his every sartorial whim a reality, as well as the self-assurance to wear what he liked. In short, as a style icon he was a sort of male, nineteenth-century Princess Diana – the ironic thing about this being that he had originally learnt his fashion sense from the very people who now admired him for it.

Bertie had first witnessed the French in all their finery when he came to Paris with his parents in 1855. However, the real importance of being sharply dressed would only have dawned on the Prince when he began visiting Napoléon and Eugénie as a young man, and realized how high the fashion bar was set.

The imperial couple were strict taskmasters, demanding precisely the right dress for each occasion. It was a fashion dictatorship. At each of their six annual balls, the invitation specified that men should be 'en uniforme', so that all the officers turned out in their regimental colours, sporting the kind of braided jackets that the Beatles and Jimi Hendrix would adopt a century later as their own psychedelic uniform. Meanwhile, at every official function, the foreign dignitaries would be smothered in sashes and medals, and usually dressed up in some kind of national army uniform, even if they had never drawn a sabre in anger. Civilian men had to follow a strict dress code that was subtly different for each type of occasion, consisting of a variation on black tails, tight white waistcoat and high collar, black knickerbockers and knee-length stockings – all of which spawned a highly profitable costume rental industry in Paris. Bertie was a guest of honour at almost every Parisian reception he attended, and would therefore have received a detailed briefing before each event so that he would be perfectly attired. For men at the imperial court, there was no room for improvisation.

Standards of dress were just as demanding for the women guests, though they were freer to personalize their costume, because the principal role of a female at Napoléon's court was to look stunning (though not quite as stunning as Eugénie, of course). A single ball gown could make or break a woman's reputation. In his memoirs of life during the Second Empire, the Comte de Maugny describes a countess who shone at court because of 'the perfection of her features, the academic purity of her curves . . . and her brilliant choice of lovers'. This lady once arrived at a fancy-dress ball at 2 a.m. (after the imperial couple had left, so as not to eclipse the Empress) dressed as a Roman goddess. Her skimpy dress was slit down one side from top to bottom, revealing erotic expanses of outer thigh and what de Maugny calls 'a foot of unreal perfection' left half-naked by an open sandal. Yes, a woman was showing her toes in public. It is hard to imagine anything similar happening at one of Victoria's sober gatherings.

When the young Bertie first ventured outside the imperial palace, he would have seen that well-off Parisians about town were also stylishly dressed. Daytime wear for chic men at that time was a long, buttoned-up jacket, a stiff high collar, a very tall top hat, accompanied by gloves worn thin and tight to prove that you didn't need to use them for anything practical. The outward style was similar to that of rich young men in London, but in Paris this playboy set reigned as uncontested masters over whole sections of the city, strutting along every boulevard as if they were in the grounds of their châteaux. And as we have seen, many of these wealthy Parisians did possess châteaux – the *hôtels particuliers* – in the city.

As soon as Bertie had got the measure of these Parisian high standards, he took them back to London and adapted them to his life there, getting his tailor, Henry Poole of Savile Row, to add what the French now like to call 'le British touch' and creating his own personal style – which he then re-imported into Paris. The French loved it, and the adjective most frequently used about Bertie was 'impeccable'. Here is Xavier Paoli, the French police *commissaire* who would later be his official bodyguard, catching sight of him for the first time in the 1870s:

Beneath the impeccable cut of a navy-blue tweed suit, his gait was fluid and remarkably relaxed. From the expertly tied knot of his tie to the fine silk handkerchief peeping from his breast pocket; from the gold-handled bamboo cane tucked under his arm to the perfumed Havana between his lips; from the light-grey felt hat that he wore tipped slightly to the left to the yellow suede gloves with black trimming, everything suggested sober elegance and subtle refinement.

The French policeman, a representative of the Republic, was instantly under the suave Prince's spell.

Bertie is credited with several sartorial inventions. If we are to believe some sources, he was the first man in the world to have turn-ups on his trousers, after going for a walk in the country and shortening his trouser legs so they wouldn't get wet. He is also said to have started the fashion for leaving one's lowest waistcoat button undone when he began loosening his clothes to accommodate his burgeoning waistline. This plumpness then led to him leaving his jacket completely unbuttoned, a fashion that Parisian men of all girths adopted. And proving that he was always open to new ideas, Bertie also began a craze for uncreased trousers after a valet accidentally ironed along the seams instead of putting a sharp crease in the front and back of the leg.

His greatest invention, though, was the dinner jacket. Legend has it that it was Bertie who first requested a short jacket for evening wear from Henry Poole. This may not sound as ground-breaking as the discovery of penicillin or the invention of the steam engine, but it is surely no bad thing that a British royal once conceived an idea more universal than marrying six wives or invading France.

As the story goes, the long frock coat with tails was becoming less and less popular in London for informal wear in the 1850s and 1860s. The tails were first removed for horse-riding in Hyde Park, for practical reasons, and then for general town wear. In the evening, though, tails were a must for anyone who wanted to look chic. Men got into the habit of putting a straight-collared velvet jacket over their evening suit when they went off to smoke after dinner so that their clothes wouldn't stink of stale cigars, and this smoking jacket* gradually became shorter. Apparently it was Bertie who first asked Henry Poole to make a smoking jacket out of black wool, with a silk collar so that it could be worn all evening at more informal get-togethers with friends (like Napoléon and Eugénie, he had innumerable sub-divisions of formality in his various residences). Perhaps Bertie was just too lazy to change into and out of a smoking jacket, or – more probably – he wanted smoking to be a permanent fixture of the evening rather than limiting it to a post-prandial puff. Either way, the James Bond jacket was born, and has survived to this day.

Incidentally, Bertie also conspired to give the dinner jacket its other name, the tuxedo. In the summer of 1886, a rich American coffee merchant called James Brown Potter

---

* Interestingly, the French word for a dinner jacket harks back to these origins – it is *le smoking*. The fact that it is an English term is probably not only a homage to Bertie. Even though the activity of smoking is still considered fairly chic by many French people, their word for smoking, *fumer*, and anything associated with it, sounds rather vulgar. *Fumier*, for example, means dung.

and his wife Cora came to London and were invited to a ball attended by Bertie. The beautiful Cora caught his eye and he invited the couple to dinner. When James asked what he should wear to such an occasion, Bertie told him to consult his tailor.

Perhaps Bertie had secretly designed a cuckolded husband's costume equipped with earmuffs and a blindfold, but in the event Henry Poole fitted the American out in one of Bertie's short dinner jackets. Mr Brown Potter took the jacket home and wore it to a function at his New York country club, Tuxedo Park, from where it spread right across America, branded with its new name. If only Bertie had thought to patent his invention, his gambling debts would have been a thing of the past.

II

Bertie was just as influential on women's fashions in Paris, mainly thanks to his choice of lovers. As we have seen in a previous chapter, his mistresses would sometimes begin dressing like Princess Alexandra as a badge of honour. And because the smartest thing to be in Paris was an English prince's lover, other women began to adopt the same fashion.

Alexandra's sober style led to the abandonment of the crinoline, the parasol-like dress that had turned mid-nineteenth-century women into walking lampshades. This fashion for ultra-wide skirts held out by layers of stiff petticoats had begun in the 1830s, and by the 1850s had become so extreme that the most fashionable women could hardly walk beneath the weight of their underwear, inspiring an American to invent a hooped frame that gave the dress its shape without obliging the woman to wear so many petticoats. The crinoline reached the height (or breadth) of its popularity at Eugénie's court, where the low-cut bodice left the top half of a lady's torso enticingly exposed while the domed skirt kept men at arm's length – at least until a lady stepped out of her evening gown and invited him closer.

After the collapse of Eugenie's court and her inflated skirts, things changed. Princess Alexandra was amongst the leaders of a new fashion for a flatter-fronted dress which extended at the back in a sort of train, eventually evolving into a full bustle. Because Alexandra had a scar on her neck from a childhood operation, she would usually wear a choker necklace in public, which also became very fashionable. As her marriage wore on and she became even less sensual than she had been as a young bride, her cleavage disappeared behind higher collars, and, strangely, the eternally sensual *Parisiennes* adopted this fashion too. In the 1880s Alexandra even inspired Parisian *cocottes* to imitate her immobile face that one painter of the time, Paul Helleu, described as 'a silver mirror'.

These extremes were part of a general French Anglomania largely created by Bertie. Forever turning up in amusing but chic new street fashions, he had shown France that the odd siege or massacre was no reason to abandon a life of fun, and he now became a kind of ideal man for many Parisians – despite (or perhaps because of) the fact that the newspapers back in London were constantly complaining about his overspending, his political indiscretions and his fondness for other men's wives.

It was for Bertie that the French imported the English style of hunting – that is, driving creatures towards shotguns and massacring them. In the autumn of 1874, Bertie's friend the Duc de La Rochefoucauld-Bisaccia organized a pheasant hunt at Esclimont, his château in the forest just outside Paris. Journalists from the newspaper *Le Figaro* were invited along to witness the novel event, and reported that the Duc and the other French royalists were mostly rotten shots, but that Bertie was a fine marksman, personally bagging eighty birds. They were too diplomatic, or too ill informed, to reveal that the Duc had wisely ordered several hundred dead pheasants from a poulterer to make sure that the hunt flattered his guests.

On Bertie's next visit to France in March 1875, he was invited to another *chasse à l'anglaise* at the Château de Serrant on the Loire, home of another French royalist friend, the Duc de La Trémoille. Here, Bertie reportedly bagged 300 pheasants in a single Monday morning. How many of them were dead before he shot them is impossible to know.

The guns naturally had to be accessorized with Bertie-style tweeds, and occasionally this new French taste for the English-landowner look caused confusion. There is an anecdote about a French aristocrat who took to dressing up as an English country gent at his château. One day, he showed some English visitors around his stables, and at the end of the tour, one of them gave him a tip. Because of the way he was dressed, they had all assumed he was a stable lad (for which the French have an English name, incidentally – *un groom*). The *aristo* thought this was so funny that he had the tip framed and hung it in his family gallery alongside his noble ancestors.

It also became fashionable in the chic parts of Paris to speak like Bertie and pepper one's French with English words. The biographer Philippe Jullian tells a story about a snobbish Parisian being served a bad wine in a restaurant, and declaring that from now he was only going to eat at the Café Anglais where he would be sure of getting 'un bon claret' – claret being the exclusively English word for what the French would call a *Bordeaux rouge*.

Bertie's personal appearances in Paris became highly important events in the city's cultural life. The best evidence for this is an opera written by Jacques Offenbach and his librettist Albert Millaud in 1874, when they were still rebuilding their careers after the Commune. The opera was *Madame l'Archiduc*, a typically fluffy story about an archduke who falls in love with a servant, into which Millaud had (very fashionably) inserted a duet sung in Franglais. Two characters at an inn are pretending to be English, and sing a song with lines like 'Oh yes! Come, come, boivez wine, so beautiful, divine' and 'Very well, I tank* you, oh my dear'. Deliberately ungrammatical

* This misspelling reflects, of course, the French inability to pronounce the 'th' sound. Mispronouncing 'thank you' is a favourite

nonsense that a Parisian audience would have found hilarious.

When Bertie visited Paris in March 1875, he went to see *Madame l'Archiduc*, helping to make it a hit after a slow start at the box office. And he probably got a great kick out of the Franglais song. If he had any literary sensibility at all (which is arguable), he might have noticed one telling line in the duet: 'Oh! Ce rosbeef very fine.' In the context of the scene, this could be taken literally to mean that the roast beef served at the inn is excellent, but 'rosbif' (as it is usually spelt nowadays) is also a slang term for an Englishman. Everyone in the theatre that night would have known that *le prince anglais* was in attendance, and it's easy to imagine the singer bowing towards Bertie as he sang the line. And it may not be going too far to surmise that Offenbach and Millaud inserted the Franglais scene with the precise intention of attracting Bertie along to hear it. If so, their strategy worked perfectly, because the first time Bertie visited Paris after the opera opened, he went along.

Naturally, during the performance Bertie was seen to spend most of his time gazing through his opera glasses at beautiful women in the audience, but then most of the audience would have gone there in the hope of being gazed at. And there would have been plenty of opera glasses trained on Bertie, too, to see what he was wearing that

---

French game, and variants include 'Saint Cloud' – the suburb of Paris, pronounced 'san cloo' – and 'ton cul' ('ton coo'), which means 'your arse'. In fact, in *Madame l'Archiduc*, the singer might well have pronounced the line 'Very well, I *ton cul*, oh my dear' to get an extra laugh.

night. In the 1870s and 1880s, Paris was a republic, but in terms of style its ruler was a prince.

III

Bertie and Alexandra can't claim all the merit for the English influence on Parisian fashion – at least where women's clothing was concerned. A lot of the credit has to go to an Englishman called Charles Worth.

Worth first came to Paris in 1845 as an ambitious twenty-year-old fabric salesman to work for the Maison Gagelin, a popular shop selling both cloth and ready-made clothing. Worth began designing dresses, and was soon promoted to head his own department in the business. When the Maison Gagelin was invited to provide clothes for the wedding of Empress Eugénie in 1853, Worth contributed some of his dresses, which were noticed by Paris's new First Lady. After winning a prize at the 1855 Paris Exposition Universelle (where he exhibited in the French section, of course, for Gagelin), the Englishman found himself a financier – a Swede called Otto Bobergh – and opened his own shop in the chic rue de la Paix, between Opéra and Concorde.

It was a canny move – this was exactly the right time to be starting a luxury business in Paris, because in Napoléon and Eugénie's capital, impressing people with your dress sense was a key part of a woman's social success. What was more, Worth's shop soon had the city's number-one customer on its books, the *maîtresse* of style, Eugénie herself. Once it became known that the Empress shopped *chez* Worth, any Parisian lady worth her *sel* was dying to get on to his client list – and being turned away if she wasn't important enough. Interestingly, amongst the élite customers accepted by Worth were the famous *cocottes*, notably the two English stars of Paris's sex-for-money scene, Cora Pearl and Catherine 'Skittles' Walters. And this in no way drove away the more respectable ladies – in the Second Empire, the high-class prostitutes formed a parallel aristocracy.

As well as a keen eye for business and a sense of style, Worth had come up through the ranks and therefore possessed a true working knowledge of new fabrics on the market and the way they behaved when cut. His success was no coincidence – his customers knew that their dress would fit perfectly, and we have seen how important that was when it came to the plunging necklines at Eugénie's court. Any bit of bad tailoring would have caused an embarrassing fashion accident.

Worth was a true craftsman-artist. His skill, and his unbeatable client list, helped him impose his own dictatorial rules. The most imposing Parisian aristocrat could no longer come and tell the tailor to carry out her instructions – she would wear what he told her. She had to buy dresses for the morning, afternoon and evening as well as more relaxed tea gowns and nightgowns to be worn at home. She would also buy new designs each season, because fashions would change, by order of Worth – although she could also be sure that her particular version of the design would be unique. Furthermore, the lady would accept Worth's choice of accessories, made by his associates in the shoemaking, bagmaking and millinery trades. In short, he was creating what the French call *le total look* as well as inventing the business model followed by all the best *haute couture* houses today.

Understandably, Worth closed up shop during the Franco-Prussian war when most of his clients left the city, but he returned after the Commune – minus his Swedish business partner, but with new designs in mind. It was when he made this Parisian comeback that he put an end to the crinoline.

The reopening of his shop was taken as a key sign of regeneration in the city. In a diary entry for January 1872, the writer Edmond de Goncourt records seeing a traffic jam in the rue de la Paix, caused by carriages jostling to get into the courtyard of a building. He walks closer and: 'Looking above the entrance to the courtyard, I read: Worth. Paris is just as it was during the Empire.' What he meant was that the rich, fashionable women were back in town and the first thing they were doing was rush to get the latest English designs.

It would of course have been a miracle if everyone in Paris approved of this Anglo influence. Goncourt's diary for 1875 contains a hilarious description of English tourists eating at the chic Café Voisin, one of Bertie's haunts: He writes:

The joy with which the *Anglais* stuff themselves is a truly disgusting thing that you don't see in any other civilized people. As they eat, their whole brain is concentrated on chewing and gulping. The men utter little grunts of animal satisfaction, while their pink-and-white-faced women glow with mindless intoxication. The sons and tomboy daughters grin lovingly at their meat. All of them – men, women and children – put on a show of bestial obsession, mute reple-tion and imbecilic ecstasy.

What Goncourt was witnessing, of course, was a family of English tourists who had come to a fashionable Paris café to enjoy the food, rather than look around to see who was with whom and gossip accordingly. In this respect, Bertie would never have 'disgusted' Goncourt – he was an *Anglais* in Paris who always behaved exactly like a Parisian.

10

BERTIE MAKES AN EXHIBITION OF HIMSELF . . . AGAIN

~

'He loves France both in a fun-loving and a serious way.'
Léon Gambetta, French politician, talking about Bertie

I

There was now a hiatus in Bertie's Parisian expeditions while he went on a long trip to India and Sri Lanka. The seven-month voyage – which was basically a big-game hunting trip at the state's expense – was his idea, and was approved by Victoria as a good diplomatic move, although she objected when Bertie said that he wanted to go without Alexandra. The Empress of India had probably not read the *Kama Sutra*, but knew all about the effects on her son of sultry foreign women.

Bertie successfully argued that his wife's health wasn't

up to the tropics (though Alexandra herself was bitterly disappointed at being left behind), and even managed to put together a travelling party consisting mainly of his friends, including his roistering sidekick Charles Wynn-Carrington. But Victoria had a word in certain ears and Canon Arthur Stanley, Regius Professor of Ecclesiastical History at Oxford, was sent along as Bertie's chaplain and guide. Just before the party left on their eastern jaunt, Stanley preached a sermon at Westminster Abbey aimed at his fellow travellers, imploring God to ensure that: 'Wherever they may go, may they see that the name of England and English Christendom may not be dishonoured, that morals shall not be relaxed, that the sensual flag* shall not be raised, and that the standard of national morality shall not be lowered but raised aloft.' Which would have been an ideal prayer every time Bertie left for Paris.

Of course, before leaving, Bertie found time to dash across the Channel to revisit a few royalists and make sure that Mesdames Standish and de Sagan weren't feeling lonely. He was also seen at the Jockey Club, and spotted steering a pair of *cocottes* around town. All in all, a refreshing Parisian break before the rigours of a state visit in the Orient.

While *en voyage* from October 1875 to May 1876, Bertie apparently stayed away from the local ladies, but let himself go with the wildlife, blasting at all creatures great and small

---

* Presumably, in Bertie's case, a pennant featuring two pearl earrings and a cigar rampant on a background of gambling-table green.

and doing his personal best to turn the subcontinent's tigers into an endangered species.

More to his credit, he also took a potshot at some of the racist Englishmen of the Raj. While in India, Bertie wrote home to complain to the Foreign Secretary about the bad treatment of Indians by the British military – he suggested that the locals should be 'treated with kindness and firmness at the same time, but not with brutality or contempt'. He even seemed to be contradicting the whole ethos of colonialism when he added that, 'Because a man has a black face and a different religion from our own, there is no reason why he should be treated as a brute.' Bertie was a snob, but he was usually a polite one. And these were not mere theories – as a result of his complaints, the British governor of the city of the southern city of Hyderabad, the so-called Resident, was sent home in disgrace. In colonial clubs across the subcontinent there must have been much spluttering into gin and tonics about moralizing by dissolute young pups.

And before Bertie had even reached England again, he was being accused of immorality at home. One of the friends on his Indian trip, Lord Aylesford, had returned early after receiving a letter from his wife informing him that she was planning to elope with her lover, Lord Blandford. (She clearly didn't understand the word 'elope'.) In the 1870s this was scandalous because it meant divorce, which, as we have seen, was then a more heinous social misdeed than publicly shooting ponies. When Bertie's sympathy for Aylesford became known, Blandford's younger brother,

Randolph Churchill (father of Winston), was furious and announced that he had letters from Lady Aylesford proving that Bertie himself had been one of her lovers. The scandal was developing like the plot of an Oscar Wilde play, and Bertie added to the melodrama by challenging Churchill to a duel with pistols on the north coast of France – an offer that Churchill rightly scoffed at as pure fantasy on Bertie's part.

In the end, this absurd upper-class Pandora's box had the lid put back on it by the Aylesfords deciding not to divorce after all, but the feud between Bertie and the Churchill family would linger on until the mid-1880s. All in all, it was not a great homecoming for Bertie.

II

Luckily, France would come to his rescue. Despite the power struggle going on in Paris between the republicans and the different royalist factions, by 1876 all parties had concurred that the best way to celebrate France's recovery from war was another Exposition, to be held in 1878. It was to be a massive enterprise, with a vast showground straddling the Seine at Trocadéro and taking up all of the Champ-de-Mars from the riverbank to Napoléon Bonaparte's old school, the École Militaire. And, proving that despite all its recent turmoils, France had not forgotten its most faithful English friend, the President of France, Patrice de Mac Mahon, asked Bertie to become Honorary President of the British section of the Exposition, as he had been in 1867.

Mac Mahon must have been shocked when Bertie refused the honour. What? Had the Indian trip erased all his fond memories of France? Hadn't he enjoyed himself at the 1855 and 1867 exhibitions? Didn't he want to come to Paris, admire a few machines, sit on a podium or two and then sneak off to the theatre?

But Bertie had good reason to refuse the honorary president role: he preferred to be an executive president, while also taking on the job back home in London as the President of the Royal Commission for the Paris Exhibition of 1878. In other words, he was to be one of the team overseeing preparations for the whole Expo as well as being the active head of the British delegation. As such, not only would he attend the opening and closing ceremonies, and a few in between, he would also have to come to Paris regularly to check on the progress of his British 'pavilions' and the rest of the exhibition site. He would be over there non-stop. It was Bertie's dream job.

It must have also been a key moment for him. Here was a chance to be *involved* in something for once, and to take on the official diplomatic role that he had been yearning for for so long. It was no sinecure, either – the exhibition space to be filled by the Brits was second in size only to France's own. Bertie would have to supervise the building of the British exhibition halls, as well as overseeing the selection and approval of all the exhibitors, not only for the British Isles, but also for the colonies, including Canada and Australia. It was an enormous task that he would embrace wholeheartedly for the next two years.

The curious thing is that the thoroughness with which Bertie now undertook the job, and the success he made of it, are achievements that are almost entirely overlooked in most of his biographies, perhaps because his biographers are captivated by the other passion that entered his life at this time – his most famous and most beautiful mistress, Lillie Langtry.

Lillie's story and the details of her affair with Bertie are very well documented. She was the daughter of a womanizing clergyman in Jersey, and came to London at the age of twenty-three, where she suddenly discovered that she was beautiful. After one society *soirée* in May 1877, at which practically every fashionable artist in England fell swooning at her feet, Lillie became an instant celebrity. Heavy-jawed, she would probably not have made such a splash in modern London, but she was idealized by the pre-Raphaelite artists, and captured everyone's hearts. It was only a matter of time before the 'Jersey Lily' came to the notice of the city's chief talent scout, Bertie, and once rumours about the pair began to circulate, her status was settled. After Queen Victoria and Princess Alexandra, Lillie was suddenly the most famous woman in England.

As a candidate for royal mistress, Lillie didn't need idealizing. She was young, married and possessed a nondescript husband who seems to have resigned himself very quickly to his wife's sudden independence. More than this, though, Lillie was the type of woman Bertie loved most – spirited and witty, aware of his status and respectful of it, but willing to speak her mind. She could almost have been French.

In Paris, Lillie would probably have become a *cocotte*, but in England there was another way for a poor girl to buy the dresses and rent the house that she needed if she was to impose herself on glamorous London life. She became a 'professional beauty'. Reproductions of the paintings of Lillie and postcards of her photographic portraits began to sell like hot cakes, and must have brought in a tidy income. In this, she was like the other category of person that Bertie always warmed to – the self-made man. And just as he had done with bankers and industrialists, he supported Lillie's ambitions with introductions to the right people, invitations to the right parties (the only caveat being that Princess Alexandra must never be embarrassed by Lillie's presence), and the odd gift. He even went as far as having a love nest built for them in Bournemouth on the south coast, which was then a quiet health resort rather than the beach metropolis that it is today. However, Bertie wasn't quite as generous as some of his biographers make out, because the house was not, as some have suggested, on the seafront but a good ten-minute walk inland, set in an avenue where other similar houses were being built.

Biographers also point out that at this time, Bertie's trips to Paris suddenly stopped looking like stag parties. He was spending less time chasing after the latest *cocottes*, and fewer evenings in the upstairs rooms at cafés. But this was not because his wayward soul had been calmed by his love for Lillie. Bertie was now a man with a mission, a prince – at last – with a purpose. He was working on his Exposition.

III

The Bibliothèque Nationale (France's national library) possesses a full collection of a magazine called *L'Exposition Universelle de 1878 Illustrée*. It was created in 1876 as soon as the planning for the exhibition began, and ran until the show closed at the end of October 1878. Its purpose was to drum up public excitement for the occasion and keep everyone abreast of progress. It published designs for the various buildings, explained who was who, and trumpeted the government's view that this was to be a celebration of the new France. The magazine was a weekly, and Bertie features in almost every issue. The articles about him give an idea of how dedicated – and important – he was to the whole project, and to France's image in a decidedly stormy Europe.

An early issue in May 1876 sets out the Exposition's ethos and shows a decidedly pro-Anglo bent, no doubt in part thanks to Bertie. A writer is describing the cafés and restaurants that will be built on the exhibition site, and adds that 'taking a lesson from our English and American friends, there will also be well-stocked buffets. On y lunchera,' he says – we will lunch there. The writer has coined a new Franglais verb, *luncher*, the kind of invention that enrages modern-day protectors of the 'purity' of the French language, but which proves that back then, this Anglo influence was welcome, something to be affectionately joked about.

In October 1876, the magazine announces with evident pleasure that Bertie is to be 'le Président executif' and that he has formed a Royal Commission to manage Britain's contribution to the Expo. He will, it says, be 'putting his hands to the pastry', meaning getting them dirty.

Looking through different issues of the magazine, one gets an idea of Bertie's enthusiastic hands-on participation over the next two years. We see him presiding over a meeting in London and issuing a request for the space attributed to British exhibitors to be tripled. He comes to Paris and spends half a day visiting the exhibition site with members of his Royal Commission and the French politicians and architects behind the project. He announces that he will be creating a personal exhibition consisting of the gifts – especially the carpets, cashmeres and jewels – that he received during his tour of India, and comes to inspect the new pavilion commissioned specially for his show.

There are dozens of similar references to the Prince's hard work. And not all the VIPs involved in the project get the same treatment. While Bertie is being praised for encouraging his architect to design a new façade for the expanded British exhibition space, other European countries get mere one-line mentions. A trainload of Austrian machinery is reported to be on its way, or the Danes are going to send a special consignment of pickled herring.

In February 1878, it is reported that the British section is 'the most advanced of all' and the Expo's French spokesman declares that: 'We must pay homage to the activity deployed by the Royal Commission and its delegates under the powerful impulsion of HRH the Prince of Wales.'

Of course there is a dose of obsequiousness in all this, but the sheer number of matter-of-fact reports about telegrams written, requests made and visits paid tells a story of real involvement on Bertie's part.

And he was more than the head of a working committee. He was also, for the first time in his life, playing a serious diplomatic role. As Russia went to war with Turkey and the European nations declared their conflicting allegiances, Bertie was quoted in *L'Exposition Universelle de 1878 Illustrée* reassuring French readers that 'despite the gravity of political events in the Orient, the attention of England will never be distracted from this great work of peace to which France has invited it'.

At the banquet on 3 May 1878 to mark the opening of the Exposition, Bertie went even further. He had been in Paris for a week overseeing the finishing touches to the British exhibits, when, in front of his Royal Commission, the French Minister of Commerce and the entire British press, Bertie made a diplomatic gesture that the magazine reported in breathless terms: '[The Prince's] short stay in Paris was marked by an event that no one in France will ever forget.' Bertie's speech (which he gave in French, without using notes) is then reprinted at length, and it is worth quoting a large section because it is one of the most eloquent pieces of public speaking he ever did. It sounds so personal – and so un-English – that it can only be his own work.

After thanking the organizers for their help, Bertie reminds his audience that the banquet is being held in a country:

. . . which has always received Englishmen with hospitality. Many years ago there was, it was true, a time when the two nations were not so friendly, but these times are past and forgotten. The jealousies from which enmity arose have now, I am sure, ceased to exist, and have been replaced by a cordiality of feeling that is not likely to be changed. Today we can already affirm that the 1878 Exposition Universelle will be a great success. Therefore permit me to say to everyone in France that the prosperity of this country and Great Britain are interwoven here, and that the cordial participation that we have contributed to the triumph of industry and the arts in this peaceful enterprise is of the highest importance for our two nations and for the whole world. The part that we have played in the Exposition Universelle is the best proof of friendship that we can give to the French people, to whom we owe so much and whom I love with all my heart, and I hope that this Exposition will live on in all memories as an emblem of work, concord and peace.

Granted, there may be more than a little champagne speaking, and when Bertie says that 'we owe so much' to France, it is probably a royal we – he must have been thinking of everything he had learnt from Napoléon III and the *cocottes*. The speech also reflects the mixture of self-satisfaction and relief that colours any inauguration dinner. Even so, for once in his life, Bertie is sounding like a cross between a foreign secretary, a minister of development and, yes, a king.

Various biographers underline the Prince's naïvety and ignorance about the Russian–Turkish crisis – it is said, for example, that he got all his opinions about it from a colonel in the 10th Hussars who had been discharged from the army after raping a Turkish girl. But articles published in the international press at the time of the Exposition paint a very different picture. A correspondent for the Australian newspapers reported that Bertie had single-handedly changed the French government's mind on European policy. Previously it might have sided with Russia, the reporter says, but since his speech, the French have:

> . . . recognized the old identity of interest between England and France, and the Prince's popularity in Paris has sealed the change. In that respect the Exhibition may turn out to have been an important factor in smoothing away Eastern complications. In the Congress [of Berlin, the international talks to end the Russian–Turkish conflict] we* are now practically sure of the support of France as well as of Germany, and Italy if not our partisan will be at least a friendly neutral.

Bertie the international peacemaker, as seen by his contemporaries.

Bertie also made an impact on French domestic politics, according to another British newspaper correspondent, Broadbrim, who noted in one of his regular 'Letters from France' that:

---

* Australia was at the time a loyal British colony, so that this 'we' would have referred to Britain and its whole empire. Also, the writer was almost certainly British, and syndicated in newspapers in the colonies.

Only a few days before the opening [of the Exposition] a band of rioters were arrested by the gendarmes shouting for Napoléon and the Empire. It was evident that another coup d'état was anxiously expected and hoped for . . . All these expectations have been doomed to a cruel disappointment.

Thanks to Bertie.

And what about the Expo itself? Well, the French were justifiably proud of themselves for an exhibition that introduced such Gallic innovations as the first solar oven and a gold-medal-winning fizzy drinks machine, but the British press was clear about who had put on the best show. One correspondent boasted that: 'The exhibit of England stands out with a regal magnificence which has distanced all competition, and which silences even the voice of envy.' Bertie and his Royal Commission had put together 40,000 square yards of British exhibition space, occupying more than 120 pages of the 400-page catalogue listing all the foreign exhibitors. The British buildings were a row of five small houses, including a mock-Tudor cottage and a neo-Gothic urban villa decorated with Doulton ceramics, a British buffet, a greenhouse, the Prince of Wales's personal exhibition space and the much larger galleries containing the various industrial, agricultural and commercial exhibitors.

The British firms selling their wares read like a portrait of Victorian Britain tinged with Bertie's own tastes – there were suppliers and makers of hunting rifles, fishing rods, silver sandwich boxes, waterproof overcoats, heaters for use on yachts, and, thanks to Bertie's trendiness, literally dozens of tweed merchants. There was also a manufacturer of water filters, perhaps a recommendation from the recent typhoid sufferer.

Looking outside Bertie's own interests, there were British firms offering to supply the world with railway ambulances, school furniture, English bibles and stained-glass windows, cricket equipment, police helmets, canal lock gates and an impressive-sounding device for protecting undersea telegraph cables against damage by marine creatures. There was even a company hawking tapestry portraits of Queen Victoria, and, amongst the many photography stands, there were doubtless a few selling pictures of Lillie Langtry, too.

Despite British pride, however, this is an Expo best remembered for a French exhibit. France had recently signed a contract with the Americans to build a monumental statue called *Liberty Enlightening the World*, and construction was well under way. The hand holding the torch had gone on show at the Philadelphia Centennial Exposition in 1876 and now the Parisians exhibited the huge crowned head, into which spectators could climb and get an idea of how the 140-metre-tall Statue of Liberty would one day look when it was erected in New York. However many Bertie-style tweed suits were ordered, this had to be the biggest commercial project of the Expo, and represented a French triumph on the international scene.

Even so, it was a monument that was seen by Bertie's royalist friends in France as a provocation, a celebration by one republic of another's successful revolution. The fact that, after a period of uncertainty caused by the Franco-Prussian War, the joint Franco-American project was going ahead was a sign that the republicans were taking control of France. And despite his previous allegiances, Bertie was now perfectly at peace with this idea, and was busy forging a friendship with one of the unlikeliest people in Paris.

IV

Bertie described his first meeting with Léon Gambetta to Xavier Paoli, his police bodyguard, who quoted him saying that: 'He [Gambetta] seemed so vulgar-looking and carelessly dressed that I thought to myself, is this really the man who exerts such irresistible power over the people?' Bertie judged everyone by appearances, as he expected to be judged himself, so the relationship was getting off to a very bad start.

Léon Gambetta was the Member of Parliament for Paris's 20th arrondissement (one of the poorest parts of the city). He was a grocer's son who dressed like the intellectual ex-student that he was. And as well as this inherent scruffiness, Gambetta had a highly noticeable physical disability – he had lost an eye in childhood after getting hit by a metal splinter while watching a knife grinder.

But despite his appearance, Gambetta was acknowledged as the most influential man in France. In the middle of the siege of 1870–1 he had famously escaped from Paris in a hot-air balloon to represent the city at the exiled parliament. Staunchly republican, he was now a tireless powerbroker guiding the country through its tricky post-empire period. Travelling the country delivering rousing speeches, he had managed to rally the republican electorate and win the parliamentary elections at the beginning of 1876, effectively depriving President Mac Mahon and his allies of any excuse to engineer a return to monarchy. After Mac Mahon used his presidential powers to dissolve the new parliament, Gambetta went out on the soapbox again, and the republicans won even more convincingly in October 1877, weakening the royalists still further. This one-eyed, scarecrow-like politician was acknowledged as the great architect of the peaceful transition towards an enduring Third Republic, and Bertie wanted to meet him.

On 6 May 1878, three days after Bertie's banquet speech, the two men were introduced and spoke for what a British reporter called 'a considerable time' but which the *Courrier de Paris* newspaper described as three-quarters of an hour. They agreed that Britain and France should unite in their distrust of the Germans. 'Gambetta explained his ideas and his projects,' Bertie told the policeman Paoli, 'and the lucidity of his intelligence, the breadth of his opinions and his charming eloquence made me forget the disappointment of his physical appearance. I was won over, just like everyone else.'

Gambetta, too, seemed to have been seduced, proving that Bertie really was the only man in Britain, if not the whole world, who could be on friendly terms with all sides of the unstable and conflictual political scene in France. Only a few ultra-nationalists who still bore grudges about the *Anglais* burning Joan of Arc and sending Bonaparte to St Helena were immune to Bertie's charms.

In July 1878, at the Congress of Berlin, Britain made a peace deal whereby it received Cyprus from Turkey in exchange for signing an alliance with the Turks. This in turn annoyed the French, who saw their domination of the Eastern Mediterranean threatened by a British naval base. Anglo-French relations were so tense that Lord Lyons, the British Ambassador in Paris, warned Bertie not to return to the exhibition. Previously, Bertie would have ignored the advice on the grounds that he didn't want to be deprived of his French holiday, but now his determination to come and show his continued support for the Exposition – his 'great work of peace' – really can be seen as a political decision. He seems to have come to a personal realization that the best people to run France weren't necessarily those with the biggest châteaux.

Bertie made it known that he wanted to see Gambetta again in July, this time at one of his usual haunts, the Café Anglais. There, the two men had another friendly meeting, discussing amongst other things a permanent *entente cordiale* and a Channel Tunnel.* Afterwards, Lord Lyons sent a report to London saying that Bertie had 'acquitted himself with great skill'. In other words, Bertie was now Britain's chief negotiator with the most powerful man in France.

---

* Three years later, in 1881, serious talks about a Channel Tunnel began. Bertie was of course enthusiastic about any way of speeding up travel to France, and went to visit the proposed tunnel opening near Dover. But when opponents of the project lobbied against any breach in England's ancient sea defences, he changed his mind. In any case, it was much more discreet to cross the Channel by yacht.

Bertie kept up his dialogue with Gambetta, and even invited the scruffy republican into the chic homes of his royalist friends. In March 1881, the two men met for lunch *chez* the Marquis de Breteuil, a royalist MP, who gave an account of the meeting in which he said that Gambetta had a 'heavy, vulgar walk' and seemed to 'spread himself across the elegant floor of our living room like an oil stain on a piece of silk'. (Not snobbish at all, then.) This time, the talk was again of the need for continued *rapprochement* with Britain, although Bertie's main contribution to the conversation seems to have been a return to his old, super-ficial concerns – he told Gambetta that France ought to get rid of its ambassador to London because he was 'living with his cook'.

But it was in October 1882, just two months before Gambetta's premature death at the age of forty-four,* that the Prince and the Parisian had their most famous and most affectionate meeting. The former British republican Sir Charles Dilke was now Under-Secretary for Foreign Affairs and on excellent terms with Bertie, and he set up a lunch at a restaurant called the Moulin Rouge on the boulevard at Chaussée d'Antin – not the famous cabaret of the same name. The lunch went well, and Bertie decided that he would like Gambetta to meet one of his closest but most controversial friends, the royalist soldier Gaston de Gallifet, who was still known in Paris as the 'assassin' of

* Gambetta died of an infection after wounding himself in the hand while pistol-shooting. He was with his mistress at the time, and it was rumoured that he sustained the gunshot wound when he stopped her committing suicide.

the Communards. So Bertie invited Gambetta to the Café Anglais, where Gallifet would be dining.

For obvious reasons, Gallifet and Gambetta didn't become bosom buddies, but Gallifet has left us with what reads like an admirably even-handed account of the conversation between Bertie and Gambetta.

Bertie asked why French republicans seemed so determined to keep royalist aristocrats like Gallifet out of politics. Gambetta replied, 'There is no longer an aristocracy in France. There are only dukes who have no army to lead.' (This sounds very much like a jibe at Gallifet.) He added that French nobles 'have no desire for employment. They just sulk. That is their occupation.' Here, Bertie must have recognized a description of frustrated friends like Henri d'Orléans who had seen their hopes of a return to power crumble to dust over the previous few years.

Gambetta's ironic jibes kept coming, and Gallifet was fair enough to record them. 'You can see [the aristocrats] in our army and navy,' Gambetta said, 'or in the diplomatic service. In those professions they look very good, I admit.'

Bertie then asked, 'Why not do as we do in my country, where we ennoble the most distinguished men in industry, science, literature, commerce, and so on?' Again, we see Bertie's belief in the self-made man – he was a truly modern king in the making.

Gambetta was worldly enough to know that this English system wouldn't work in France: the traditional aristocrats would not be willing, he explained, 'to rub shoulders with the Duke of Industry, the Duke of Science and the Duke of Arts . . . As a republic, we can have only one aristocracy, that of knowledge and merit. And it doesn't need titles.'

Bertie conceded: 'You are a real republican, Monsieur Gambetta,' to which the man at the opposite end of the social and political scale replied, 'And I consider it logical that you should be a royalist.'

Not since Napoléon III's brief reign had Britain and France expressed such an amicable acceptance of each other's political differences, and even then, the maverick Emperor had been viewed with suspicion by the Brits. In the past, the idea of having a republic on the other side of the Channel had always been seen as a direct threat to Britain's monarchy. Suddenly that fear seemed to have dissipated, and the seeds of the lasting friendship that would later unite the traditional enemies in two World Wars were being sown by Bertie, who, until now, had been thought incapable of sowing anything except wild oats.

Gambetta summed up Bertie's affinity with France perfectly when he told his friends later that: 'It is no waste of time to talk with him over a cheerful supper at the Café Anglais. He loves France both in a fun-loving and serious way, and his dream for the future is an *entente* with us.'

Gambetta's actual words to describe Bertie's loving France were 'gaîment et sérieusement'. The French word *gai* means happy and light-hearted, while *sérieux* implies frankness, trustworthiness and real dedication. For example, the last thing you want in life is a plumber who is *pas sérieux* – your pipes will be leaking forever. In choosing this word, Gambetta hit the nail on the head – Bertie's relationship with France had evolved from a teenage crush into a deep, protective affection founded on mutual trust, understanding and admiration.

Fortunately this 'seriousness' didn't mean that the original spark had died. On the contrary, Bertie still found France incredibly sexy, as he was about to prove . . .

11

THE FRENCH MAKE WORK
FOR IDLE HANDS

～

'Mademoiselle La Goulue, you have the prettiest legs in Paris.'
Bertie flatters Paris's most notorious
can-can dancer, in public

I

As the 1880s began, and Bertie turned a plump, unhealthy forty, two influences came to bear on his life. First, Britain's mainstream journalists, who had until now been fairly discreet (unlike their republican colleagues), became more like their modern descendants – prying and prurient. There had always been a public appetite in Britain for royal gossip, but now, with literacy on the rise, there was more money to be earned selling juicy stories about the upper classes. Later, in June 1891, *The Times* would set out this new attitude in black and white – Bertie had no right to a private life, an editorial said, because he was 'the visible embodiment of the Monarchical principle', a slightly pompous way of saying that it was in the public interest to tell people if he was caught with his trousers down in a married lady's sitting room. In the 1880s, though, the self-justification was less well formulated, and the British reading public simply enjoyed scandal about high society, and especially the highest socialite, Bertie.

Far safer to go to Paris, where a man's private life was his own affair – and that of the madams and prostitutes he chose to spend it with. Consequently, during this period of disapproval at home, Bertie's Parisian escapades rose to new heights (or lows, depending on one's moral point of view).

The second theme in Bertie's life during this period was a heightening social conscience. This grew partly out of frustration that, despite his success as an Anglo-French negotiator, his mother refused to trust him with anything that really interested him – foreign, and especially European, politics. But Bertie also seems to have become increasingly aware that there were people around him who had no money for fresh cufflinks to meet every occasion, who drowned their sorrows in cheap gin when he was crowning his pleasures with champagne, and who didn't need to take annual spa cures to lose the pounds they had put on by eating four or five meals a day.

In 1884, Bertie became the head of a Royal Commission on the Housing of the Working Class, and had to be prevented from causing a riot by doling out money in the slums he visited. At the same time, his appointments diary, and that of his wife Princess Alexandra, began to fill up with hospital openings, most of them new institutions designed to care for the poor. Bertie would often twist friends' arms to contribute to these charitable causes, and rich men knew that if they made a donation to one of the Prince's schemes, they would be invited into his circle of friends and might even earn the privilege of lending him money to cover his gambling debts.

These public shows of concern for the needy had the added advantage of making Bertie increasingly popular with his future subjects, so that they became more forgetful about any indiscretions that might leak out into the press. When he acceded to the throne in 1901, he would continue these frequent public appearances in aid of the poor, and they would help him gain a reputation as a real people's monarch – a sort of plump, bearded, cigar-smoking Princess Diana.

And like so much in Bertie's life, it seems to have been Paris, and more specifically his newly discovered taste for the city's poorer neighbourhoods in the late 1870s and early 1880s, that sparked his new awareness of social issues. This was the time when the working-class areas of Montmartre and Pigalle came into their own, and when top-hatted toffs like Bertie made their first forays outside the realm of opera houses and expensive cafés and into the shadier world of street singers and straight-talking can-can girls.

II

By the end of the 1870s it was clear that France's young republic was going to survive. The final proof came in June 1879, when the last credible contender from the Bonapartist clan met a grisly end – thanks to the Brits.

Louis-Napoléon was the 23-year-old only child of Eugénie and Napoléon III, and, since his father's death in 1873, he had been making preparations to return to France and seize power. Like Henri d'Orléans, who went away to get battle experience in the American Civil War, Louis-Napoléon decided that the ideal training for a *coup d'état* was to see some action in uniform.

If all the adult French males with imperial or royal blood and political ambitions had actually got on their cavalry horses and charged on Paris, they might well have stood a chance of conquering their country, but in true French fashion, they seem to have spent more time talking about action than taking it, which explains why they were all destined to fail. At least Louis-Napoléon did so in spectacular style.*

Anticipating the day when he would march off the cross-Channel ferry and regain possession of his father's châteaux (those that hadn't been destroyed by the Parisians, anyway), Louis-Napoléon badgered his mother and Victoria to let him join the British army. After much resistance, they eventually gave in and let him board a troop ship bound

* For the full story of the young Bonaparte's unfortunate demise, see *1,000 Years of Annoying the French*.

for Southern Africa, where Britain was trying to convince the Zulus that they did not own any of their homeland.

Louis-Napoléon's commanding officers had been briefed not to let their imperial charge get into any physical danger, but he was Parisian and, as such, a persuasive (or at least irritating) talker, and parleyed his way on to a scouting mission into enemy territory. The small British troop was surprised by Zulu warriors, who put an end to France's chances of having another emperor with seventeen blows of their spears.

The decaying body was shipped back to England, where Bertie grieved with his friend and spiritual mother Eugénie, and even served (along with his brothers) as a pallbearer at the Catholic funeral – an unheard-of breach of Anglican royal protocol.

The two families had been closer than most people realized – when Louis-Napoléon sailed for Africa, there were plans afoot to make him Bertie's brother-in-law. Victoria and Eugénie had agreed that it would be a good idea to marry Louis-Napoléon to the Queen's youngest daughter, Beatrice. It was an intriguing prospect – Britain allied by marriage to the family of its greatest rival, Bonaparte. The match never happened, but if the Duke of Wellington had not died some twenty-seven years earlier, the shock of the idea alone would have killed him.

Bertie had helped with the complex protocol problems surrounding Louis-Napoléon's funeral – deciding, for example, when and where Queen Victoria could be seen paying her respects to the Catholic son of a former French emperor. But Victoria was still adamant that he couldn't be trusted with more serious affairs of state. After the general election of March 1880, when Bertie dared to express an opinion about who should be the new Prime Minister, Victoria responded furiously that he had 'no right to meddle'.

He was almost forty years old and being treated like a teenager. It must have become even clearer than ever that the only subject on which he would ever be taken seriously was France – and for the moment, the only people taking him seriously on that subject were the French themselves. Not surprising, then, that in between domestic chores like holding dinners for foreign dignitaries and opening new hospitals, Bertie now threw himself into an even deeper exploration of the good French things in life.

III

When he couldn't be on the other side of the Channel, Bertie imported French amusements into London. Chief amongst these in the summer of 1879 was the 34-year-old actress Sarah Bernhardt. She was a *cocotte* in the great tradition of Hortense Schneider and the fictional Nana. In 1874, while starring at the Comédie Française in Racine's classic tragedy *Phèdre*, Sarah had been put on the official police register of Parisian courtesans and was known to have the *crème de la crème* on her client list. In her police file, one of her customers, the politician Charles de Remusat, is quoted complaining that 'when he arrived *chez* Sarah at number 4, rue de Rome, he sometimes had to wait in an anteroom while another gentleman left the premises'. *La divine* Sarah was a very popular lady. She liked to shock people by boasting that she was unsure whether her illegitimate son – conceived when she was nineteen – belonged to the writer Victor Hugo (author of *Les Misérables*), the left-wing politician Léon Gambetta or the royalist general Georges Boulanger.

Sarah also courted scandal by her appearance. Refusing to bow to contemporary tastes for the busty, corseted classic female form, in public she wore waistless robes that emphasized her boyish figure. She was even photographed by the British press sporting trousers and a jacket, though these were in fact the overalls she wore when painting. Her make-up, too, was decidedly unlike the delicate natural blush of Lillie Langtry and her imitators. Madame Sarah went in for white face-paint, bright lipstick and kohl-black eyelids, as if she were permanently on stage.

When she was performing, she was said to be entrancing. Even Lillie Langtry, her main rival for Bertie's affections, acknowledged this, remembering in her memoirs that Bernhardt's 'superb diction, her lovely silken voice, her natural acting, her passionate temperament, her fire – in a word, transcendent genius – caused amazement'.

Like so many of Bertie's mistresses, Bernhardt also had real character. She had stayed on in Paris during the siege and helped to turn a theatre into a military hospital. And having been expelled from the prestigious Comédie Française troupe for slapping a star actress, she was recalled on the strength of her performances when the theatres opened again after the Commune.

Hardly surprising, then, that Bertie was to be seen at

the first night of every one of the productions put on by the Comédie Française in London in the summer of 1879, and paid a visit to an exhibition of her paintings in Piccadilly. Not only this, he also announced that the shocking Miss Bernhardt was to be invited into London society, including his own Marlborough House, where he is known to have 'entertained' her. She once sent a note to her director at the Comédie, apologizing for missing a rehearsal: 'The P. kept me occupied.' A euphemism if ever there was one.

Not everyone in London shared Bertie's Parisian tastes, however. Lucy Cavendish, a close friend of the royal family, and one of the Queen's maids of honour before her (Lucy's) marriage, was outraged. In her diary for 30 June 1879, she says that:

London has gone mad over the principal actress in the Comédie Française who are here: Sarah Bernhardt – a woman of notorious, shameless character . . . Not content with being run after on the stage, this woman is asked to respectable people's houses to act, and even to luncheon and dinner; and all the world goes. It is an outrageous scandal!

The aristocratic Lucy went to see the French company, but made a point of snubbing its star. On 8 July, she announces to her diary that: 'Had the delight of my one and only Comédie Française at the Gaiety; N.B. without the notorious woman.' And this was an attractive 37-year-old talking, not some ancient dowager.

Bertie ignored society's disapproval, and got his royal French friend Henri d'Orléans, aka the Duc d'Aumale, to arrange a dinner in London at which Sarah Bernhardt was to meet a selection of English ladies hand-picked by Bertie himself. However, things didn't go to plan. Charles Dilke described the awkward *soirée*: 'As they [the society women] would not talk to Sarah Bernhardt and she would not talk to them, and as the Duc d'Aumale was deaf and disinclined to make a conversation on his own account, nobody talked at all . . .'

Bertie, social animal that he was, must have suspected that this would happen, and probably laughed with Sarah afterwards about the contrast between this stuffy London gathering and the riotous nights they had spent in Paris society. Like Sarah's performances at the theatre, the dumb dinner would have reminded Bertie even more keenly why he enjoyed so much going to France. And at this time, he was enjoying himself there more than ever . . .

IV

As Bertie himself had proved, the contrast between Parisian and English attitudes to sex was becoming increasingly – laughably – clear. Sarah Bernhardt might be snubbed in London, but when Bertie went along to the Théâtre des Variétés to see the actress Jeanne Granier, a star of the operetta scene who was known to be his lover, the French audience applauded her performance and cheered Bertie as if to congratulate him for his good taste in mistresses. The London newspapers would have splashed the scandal across their front pages and caused duchesses to faint in their breakfast rooms, but in Paris he received public praise for indulging in adultery with a painted lady.

Perhaps it was the apparent banality of extra-marital affairs that led posh Parisians like Bertie to go in search of even edgier thrills. As the Third Republic matured, a spirit of democracy began to seep into the city's nightlife. The excitement was no longer restricted to rich gents who could afford theatre tickets every night and private rooms at the Café Anglais. The nightspots on the boulevards were still very much in business, as were élite private places like the Jockey Club, but the well-heeled men about town started to stray up the hill towards Pigalle and Montmartre where a bohemian community of artists, musicians and intellectuals had established a new in-crowd.

Two writers of the time, Georges Renault and Henri Château, combined their anecdotes from 1870s and 1880s Montmartre in a joint memoir. Their book, called, succinctly, *Montmartre*, attributes the area's sudden popularity to Napoléon III's revamping of the city centre. With so many of the medieval alleyways in the old Quartier Latin being flattened by Haussmann's roadbuilders, students and arty types migrated to the hilltop village that had become synonymous with the anti-establishment spirit of the Commune. Here, the housing was cheap but cramped and badly heated, so everyone gathered in the bars and cafés. Lots of the poorer prostitutes also lived in Montmartre, and when they began to mingle with the artists and poets, the combination of hardship and hedonism spawned a whole new subculture of risqué cabarets and pay-per-dance *bals populaires*.

Venues with names like L'Enfer (Hell), Le Ciel (Heaven), La Truie qui Chante (the Singing Sow) and the Cabaret des Assassins (which was decorated with pictures of real murderers) sprang up in every available building. It wasn't long before this frenzied new nightlife attracted the attention of the city's richer thrill-seekers, and by the early 1880s, according to Renault and Château, 'high society and the *demi-monde* [the *cocottes* and their clients], the bourgeois and everyone else met in Montmartre in search of fun'.

Bertie and the silk-scarf set would come up the hill accompanied by bodyguards. The police, who until then had been keeping an eye on the English Prince to make sure he wasn't planning to overthrow the Republican régime, now acted as his unofficial guides to Paris's underworld. Protection was a real necessity for anyone slumming it while wearing an expensive pocket watch and carrying a gold-topped cane. Renault and Château say that the Moulin de la Galette, which was painted by Renoir in 1876 and Van Gogh in 1886, was a 'badly frequented workers' place' that specialized in dancing and drinking: 'Who knows how many temporary marriages, quickly consummated and just as quickly dissolved, took place between two quadrilles in that stifling atmosphere?' It was unwise for a chic Parisian to venture in unprotected.

Bertie was seen at the Chat Noir, a club that was founded in 1881 on the boulevard de Rochechouart, at the foot of Montmartre, its initial aim according to Renault and Château 'to serve bad wine to poets and painters'. The décor was meant to be arty and history-themed, but turned out more like an antique shop or a 'baroque museum', with stuffed birds and obscene nudes alongside religious stained-glass windows. To preserve this iconoclastic atmosphere, a bouncer dressed in a gold costume would 'make sure that dastardly priests and soldiers' stayed away. The club's owner, Rodolphe Salis, also created an artistic movement, Les Incohérents, an apt name for a bunch of artists and writers tanked up on absinthe.

Salis was a shrewd businessman, though, and quickly developed the Chat Noir into a place where 'the gentry, the bourgeois and the vulgar [could] drink Victor Hugo's absinthe in golden goblets'. Soon, gents like Bertie were pulling up outside in their horse-drawn cabs, often accompanied both by a bodyguard and a woman they had picked up at the theatre or in a boulevard café. They would be whisked past the bouncer and squeeze into the smoky den populated by raucous, chain-smoking artists and their models, and a piano bashing out singalong tunes. The best-dressed customers, often princes and visiting heads of state, would be welcomed by Rodolphe Salis himself with what Renault and Château describe as 'humility that was not entirely free of insolence'. On one occasion, Salis is said to have greeted Bertie with an enquiry about Queen Victoria's health, asking loudly, 'Et cette maman?' – 'And how's Mum?'

The singers on stage would add to this spirit of irreverence, welcoming chic new arrivals with comments like: 'When did you get out of prison?' or: 'Where's that tart you were with last night?' Bertie himself became the butt of these jokes at the Chat Noir. One night, when he was being ushered to the best table, a performer called out: 'Look at him. He's the spitting image of the Prince of Wales.' In French, it was much more risqué: 'On dirait le Prince de Galles tout pissé'; literally a 'pissing image'. Bertie, though, would surely have loved this sign that he had been accepted here – as he was in palaces and Paris's finest restaurants – as one of the locals.

The songs performed in these places went a stage further than the farces and double entendres of vaudeville and the operettas. The Montmartre singers told true stories drawn from the life of Paris's underclass. One of the most popular performers, Aristide Bruant, whose red scarf and wide-brimmed hat were made famous by Toulouse-Lautrec's poster for his show, wrote a song about a real streetwalker called Nini Peau d'Chien,* a 'sweet, kind' girl who was to be found touting for business around Bastille 'with love sparkling in her mousy eyes'. Another of Bruant's songs began with a lament that it had become impossible to find a prostitute in Paris who hadn't become 'un débris' (a wreck) because of her job. There was only one place where you were always in luck, he went on: the Bois de Boulogne, where 'there were even royal birds' touting for 'rich old bastards'. Bertie might not have laughed at that.

Another of Toulouse-Lautrec's favourite models was the can-can dancer La Goulue, who had a well-documented encounter with Bertie. She was typical of the girls who

---

* 'Dog-skin Nini' – a name that probably referred to her cheap coat rather than her personal hairiness.

found themselves dancing in Pigalle. She was born Louise
Weber in the suburbs of Paris and raised by her elder sister,
a washerwoman. Young Louise caused her first scandal
when only twelve by taking communion dressed in a tutu
and ballet shoes, and left home at fifteen to live with her
boyfriend, a soldier. She then progressed to a rich lover
with a house near the Arc de Triomphe, before leaving (or
being dumped by) him and earning money dancing in
cabarets and posing for paintings and nude photos.
Toulouse-Lautrec depicted La Goulue entering the Moulin
Rouge in a dress cut so low that you can see her navel.
Renoir chose a more romantic image for his picture *Danse
à la Ville*, in which La Goulue is in the arms of a white-
gloved gentleman.

Her photos, meanwhile, often show her wearing nothing
but stockings, see-through knickerbockers or, in one case
of bizarre fetishism, what looks like an ancient Roman
helmet. Making money from pornographic photos was an
accepted sideline for the can-can dancers, whose speciality
was, naturally enough, to be photographed doing the splits
and advertising their sexual flexibility.

The can-can girls' main job at a cabaret was to *chauffer
les messieurs* – get the men hot under the collar – and La
Goulue was one of the most gifted *chauffeuses*. Like a
modern footballer, she switched employers in exchange for
ever-increasing wages, and became the best-paid dancer on
the circuit, headlining at the Moulin Rouge for six straight
years. She earned her nickname, which means something
like 'the glutton', by leaning out into the front row as she
danced and grabbing men's drinks, which she would then

swallow in one gulp. Her most popular trick amongst her male fans, though, was her skill at high-kicking right over their heads and knocking their hats off. Given that her outfit was usually a flouncy skirt that exposed bare thighs between her loose knickers and over-the-knee stockings, at a time when most women were loath to reveal anything below the waist except their shoe, the effect on a well-oiled audience – including Bertie – is not hard to imagine.

Bertie apparently met La Goulue in 1893 at a *café-concert* called Le Jardin de Paris, and she instantly proved that she knew how to attract a man's attention even if he was a little too grand to have his hat kicked off on a first date. As soon as she saw Bertie, so the story goes, she called out, in an accent that would have been the Parisian equivalent of the broadest Cockney: 'Hey, Wales, you paying for the champagne? Are you treating me, or does your mother have to pay?' She called him 'tu', as if they were best friends or lovers.

Bertie came back with one of his trademark pieces of public French repartee: 'Mademoiselle La Goulue, you have the prettiest legs in Paris,' he is said to have replied. He then invited her for supper after the show, which was apparently followed by what the French picturesquely call *une partie de jambes en l'air* – a legs-in-the-air party. Very appropriate for a can-can dancer.

Another famous cabaret founded around this time was the Divan Japonais, in a side street leading up from Pigalle to Montmartre. It was the first-ever French striptease joint, and is yet another venue still known today because of a Toulouse-Lautrec poster – his decadent picture of the black-dressed dancer Jane Avril watching a concert while a blond-bearded dandy peers lustfully over her shoulder. Lautrec designed his poster in 1892, but before that the Divan had used more conventional advertisements – for example, a flyer featuring a man in evening dress with a topless beauty draped across his shoulders.

Incidentally, the Divan Japonais got its name because of the oriental décor that was already in place when it was bought in 1873 by an entrepreneur called Théophile Lefort – though in fact the furnishings were originally intended to be Chinese. But then the men in the audience didn't go there to quibble about interior decoration.

The Folies Bergère (Shepherdess Follies), which is of course still operating today as a semi-naked dance revue, was not in Montmartre at all. It opened down in the boulevard area of the 9th arrondissement as an opera house, and only switched over to more fashionable *café-concert* shows in the late 1880s. At Bertie's time there wouldn't have been any semi-naked dancers – they didn't arrive until around the time of the First World War.

Similarly, the Moulin Rouge was another latecomer to the scene. It was founded at the foot of the hill in 1889 as a deliberate ploy to attract rich people into the neighbourhood, and charged much higher prices for food and drink than its older neighbours. In fact it was a pastiche of the goings-on in the real windmills like the Moulin de la Galette, a sign that Montmartre was already going mainstream. It was dreamt up by a Spanish-born entrepreneur called Joseph Oller and his partner Charles Zidler, who opened another *café-concert*, the above-mentioned Jardin de Paris, right down on the Champs-Élysées. Places like this, along with the Folies Bergère, were completing the circle – by the end of the 1880s, the edgy Parisian cabaret had left the hilltop and come down to the rich boulevards so that men like Bertie didn't need bodyguards if they wanted to listen to songs about low-class prostitutes.

Bertie had been present at the birth of this phenomenon that is still at the heart of Paris culture today, and stayed long enough to watch it grow tame. At which point, like an experienced pearl diver, he knew where he had to go when the pickings grew lean – even deeper down . . .

V

Back in the 1860s, when Napoléon III's court was still at its brightest, one of the most brilliant stars of his entourage was Pauline von Metternich, glamorous wife of the Austrian Ambassador. She was famous for her perfect shoulders, her excellent taste in all things artistic, and her independent spirit. As we saw earlier, it was Pauline who introduced Parisian ladies to two pastimes that had previously been reserved for men only – smoking and ice-skating. But she also sought thrills elsewhere, and started a trend for what became known as *tournées des grands-ducs* – grand dukes' tours – which sound like outings to visit friends' palaces but were in fact night-time excursions into poorer areas of Paris. We have seen earlier examples of aristocrats slumming it – women going to the upstairs rooms of boulevard cafés, the Empress Eugénie herself pretending to be a peasant at a country dance – and Pauline's *tournées* were similar, the *crème de la crème* descending a few levels in society and giving themselves something to gossip about next day.

After the fall of Napoléon III, however, with Montmartre giving anyone with a bodyguard and a sense of adventure the chance to see the working classes close up, new thrills were harder to get. Men with a real need to see how the other half lived were forced to find oases of depravity that hadn't been cleaned out by Baron Haussmann's demolition men.

And it is known that Bertie frequented at least one of Paris's louchest dives.

This was a notoriously sordid cabaret called Le Père Lunette, appropriately situated at 4, rue des Anglais, a narrow alley in the old Latin Quarter named after the English students who had colonized it in the thirteenth century, when they came to study at Paris's university. In Bertie's day, demolitions were taking place all around this dismal corner of Paris, and today the rue des Anglais is set between two wide, post-Haussmann streets, but in the early 1880s, rich visitors would have had to walk for several minutes after leaving their carriage in the new boulevard Saint-Germain, with their bodyguard pushing aside lolling drunks and potential muggers. The writer Oscar Méténier described the street in 1882 as 'dirty, stinking and pitch-black'. Bertie's impeccable shoes would definitely have stepped in substances they weren't designed for.

Méténier, a former policeman, was writing an article about Le Père Lunette and its rich patrons for a magazine called *Panurge*, named after the quack doctor in François

Rabelais's story of over-indulgence, *Pantagruel*. Méténier's description of the rue des Anglais seemed designed to put off all but the most curious. He wrote:

> When night falls, the place swarms with shabby, tattered people . . . they gesticulate, shout, yell, swear, whistle, yap. The dim light of the lanterns outside the shady hotels . . . lights up pale, sinister faces. Number 4, a door reinforced with bars and set below a drawing of a giant pair of glasses, is a meeting place for aristocrats of crime and poverty. As you enter, a warm fug made up of the foul breath of the drinkers and the vapour of cheap eau-de-vie makes you retch.

Not Bertie's usual kind of hang-out.

The women *chez* Le Père Lunette didn't look much like Lillie Langtry or Sarah Bernhardt, either. They even made La Goulue look classy. Méténier says:

> Around a horseshoe table sit nameless creatures, the establishment's female customers. Anything goes. All of them, young and old – because there are young girls, too, toothless and prematurely wrinkled – beg for a consolation drink from the unknown lovers that fate throws their way, and, drunk, slumped, blank-eyed, swearing, they reward their benefactors with hideous caresses and repugnant kisses.

At the back of the café, behind a rough wooden partition, was a room called Le Sénat (the Senate), named after its amphitheatre-like benches where prostitutes sat waiting for customers. Any man wandering in here would have to be desperate, and either already infected with a sexually transmitted disease or willing to catch one. The poor women here were at the bottom of the heap, and might have been thrown out of a legal brothel, where the prostitutes were obliged to undergo regular medical examinations, for showing too obvious symptoms of, say, syphilis.

It is impossible to believe that Bertie would have succumbed to temptation here. He knew all about syphilis – some of London high society's biggest names had turned into raging lunatics and died atrociously because of it. There was nothing romantic in the rue des Anglais. This was sex at its most sordid. The attraction to the chic voyeurs who came here must have been that the horrific squalor was only a matter of yards away from the glittering new lights of Paris. It was a living zoo of sleaze that would soon be cleared away – both buildings and people – by Haussmann. The more heartless visitors must have seen it as proof that the uneducated lower classes were no better than animals. Worse, even, because at least animals don't get drunk and catch 'immoral' diseases.

On Bertie, though, the effect of this morbid sex tourism seems to have been different. Parisian poverty appears to have made him more acutely conscious of the similar conditions that existed back home. He had done his share of slumming in London as a younger man, but that had been in music halls which were palaces compared to Le Père Lunette. There was no way that Bertie could go on a tour of the slum brothels in London, even if he didn't plan to indulge, but he felt that he should do something to alleviate the poverty. And it was in conditions very similar to these

Parisian *tournées des grands-ducs* that Bertie visited the filthy, overcrowded streets of Holborn and St Pancras in 1884, when he joined the Royal Commission on the Housing of the Working Class. He dressed in what he regarded as poor clothes (no doubt cleaner and smarter than most Londoners had ever worn in their lives) and, accompanied by a detective, went on a tour of the slums. The locals must have guessed that these well-scrubbed, overfed people were do-gooders, but Bertie seems to have found the visit very illuminating all the same.

A landlord took him to see an emaciated woman slumped in a room with three naked children. She had a fourth, she told them, but it had gone out a few days ago and never returned. This was when Bertie had to be persuaded not to start doling out money and thereby provoking a riot. To his credit, he also went back to the House of Lords and made a speech about the 'disgraceful' conditions of the poor.

Of course Bertie wasn't going to take a room in one of the hotels in the rue des Anglais and set about upgrading the neighbourhood from the inside. After all, his main purpose in Paris was to escape the suffocating moral atmosphere of London, not to bring about social change. After a visit to a Paris flophouse like Le Père Lunette, he would go and clean up at the Bristol, or drop in to see his rich friends for some gambling at the Cercle de la rue Royale club, no doubt regaling them with stories of toothless hags and unmentionable odours.

He would almost certainly not have admitted that, somehow, he had also got a thrill from seeing these

Hortense Schneider, star of the Paris stage in the 1860s, whose 'heart was as open to visitors as her house'. Bertie was a keen visitor.

When Bertie watched his lover Jeanne Granier at the theatre, the Parisian audience applauded him for his taste in women.

Can-can dancer La Goulue. One night at the cabaret, Bertie called out: 'You have the prettiest legs in Paris.'

Pauline Metternich, socialite wife of the Austrian ambassador to Paris. She introduced Parisian women to the pleasures of ice-skating and smoking.

Bertie invited actress Sarah Bernhardt to chic dinners in London just to shock prudish society ladies.

Bertie often enjoyed private performances by Yvette Guilbert, singer of crude Parisian songs.

Caroline 'la Belle' Otero, a
singer whose ample chest
is said to have inspired the
domes on the roof of the
Hôtel Cartlon in Cannes.

Cora Pearl, an English
'grande horizontale'
in Paris who once had
herself served, naked,
as dish of the day at the
Café Anglais.

Thérésa, a poor *Parisienne* who earned a fortune in the 1860s from her suggestive songs and generous lovers.

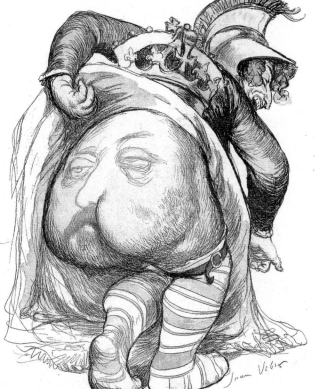

France was annoyed by British colonialism in the early 1900s, hence this rare reference in the press to Bertie's amorous antics.

Le Petit Journal

SUPPLEMENT ILLUSTRÉ

Le Petit Journal
5 Centimes

ABONNEMENTS

Le Supplément illustré

L'AGRICULTURE MODERNE, 5 cent.

Quatorzième année

DIMANCHE 17 MAI 1903

Numéro 652

LE ROI D'ANGLETERRE EN FRANCE
Le départ de Cherbourg

It was thanks to Bertie's gift for smooth-talking the French that the Entente Cordiale was signed in 1904.

On the beach at Biarritz, where Bertie went in old age to soothe his damaged lungs. And to smoke cigars.

Bertie was the only man who could control his temperamental nephew the Kaiser.
When Bertie died, the French acknowledged that war with Germany was inevitable.

worn-out, dangerous prostitutes who would have had sex with him for the price of a dirty glass of watered-down hooch. Though as Bertie entered his forties, he may have been in need of some extra stimulation.

VI

Bertie's biographers can be an unsporting lot. Overall, he gives great entertainment, and throughout his time as Prince of Wales, he can usually be relied upon to alternate between serious intent and absurd gaffe, between family crisis and private merrymaking. So it seems hardly fair, albeit historically justified, for several of his biographers to start casting doubts upon Bertie's virility as soon as he hits his vulnerable middle age (and in the portly Prince's case 'middle' was certainly the operative word). But from the time of Lillie Langtry onwards, there is frequent speculation about whether or not Bertie was actually having sex with such-and-such a female favourite, and if so, how often.

There is even one story which has him in a yacht cabin with a lover when he hears approaching footsteps. 'Is somebody coming?' he asks. 'Well, it certainly isn't you,' replies the witty lady – who must have been the one to tell the story in the first place, unless Bertie pushed the English talent for self-deprecating humour to its extreme limit.

But if his libido was flagging, Paris was the perfect place to give it a jolt, and not necessarily with diseased, poverty-stricken hookers. At the end of the 1870s, the city was refining its sexual subculture. If a man like Bertie wanted a really sophisticated erotic experience, he no longer had to pursue an actress or a *cocotte* in the hope of squeezing his name into her crowded diary. Now the brothels and their legal prostitutes were becoming *très chic*, and were adding new variety to the pleasures they offered. Even the most jaded libido could find exactly the titillation it required. And the place with the widest selection of sexual delights for sale was a *bordel* called Le Chabanais.

Founded in 1878 by an Irish madam called simply Madame Kelly – and her financiers, of course – it was designed to attract men like Bertie who had enough money to fulfil their wildest fantasies. And it was, of course, perfectly legitimate – all the two dozen or so girls were registered with the police, had twice-monthly medicals, and paid (in theory at least) tax on their earnings.

The brothel occupied the whole of a building at number 12, rue Chabanais, in a reasonably smart section of the old city between Opéra and the Palais Royal. Today the building is a nondescript mixture of shopfront and apartments, and in those days it would have looked still more anonymous from the outside – even the most sophisticated *bordels* were obliged to protect the neighbours from seeing anything untoward by closing their doors and shutters. Hence the French name for a brothel: *maison close*. Apart from the frequent comings and goings of its customers, the only giveaway as to what was going on inside was a sign on the wall of the restaurant on the other side of the street saying: 'You can be just as comfortable in here as opposite.'

That was a bold claim, because Le Chabanais was

designed at a cost of 1.7 million francs – about £3.5 million at today's values – as the (whipped) *crème de la crème* of Paris brothels. A writer called Paul Reboux, author of a lament for France's classic pleasure houses called *Le Guide Galant*, dubbed it 'the Château d'Yquem of the wine list', this being a sweet, golden Sauternes, vintage bottles of which can fetch thousands of euros at auction.

The new brothel prided itself on offering something luxurious for all tastes, both in the selection of beautiful women available and the setting in which they could be enjoyed. The naked or skimpily dressed prostitutes would mingle with clients and serve them refreshments in a downstairs *salon*, and after a glass or two of champagne, some nibbles and flattering banter, the moneyed male 'guest' would have the girl of his choice delivered to one of the fabulous bedrooms upstairs.

On the upper floors, there was a sultry Arabian harem, a Pompeii room with pictures of coupling centaurs painted by Toulouse-Lautrec, a pirate's den, a medieval bedchamber for men wanting to get a damsel into distress, as well as classical French boudoirs fitted out with authentic antique furniture and wall-to-ceiling mirrors. Le Chabanais was such an institution that its Japanese room was displayed at the 1900 Exposition Universelle, and won a prize for interior decoration.*

Bertie was a regular in the Hindu room – perhaps

---

* Bertie must have been sad because this was the only Expo in his lifetime that he missed – for a reason that we shall see in Chapter 13.

because, like his mother, he was sentimentally attached to that part of his family's empire. The *chambre hindoue* was famous for its 'gold' bath – though in fact it was silver-plated copper. Here, Bertie is rumoured to have cavorted in champagne with the good-time girls, though why anyone would get an erotic thrill from sitting in a chilly tub of rapidly flattening wine is hard to imagine. Probably even more dissuasive would have been the enormous cost of emptying out several dozen bottles of bubbly for a quick dip. But the above-mentioned Paul Reboux offers a solution to this enigma – Bertie probably did nothing of the sort. According to Reboux, who seems to have tested many of the establishments he describes during the research for his book, the bathtubs at the Chabanais were more often used by clients cleaning up after their sessions, ridding themselves of the bordello scent before returning to the respectable outside world. A hot, soapy sponge bath at the hands of a skilled professional *Parisienne* sounds much more like Bertie's cup of tea than a soak in cold wine.

The Hindu room was also well known for Bertie's own contribution to the science of sex – the love seat that he is said to have designed himself in 1890.

This extraordinary piece of furniture was worthy of anything at the Paris Expos that Bertie attended. Its design was half gynaecologist's chair, half bobsled. It was Louis XVIII-style, sculpted in curved and gilded wood, with cushioned areas covered in a pale-green, satin-like material. The lower tier was a long narrow mattress, and the upper section, mounted on four sturdy legs, was a tipped-back seat with vertical armrests rather like thick ski poles. At the front edge of this upper tier there were two gynaecologist's stirrups – gilded so as not to look too medical.

There has been a lot of speculation as to how the seat was used, but there probably was not one single answer. It is obvious that the armrests and stirrups of the top section could have been used by a woman sitting with her legs apart and receiving the attention of a man standing or kneeling in front of her. Meanwhile another woman could have been lying on the bottom section watching, or joining in somehow. Alternatively, Bertie himself might have sat on top and been attended to by a woman kneeling before him. Then again, maybe sometimes he enjoyed just lying down below and watching things going on above. With all the time and money he had at his disposal, Bertie was free to explore every angle.

It is said that Bertie commissioned the seat from a chairmaker called Louis Soubrier in Paris's furniture-manufacturing district around the Bastille. Soubrier was a specialist in antique reproductions (no pun intended), and may well have contributed other pieces to the themed rooms at the Chabanais. According to Reboux, Bertie's love seat was not the only piece of imaginative furniture in the building. In the so-called Louis-Philippe room, named after the corpulent French king of the same name, there was also a chair where overweight clients could enjoy themselves 'before taking the rest that follows such unaccustomed exertion'. Tubby Bertie might well have needed that.

All these furnishings were sold off at auction in 1951 after France passed a law outlawing its *maisons closes.** This was not done to protect women from exploitation but because the brothels had been tainted by collaboration during the war. Many of them had been set aside for German soldiers, while black marketeers and Nazi sympathizers had used them as meeting places. The famous 'gold' bathtub was acquired by some fans of Salvador Dali, who had it installed in his suite at the Hôtel Le Meurice. Bertie's seat was bought by the brother of the writer Boris Vian, and after being sold on twice more, it was bought back by the original furniture maker's great-grandson.

Bertie was by no means the only prince to find his way to the Chabanais in the late nineteenth century. It became so well known abroad that foreign royals often had a trip to the brothel inserted into the official programme of their state visits to Paris. A quick romp would appear on the agenda in code as a 'visite au Président du Sénat'. It is said that on one occasion, a 'visit to the President of the Senate' was accidentally included in the diary of the Queen of Spain, and embarrassed Parisian officials covered up their gaffe by taking the lady on a pointless courtesy call to the man in question.

* Reboux tells a story about an Englishman wandering forlornly around the neighbourhood a few years after the Chabanais closed. An antique dealer asked him what he was looking for. 'Une vierge,' the Englishman replied. Thinking the tourist wanted a statue of the Virgin Mary, the antique dealer asked him, 'Sixteenth, Seventeenth, Eighteenth?' (Referring to centuries.) 'Oh, I don't care what arrondissement she comes from,' replied the Englishman.

VII

The living conditions of the girls at the chic Chabanais were far less luxurious than the rooms where they performed their services. In fact, the prostitutes' quarters were less than basic – after all, a good proportion of them were expected to spend their nights with clients, so they didn't need much personal space. The clients' bedrooms often had large bathtubs, but the women's private facilities would have been shared and rudimentary – a shallow squat tub on the floor, the odd bidet for minimal protection from disease and pregnancy. Medical examinations were obligatory in theory, but the doctors who visited the brothels were open to bribes. Clients of Le Chabanais were lucky that the establishment had such a high reputation to defend, because it meant that any woman showing symptoms of disease would be banished immediately – but she would almost certainly end up at a less scrupulous brothel, where prostitutes could keep on working until their symptoms became too visible to hide.

There has been a lot of romanticism about the sophisticated decadence of Le Chabanais and other Parisian *bordels*, and the easy-going willingness of the *filles de joie* who worked there. It is said, for example, that when Victor Hugo died in 1885, all the capital's working girls gave their favours free of charge for a day in honour of a great 'ladies' man'. But this sounds very much like a legend to confirm nostalgic male fantasies about Paris's nineteenth-century prostitutes being big-hearted and grateful for the custom.

The women working at Le Chabanais would have been

under strict orders to maintain this myth, to laugh at Bertie's witticisms as he puffed on his cigars and drank his overpriced champagne, and then act out a pastiche of pleasure when he 'invited' them to come upstairs and see his portliness in naked close-up. He would probably not have seen any contradiction between his behaviour at Le Chabanais and his avowed concern for London's paupers. To him, it might even have seemed that these highly organized Parisian sex sessions were part of a medical programme – vitamin boosts for his libido, workouts for his ageing heart, tonics to ensure that he would have the energy to perform his good works back at home.

Because as he advanced into middle age, Bertie began using France less as a playground than as a giant health resort . . .

12

WE ALL LIKE TO BE BESIDE THE SEASIDE

~

'If there had been a medical examination for kings, as there is for soldiers, he would have been declared unfit for duty.'
Émile Flourens, French Minister of Foreign Affairs,
writing about Bertie

I

Fat cigars and fatty meals were beginning to take their toll on Bertie's body. As the French politician Émile Flourens wrote while Bertie was still alive, the closer he came to inheriting the throne, the more 'obesity deformed his body . . . and seemed, beneath the weight of bloated flesh, to paralyse all physical activity and intellectual strength'. Apparently not all French politicians of the time were fans of the English Prince.

Bertie had long been a regular at German spas like

Homburg and Baden. At the time, people believed that the body could be cleansed and recharged with a brief cure of mineral water, light meals and brisk walks – it was fashionable to stride as fast as one could along the avenues, giving quick bows and tips of the hat to important fellow curists, but stopping to talk to no one. The only problem with this treatment was that for Bertie, 'light meals' meant not requesting his usual cold chicken by the bedside in case he got hungry in the night. And a spot of over-indulgence in the evenings was not thought too damaging.

Bertie and his doctors soon began to notice that mineral water and power-walking wasn't enough. Although he had barely entered his forties, his breath was getting shorter and his veins were starting to clog. Hardly surprising, really, when he was virtually chain-smoking cigars, with cigarettes in between as light relief. He would usually light up one cigar and two cigarettes before breakfast, then fill his cigar and cigarette cases for the day, and get through twenty cigarettes and twelve cigars before dinner. In the evenings he was rarely to be seen without a cloud of smoke hovering around his head, and his less discreet mistresses complained that he stank of stale tobacco.

Seeking an additional, albeit pleasurable, remedy for his ills, from 1883 Bertie opted to spend as much time as possible during the damp English months of February and March on the French Riviera. This was the new English name for the section of France's south coast east of Cannes, rubbing French noses in the fact that until 1860 the area had belonged to Italy. The French had no collective name of their own for the Riviera until 1887, when the writer

Stéphen Liégeard said that 'this shore bathed in sunbeams deserves to be baptized the Azure Coast'. The term Côte d'Azur was immediately adopted by the patriotic French in opposition to the British name.

Bertie was by no means the first royal to winter in the south of France. Leaving aside kings like Richard the Lionheart, who didn't really go in for rest cures, Bertie's great-great uncle, the Duke of York, brother of George III, first escaped to Nice in the winter of 1764. The town had since become so popular with Brits that at the beginning of the nineteenth century it gained its Promenade des Anglais, the English prom financed by a certain Reverend Lewis Way so that the expats would be able to walk along the beach without stumbling on its large round pebbles. After all, it didn't look good if people came to the town for their health and ended up with broken ankles.

Similarly, ever since the mid-1860s, Monaco had been offering a healthy mix of seawater bathing and gambling, and in 1878 the resort felt rich enough to commission a new casino from Charles Garnier, the man who had designed Paris's opera house. This was the start of the principality's reputation as a place to lose one's excess pounds, in both senses of the term.

Menton, just along the coast towards Italy, was another resort being developed by the Brits. A Manchester doctor called James Henry Bennett arrived there in 1859, looking for nothing more than a pleasant place in which to die of his chronic lung disease, and found to his surprise that he got better. He opened a surgery there and wrote a book called *Mentone [sic] and the Riviera as a Winter Climate*. In this, he rejected towns further south – Turin was foggy, Rome full of malaria and Naples a cholera trap – and praised both Menton's clement weather and its cleanliness, which he ascribed to the locals collecting their own excrement for use as fertilizer: 'They husband their manure with jealous care, and let none escape into the sea.' Dr Bennett also had a piece of advice that Bertie might well have been wise to follow: 'It is', he warned, 'impossible to effectually pursue health and pleasure at the same time.'

The clean-living doctor quickly began to attract English patients, amongst them Robert Louis Stevenson, and in only ten years or so, Menton grew into one of the most fashionable winter resorts on the Mediterranean coast.

Cannes, meanwhile, had been transformed from a fishing village into a bustling resort by a succession of British immigrants. It had first been discovered in 1834 when a certain Henry, Lord Brougham and Vaux (pronounced 'broom and vokes', rather like some nineteenth-century house-cleaning implement) was taking his daughter to Italy for the winter to ease her lung condition. However, they found the border closed at Nice because of a cholera outbreak, so they stopped for the night at an inn in Cannes, where they apparently enjoyed an excellent *bouillabaisse*. Next morning, Lord H. B. & V. took one look at the bay and decided that he didn't need to go to Italy after all. He bought a piece of land, built a villa, and was soon inviting high-society friends to join him there. More villas sprang up on the wooded hillsides, and Brougham, a skilled orator (or rather, a determined one – he once spoke in the House of Commons for six straight hours), persuaded the French state to pay for a decent jetty. This attracted the yachting crowd, who began to flock south in search of somewhere less bracing than Cowes.

In 1837 a certain John Taylor, estate agent, arrived in Cannes, and from then on the town became a collection of 'prime seafront locations', 'dream homes in the sun' and 'stunning vistas'. The health benefits of the climate were also being touted, and before the 1830s were done, over-indulgers from all across Europe were coming for the sea air, year-round sunshine and what one French history of the town calls its 'vegetable smells'.* Thermal spas began to open in Cannes, offering cures for lung diseases, indigestion, gout and kidney trouble – in fact, almost every ill that afflicted the hard-drinking, chain-smoking, over-eating upper classes, including Bertie.

He frequented all these resorts and, according to his future French police bodyguard Xavier Paoli, was well known on the coast by the mid-1870s. In 1878, when Paoli, then an ordinary policeman, first saw Bertie getting off a train in Nice, the station master pointed him out and said: 'He knows everyone in Nice and we adore him.'

As of 1883, Bertie elected Cannes as his favourite winter hideaway, probably because he had been singing the praises of the Riviera back home, and his mother got into the habit of coming down to Nice and Menton. It was best to base himself a few kilometres away. There wasn't much fun to

---

* No doubt a reference to pine trees and lavender rather than illegal smoking materials – those wouldn't arrive in any quantity until after the film festival started in 1947.

be had if the black-clad Queen was hovering in the background.

Bertie and Victoria were by no means the only royal personages to spend time on the coast – every winter, the local papers listed visiting monarchs from as far away as Russia and Brazil, as well as the touring hordes of European aristocrats – but Paoli gives Bertie the credit for the fashionability of the whole Riviera.

'Cannes was his headquarters . . . but his realm of elegance and pleasure spread as far as Menton and Nice,' Paoli says. 'Each of these resorts competed for the honour of a visit, and he increased their prosperity by attracting a vast British colony.' Even before becoming a monarch in name, Bertie was, says Paoli, 'the King of the Côte d'Azur, and where pleasures were concerned, nothing was decided there without his assent'.

Bertie's pleasures while he was down south were (in no particular order) gambling, dining, going to the theatre, womanizing and yachting. When he started visiting Cannes more or less annually, the town was already a glittering society capital, with banquets, costume balls, gala evenings at the theatre, a regatta, and sporting events such as horse-racing and pigeon-shooting, as well as less formal get-togethers – what the French called 'le five o'clock' (a tea party) with games of 'croket'. Though in fact, as of the 1880s, the biggest pleasure of all for Bertie must have been the considerable relief of breathing warm French sea air instead of London's smog particles and Sandringham's damp vapours.

The local newspapers would always announce Bertie's

arrival, sometimes months in advance. In October 1885, for example, the weekly *Courrier de Cannes* reported that Bertie would be coming the following January and that his stay would last 'at least a month and maybe two. Let's hope the last figure prevails.' The locals knew that Bertie's presence would ensure full hotels and a crowded social calendar. In July 1888, the same paper went so far as to repeat a rumour heard by a Monaco journalist that Bertie had been telling friends in London that he intended to spend more time than usual there the following winter. The Cannes journalist deduced, with much rubbing together of hands, that 'English high society will follow him, as usual'.

And this it did. Bertie's arrival always coincided with a long 'Liste des Étrangers Arrivés' (List of Arriving Foreigners) column in the society section, detailing who had just settled in at which villa or hotel. Many of these chic tourists would reside at the Hôtel Prince de Galles – not that Bertie stayed in the hotel named in his honour. According to the papers, the Prince of Wales favoured other addresses like the Hôtel de Provence, the Réunion de Cannes, a selection of private villas and, as of 1893, his own racing yacht *Britannia*.

There were always a few lines in the Cannes papers when Bertie left England or Paris bound for the south, and when he arrived in town, usually on the train that pulled into Cannes around 1 p.m., there were speeches on the platform. However, the accounts of his various arrivals seem to imply that Bertie was in a hurry to get on with the fun – on 14 February 1888, for example, the *Courrier de Cannes* reports that Bertie arrived by 'luxury train' at 1.12 p.m., to be greeted by an official welcoming committee of twenty people and a speech from the deputy mayor.

'With a few courteous words,' the article reveals, 'the Prince thanked Monsieur Millet [the deputy mayor] for the enthusiastic and friendly welcome that the town gave him every year', and then hurried off to settle into his apartments. On that occasion, it was no wonder that he was keen – printed on the same page was the guest list of a dinner at the Cercle Nautique (yacht club) that same night, that included his lover the Princesse de Sagan.

Not that she is labelled as such, of course, and there is not a whiff of overt scandal in any article about Bertie, as there would have been back in prurient, puritanical England. The Cannes papers afforded the Prince all the discretion necessary to keep him coming to the town. For example, in 1895, we are told that Bertie paid a visit to the Grand Duke and Grand Duchess of Mecklenburg-Schwerin, but not that the Grand Duchess was a beautiful young Russian called Anastasia, unhappily married to a husband who was known for his weak heart and asthma – and who often left his wife alone in Cannes. The closest we get to gossip is after one visit to the Grand Duchess (who is named on her own this time), when we learn that 'cette entrevue a été assez longue'.

We know from the newspapers that there were often famous women of dubious reputation performing at the theatres during the winter season – in February 1889, Bertie was in Cannes at the same time as Sarah Bernhardt, who was putting on her famous production of *Fedora*, the tragic story of a princess who is in love with a womanizing count (and that is not a misprint). There is no record in the newspaper of Bertie and Sarah meeting up on this occasion, but it's hard to imagine the two avoiding each other.

Bertie was also reunited with another former lover, the actress Jeanne Granier, in Monte Carlo, where the two apparently had a fond get-together in a hotel room in 1889. It was said that Jeanne kept the Prince amused for a whole evening with hilarious anecdotes about the Paris theatre scene. But of course she may well have amused him in other ways, as well.

Similarly, another actress-*cocotte*, Caroline Otero, nick-named la Belle Otero,* was often on the coast in winter, under contract to attract clients to the Monte Carlo casino. Again, she is known to have entertained Bertie as a client/lover, but the local newspapers keep mum about it.

If there were no scandalous actresses due to perform, Bertie had them shipped down specially from Paris. Once, after dropping heavy hints to an American friend that he would like to see the shocking *chanteuse* Yvette Guilbert, she was brought to Cannes at enormous expense to sing at a private dinner. When she toned down her act for the refined company, Bertie begged her for her 'most delight-fully Parisian items'. Guilbert's repertoire included ditties like 'L'Hôtel du Numéro Trois' which talks about a squalid

---

* La Belle Otero's generous chest measurements are said to have inspired the twin domes on the roof of the Hôtel Carlton at Cannes. This seems hard to believe because the domes are very wide apart and alarmingly pointed.

hotel where 'the maid isn't very beautiful, but everyone makes love with her', and 'Belleville-Ménilmontant' (named after two poor areas in Paris), in which she reveals that 'my brother-in-law makes a fortune pimping my sister Thérèse'. Bertie was so delighted with Yvette's show in Cannes that he invited her to London to perform in front of the ladies and gentlemen of the court. Fortunately, very few of them would have understood her Parisian accent as well as he did.

Although Bertie's stays in Cannes were very public affairs, with his daily engagements published in the papers, it is possible to read between the lines and find hints of the illicit fun he might also have been enjoying. For example, on 8 February 1883, he was at a soirée given by a certain Lady Camden at her villa, and amongst the guests were 'Mistress et Miss Chamberlain'. This Miss was Jane, the daughter of an American millionaire, who was one of Bertie's favourites at the time, and who was seen with him in Paris the following year, when the police recorded her as the Prince's *maîtresse-en-titre* (his 'officially appointed mistress' – the Parisians, of course, have different grades of lovers).

A more tantalizing reference comes on 15 February 1887, when the Prince attended a seventeenth-century-themed ball *chez* Lady Murray. Bertie's costume isn't mentioned, but one of the guests, a certain Miss Townley, went as Diane de Poitiers, the notorious mistress of France's King Henri II. Diane de Poitiers was so sexy that Henri's wife, Catherine de' Medici, used to watch her husband's adulterous couplings through a hole in the ceiling in the hope of picking up bedroom tips. Was this Miss Townley sending out a message to Bertie? Did he pick it up? If so, was his chat-up line based on the fact that her costume was a century too early for the evening's theme, because Diane de Poitiers lived from either 1499 or 1500 to 1566? The newspapers don't tell us. The last thing they wanted to do was gossip and scare off their biggest tourist attraction.

Bertie was the nineteenth-century equivalent of a superstar. Just as the arrival of a world-famous football player can guarantee a club's fortunes for a season from the sale of tickets and replica shirts, so Bertie's regular residencies in Cannes helped the town, and the whole coast, to prosper.

But it wasn't all about economics. Bertie was also completing his seduction of the French people. As a younger man he had become a welcome fixture on the Parisian scene. Now, in middle age, he was winning the undying affection of the Mediterraneans, all of it thanks to his warm personality. Although he was a prince, he was also a team player, and joined in with any fun that was on offer. He regularly took part in the Nice *bataille des fleurs*, part of the carnival, during which everyone would throw locally grown daisies, mimosa and *fleurs de lys* at each other as they drove along the Promenade des Anglais in their carriages. Visitors dressed up in carnival costumes, and Bertie once went disguised as Satan, with a red cape and horns. Quite daring for a future head of the Anglican Church.

After watching Bertie at the carnival one year, the French police noted that: 'He enjoys himself like a young man, laughs at all the grotesque scenes and afterwards takes great pleasure in describing the day's events.' They sound almost surprised that he should be so human.

But Bertie's greatest strength was that he was always so personable. In March 1896, he paid a short visit – just forty minutes – to the Cannes flower show. A very brief stop, with little opportunity to admire the displays or talk to anyone. Even so, he made excellent use of his time. According to the *Courrier de Cannes*, as Bertie was leaving the showground, he caught sight of an old man wearing a medal that he recognized (Bertie was an obsessive connoisseur of medals). 'Ah,' he exclaimed, 'I see that you were among the brave men who fought in the Crimea campaign. I am happy to shake your hand.' The old man was so touched by this gesture that he was left speechless – and Bertie had won yet another friend and admirer, as well as earning himself a glowing write-up in the press.

The concrete proof of the affection he earned came in 1912, two years after his death, when a statue was erected in Cannes in his honour. He was not depicted in the usual monarch's stately uniform, but as a sailor with a yachting cap set on his head at a racy tilt, and a telescope tucked under one arm. This marble Bertie, who was torn down by Nazi sympathizers in 1943, was gazing fondly out towards the horizon – which was a pity because sprawled at his feet was a naked girl, her modesty barely covered by a sheaf of flowers. She was designed to symbolize the town of Cannes, which – like so many French females – reacted to his presence by getting undressed and prostrating herself in front of him.

II

In the early 1890s, Bertie's health took a turn for the worse. He was diagnosed with what his doctors called 'gouty muscular rheumatism', and had to give up dancing. He still went to the south of France most winters, but a sense of melancholy pervades some of the newspaper reports of his visits. He stayed on his yacht *Britannia* more often than on land, and attended far fewer functions, though the *Courrier de Cannes* managed to put a positive spin on the Prince's reduced socializing, saying: '[He] wants to live peacefully, rest and enjoy the region's delicious climate.'

The melancholy was understandable, because Bertie suffered some serious blows to his morale at this time. In 1891 his leg was so gouty that he had to cancel his trip to the Côte d'Azur altogether. In January 1892, his eldest son Eddy died of flu just after his twenty-eighth birthday. Even though the young Prince had been a dissolute throwback to the family's Hanoverian genes, the loss was a crushing blow to Bertie and Alexandra, who descended into months of gloom. During the year of official mourning, all fun was forbidden, and this inactivity, according to one of Victoria's cousins, the Duchess of Mecklenburg-Strelitz, turned Bertie 'very fat and puffed'. In March of 1892, he made a trip to Cap Martin, between Monaco and Nice, but it was a mournful exile with Princess Alexandra, as well as an attempt to avoid the rampant influenza virus that had killed their son.

After Bertie's new yacht was delivered in 1893, he

enjoyed the regattas at Nice and Cannes, and even won a few prizes, but he must have got the increasing feeling that he was losing the most important race in his life – the one to outlast his mother. She was looking immortal, especially because she was using the same health-preserving tactic as he was, and coming to the Riviera.

What was more, surprisingly for such a resolute widow, Victoria was also giving Bertie headaches because of her infatuations with male servants. First there had been the Scotsman John Brown, the kilted valet who had been by her side for more than ten years, helping her in and out of carriages, talking back to her with coarse common sense, sitting for her sketches, and sleeping at night in a neighbouring chamber.

To Bertie's relief, Brown died in 1883 of a streptococcal infection at the early age of fifty-six, but a few years later he was replaced by an Indian called Abdul Karim. Also known as the Munshi (teacher) because he taught the Queen Hindi and Urdu, Karim quickly rose from waiting at table to the role of a surrogate John Brown. The closeness between a servant and a queen had been almost tolerable when it was a Scot, but the ladies-in-waiting and male attendants were aghast when they were ordered to treat a colonial as their equal.

From 1892, the Munshi was included in the small party that accompanied Victoria to the Riviera each spring. It sometimes came as a surprise to her visitors when the turbanned Karim was introduced to them. According to a report in the less-than-respectful *Birmingham Post* in 1893, King Umberto of Italy apparently thought that the Indian was a captive prince, kept by Victoria as proof of her power over her colonies.

In March 1897, Karim's presence on the south coast of France caused a scandal in the royal household. He had been diagnosed with gonorrhoea (a disease most commonly caught from prostitutes), and the other servants threatened to resign if he came on the Queen's annual trip to Cimiez, a hilltop suburb of Nice. Victoria threw a fit, accusing her servants of racial prejudice, and the Munshi came along, but the holiday mood was spoilt by constant tensions at the villa. Bertie, who was wintering on his yacht *Britannia* at Cannes, was called in as a peacemaker by Victoria's doctor, but he didn't have the courage to confront his mother.

She, meanwhile, seems to have enjoyed the rumpus, admitting to her doctor that the arguments about Karim were a source of excitement in her old age. The Munshi inspired an almost girlish sense of mischief in Victoria: in 1899, when snobbish members of her household again demanded that Karim stay away from Nice, she left him behind, only to telegraph him as soon as she arrived, telling him to follow on.

These holidays in the sun seem to have brought Victoria out of herself. She could see foreign friends and relatives like the Emperor of Austria and the Prince of Denmark without crossing half of Europe. She even showed signs of spontaneity and energy. During that tempestuous season of 1897 Victoria organized an impromptu jaunt along the coast to Cannes to have tea with her daughter Louise, who was another fan of the Riviera, mainly because of the gambling. According to the society column in the *Courrier de Cannes*, 'the news [of Victoria's arrival in town] was immediately passed on to His Royal Highness the Prince of Wales'. It is easy to imagine Bertie grumbling into his beard at having to come ashore and make small talk with his mother – and the omnipresent Karim.

But this was Victoria's Diamond Jubilee year, and Bertie set aside any impatience he might have about inheriting the throne to play a key role in organizing the festivities. Driven by his social conscience, he suggested using the grand state occasion to raise money for hospitals. He was also determined to make sure that the poorer citizens of London would get a good view of the proceedings.

There was pressure to hold a ceremony in St Paul's, but Bertie supported an idea that would allow Victoria to sit peacefully in her carriage rather than have to climb painfully down in full view of the public. The main event was therefore a parade through London on the morning of Tuesday, 22 June 1897. First, Victoria, who had dressed up in what was for her a wild party gown – black silk with silver embroidery – was driven from Buckingham Palace to St Paul's, where her carriage stopped and she remained seated while a service of thanksgiving was held. The procession then continued through six miles of streets festooned with flowers and bunting, with onlookers leaning out of every window, and filling all the seats on specially erected grandstands.

Thanks to Bertie's influence, his mother's rare tour of her capital city also took in the poor neighbourhoods south of the river, and everywhere she went, Victoria received deafening cheers and renditions of 'God Save the Queen' as congratulations for her longevity. 'A never to be forgotten day,' she wrote in her diary. 'No one ever, I believe, has met with such an ovation as was given to me.' If anyone thought she was tired of reigning, they were wrong.

Bertie put on a glorious scarlet field marshal's uniform for the occasion, but took a back seat – literally. A short piece of newsreel film of the procession shows Victoria beneath a parasol accompanied in her carriage by her daughter Helena and Princess Alexandra. Bertie, in a plumed hat, was on horseback behind them. As he rode around London playing the guard of honour, he must have been wondering when, if ever, it would be his turn. Two of his young nephews, Kaiser Wilhelm and Tsar Nicholas, had already inherited their crowns, while he was still waiting. His mother was frail, but winters in the south of France were keeping her going. And he was no spring chicken himself, even though he was trussed up like one and broiling in the sun beneath his feathery helmet.

The celebrations were a great success. Encouraged by Bertie to come out of her shell, the normally reclusive Queen managed to be more sociable than ever, attending receptions for – to name but a few – MPs, lords, school-children and the country's mayors. She reviewed troops, attended a torchlight procession at Eton and paraded with firemen.

The only major event at which Bertie had to deputize for his absent mother was a review of the fleet at Spithead, near Portsmouth. As he stood on the deck of the royal yacht *Victoria and Albert*, the full might of Britain's navy

– more than 150 ships manned by over 50,000 sailors – rode at anchor in the Solent, firing cannon salutes and generally showing off their capacity to rule the waves. It was the greatest assembly of naval strength the world had ever seen, and the lines of warships were said to have totalled thirty miles in length. As was the custom in these cases, there was little or no sense of military secrecy, and the fleet was observed by crowds of foreign visitors – there were journalists, visiting admirals and guest vessels from, amongst others, France, the USA, Russia, Japan and Germany. For once, though, Germany's contribution to the display was a huge disappointment.

Whenever the 38-year-old Kaiser Wilhelm II, Bertie's nephew and Victoria's grandson, came to the Solent to sail one of his racing yachts in the Cowes regatta, he usually brought an escort of two immense new warships to remind his English relatives that Britannia wasn't the only force to be reckoned with on the seas. In June 1897, however, for such a grand official occasion as the Diamond Jubilee review of the fleet, he sent over a thirty-year-old refurbished frigate, the *König Wilhelm*, named after his grandfather.

It was a crude and obvious snub, intended as revenge on the British royal family. Victoria had refused to invite Wilhelm himself to her Jubilee celebrations, ostensibly on the grounds that she didn't want the nation to bear the expense of entertaining crowned heads of Europe, and he was furious. He wrote to Victoria complaining that 'to be the first and eldest of your grandchildren and yet to be precluded from taking part in this unique fete, while cousins and far relations will have the privilege of surrounding You . . . is deeply mortifying'.

It was a massive blow to his ego, and he might well have been tempted to order his most terrifying new dreadnought to steam into the Solent and deafen Bertie with its big-gun salute. Instead, Wilhelm responded with Teutonic disdain and sent over an ancient tub that was due to be demoted to service as a floating barracks almost immediately after its trip to England.

In the event, the British admirals didn't need a new German battleship to remind them that their impressive fleet might be going out of date. As Bertie and the assembled dignitaries looked on, a small steamer suddenly appeared amongst the British warships and evaded all naval attempts to intercept it as it sped back and forth in front of the surprised spectators.

This was the *Turbinia*, then the fastest ship in the world, capable of 34.5 knots (39 mph), almost double the speed of most warships of the time. Its startling power was achieved thanks to brand-new steam turbine engines, an invention that was about to revolutionize sea warfare. The *Turbinia* was British, but it was a stark sign that, as the century drew to a close, the world was changing. The exchange of snubs between the fading Victoria and her ambitious German grandson, and the appearance of an uninvited intruder at an occasion as solemn as a naval review, were proof that Europe was losing the cosy stability that had been symbolized by all those winter gatherings of aged royals in Cannes and Nice.

Bertie was not the poetic type, but even he might have seen the hint of a metaphor in the crashing thunderstorm that broke out over the darkened sea as the Diamond Jubilee naval review came to an end.

13

REACHING AN ANGLO-FRENCH ENTENTE

~

'He [Bertie] is the most powerful factor in world diplomacy, and, because he is for peace, his overall approach will serve above all to maintain harmony between the nations.'

Remark made by an Italian politician to Camille Barrère,
French Ambassador to Rome 1897–1924

I

Nowadays it is a major media event if a member of the British royal family has to give a speech in French. The Windsor in question will squint at a carefully prepared text and gargle his or her way through several minutes of tortuous vowels and unpronounceable consonants, delighting French listeners with an English accent as strong as a ten-year-old Stilton. Bertie though, both as Prince of Wales and King, was trilingual, and could

banter fluently at any social occasion from Biarritz to
Berlin and from Marseilles to Moscow (where the aristocrats all spoke French). The only time he felt slightly
awkward improvising speeches was in Danish or Russian,
but even then he was capable of learning a short text off
by heart. He was a true international. And as the sun
finally began to set on Victoria's reign, Bertie was exactly
the successor that Britain – and the rest of Europe –
needed. The fact that no one realized it, except perhaps
a few of his fans in France, was not his fault. In Britain,
unlike France, a tempestuous private life has always
blinded people to the possibility that someone might be
well suited for public service, and most Brits still believed
what Bertie's own mother had said about him when he
first started straying across the Channel: he was, she
declared in 1863, *'totally totally* unfit . . . for ever
becoming King'.

Not that being monarch actually meant very much in
the last years of Victoria's life – despite her brief showing
at the Diamond Jubilee, she spent most of her time shut
away at Osborne House on the Isle of Wight, either blus-
tering vainly about her government's policies, or dismiss-
ively rubber-stamping them. Britain's monarchy had
become the ghost in the attic. Few people thought that
Bertie would be more than another poltergeist.

II

On 19 January 1901, Bertie was summoned to Osborne.
He was fifty-nine years old. He had been aware that his

mother was slowly sinking into dementia and blindness for years, but he had been kept in the dark about the recent deterioration of her condition by optimistic reports from his sister Helena and one of the doctors. Now, though, a more pragmatic royal physician, James Reid, had insisted that Bertie be warned that his mother was dying – after all, preparations for a handover of the throne would have to be made. And Reid, an ambitious man, no doubt hoped that by showing himself as an ally of the Prince, he might become a doctor to the King.

On receiving the summons, Bertie rushed down from London as fast as the train and boat could carry him. Not that he actually spoke to Victoria when he got to Osborne – he had never seen his mother in bed before, and couldn't face it now. Perhaps he was in denial about the idea of Victoria's death, even though it was all that stood between him and the culmination of decades of waiting for a meaningful job. Seeing her lying helpless and defeated would have made his mother's imminent disappearance too real. So next day Bertie left the Isle of Wight again and headed to London where he was due to meet his nephew, Kaiser Wilhelm.

Almost no one in England wanted Wilhelm to come to England at this time, including the closest members of his English family, but everyone in the nation knew he was arriving because he had published the fact himself.

Wilhelm had been informed of Victoria's final illness by Dr Reid, who was in fact the Kaiser's man at the palace – his spy. Reid had correctly assumed that Victoria's deathbed scene was a family occasion that Wilhelm would not want to miss. And so, in typical attention-seeking fashion, the Kaiser had sent a telegram to the royal family that was left uncoded (unlike all other official communications, so this was almost certainly a personal order by Wilhelm), announcing that he would be joining the vigil at his grandmother's bedside. The message, which passed through the hands of several telegraphists, as he knew it would, was instantly leaked to the press, so that all of Victoria's subjects suddenly knew that she was at death's door.

Returning to Osborne on 20 January with the Kaiser, Bertie finally accepted that it was time to see his mother in her nightdress. When he entered her bedroom, Victoria told him 'Kiss my face' and held out her arms to embrace him. Faced with such a rare show of maternal affection, Bertie began sobbing uncontrollably.

Throughout the evening and the next day, as more family members gathered, Victoria's daughters Beatrice and Helena repeatedly told her who was in the room with her – but always omitted one name: Wilhelm.

Dr Reid, Wilhelm's secret sidekick, questioned Bertie about this, and Bertie replied that he was afraid to tell his mother about the Kaiser's presence because it would 'excite her too much' – in the negative sense of the word, of course. What he probably meant was that Wilhelm was capable of saying something inappropriate that would give her a heart attack: 'Yes, I am here, Grossmutter. You didn't think I'd miss your deathbed scene, did you?'

At one point, everyone was asked to leave Victoria's bedroom. Wilhelm took the opportunity to complain to Dr

Reid about being left out of the Princesses' list of names, so Reid asked Bertie if it was possible to take Wilhelm to the bedside alone. No doubt fearing a scene, Bertie agreed, and told Reid to inform Wilhelm that 'the Prince of Wales wishes it'.

This private audience did the trick, and from then on, Wilhelm was attentiveness personified – for two and a half hours he sat uncomfortably with his good arm under Victoria's pillow, holding her head up so that it was easier for her to breathe. He was in his place, at the heart of his family.

This protracted vigil seems to have helped Bertie come to terms with the prospect of his mother's demise. He even managed a joke about it. As Victoria was sliding in and out of consciousness, a member of staff asked Bertie whether he thought the Queen would be happy in heaven. He replied: 'She will have to walk *behind* the angels. She won't like that.'

In the end, the great Queen died peacefully, surrounded by her family and propped up by Kaiser Wilhelm, at 6.30 p.m. on 22 January 1901. As Bertie sailed back from the Isle of Wight to the mainland with her coffin, he saw that the ship's royal standard was flying at half mast, and asked why.

'The Queen is dead, sir,' he was told.

'The King of England lives,' Bertie replied, and the flag was raised.

The question was: would anyone in Europe salute it?

III

To everyone's surprise, Bertie immediately revealed the strength of character that he had been forced to suppress – in England, at least – for so many years. He announced that he was to be called King Edward, contrary to his mother's wishes. She had wanted him to succeed as Albert Edward, but Albert was to be remembered as his father's name, Bertie said. The message was clear – King Edward was going to be his own man.

At Buckingham Palace, Bertie quickly erased all signs of his mother's cloistered existence. He fired the Munshi, her Indian servant, threw out her statues of John Brown, and emptied the rooms that had been preserved as shrines for his father. He also modernized the palace, ordering new bathrooms and toilets, and converting old coach houses into garages for his motor cars. The same revolution hit Windsor Castle, where Bertie marched about moving paintings and giving instructions for the immediate installation of all mod cons.

The domestic changes cut deep. Bertie even asked Princess Beatrice, his widowed sister who had been Victoria's companion all her life, to vacate her rooms in the royal palaces and move into a cottage at Osborne. Against Victoria's wishes, Bertie gave the main house there to the nation as a naval college. The only royal residence he left untouched was Balmoral, because he loved its spartan, tartan *über*-Scottishness.

At work, too, there was a new régime. From day one, Bertie proved that when, as Prince of Wales, he had begged to be given useful employment, he really meant it. Now he personally dealt with 400 letters a day, and set about clearing a backlog of 6,600 army commissions that had built up during the final months of his mother's reign, signing each promotion himself.

He was determined to prove the doubters wrong. Out of respect for the new monarch, the British newspapers didn't openly talk about his dubious past, but *The Times* expressed the anxiety that the establishment felt about the playboy Prince coming to the throne: 'We shall not pretend that there is nothing in his long career which those who respect and admire him could not wish otherwise.' All of Victorian England's sexual angst and denial in one triple-negative sentence.

It was appropriate that Bertie's first major ceremony, the Opening of Parliament, took place on Valentine's Day 1901. And he certainly seized the opportunity to show the nation that things had changed. Victoria had attended the Opening only seven times since her husband's death, and always in her widow's weeds, never in full royal regalia. Now Bertie was driven to Westminster in the state coach, resplendent in crimson robes and wearing the Imperial State Crown that had not been seen in public since 1861. He was immediately projecting himself as the opposite of his mother – a public sovereign. His subjects had a monarchy, with all its associated palaces, jewels and costumes, and he wanted them to get the most out of it. As always, Bertie was all for sharing the fun.

In adopting this showiness, he was applying the principle that he had first seen in Paris, when Napoléon III and Eugénie took every opportunity to dress in their finest imperial costumes and stun the crowds with their magnificence. In their logic, and Bertie's, they weren't simply showing off – they were doing the nation proud. The people might not get a chance to wear the jewels or ride in the carriages themselves, but they should be able to see them, and bathe in the reflected glory. It's an idea that lives on to this day, and is the reason why TV companies all over the world are desperate to televise any British royal ceremony going. The Brits do good ceremony. And Bertie was the first modern royal to make it happen.

A cynic might say that this spirit of official openness allowed Bertie to cover up what was going on in his private life – he was at this time enjoying a long-term affair with Alice Keppel, a witty, big-busted married English lady of thirty-two, the great-grandmother of Camilla Parker Bowles, the present wife and former lover of Bertie's own great-great-grandson, Charles. But the grand ceremonies weren't all about camouflage – Bertie genuinely did want to be a public king. He was a people person in all senses of the term.

He even risked his life to be crowned. His coronation was set for 26 June 1902, but a few days earlier, he began to suffer from a searing pain in his lower abdomen. His doctor Sir Francis Laking prescribed bed rest and warm milk, even though he recognized the symptoms of appendicitis. Perhaps the doctor thought that the problem would go away of its own accord, and that Nature would not dare to interrupt the coronation of a British monarch. He was certainly afraid of seeing the new uncrowned King dying on the operating table on the eve of his succession – the other European powers might take it as a divine sign of England's weakness. In any case, Bertie was not informed of the seriousness of his condition, and insisted that the coronation go ahead.

He probably hoped that a milk-only diet would do him some good. His appetite had been misbehaving badly of late. First he had gone off his food, and then he had started craving it. He had even been overdoing the alcohol, which was very rare for him, and had been falling asleep during meals, which never happened, mainly because he spent them gobbling every dish in sight.

The press was told that the King was in bed with lumbago, but his doctors finally summoned the courage to tell Bertie the truth: he would die without an operation. Even so, the people's monarch was insistent that his hundreds of guests and millions of expectant subjects should not be disappointed, and he refused to postpone the coronation. Finally, one of Britain's top surgeons, Sir Frederick Treves, was called in to convince him that an appendectomy was both vital and survivable. Treves had performed the first-ever operation of its kind in England in 1888.*

Bertie submitted to medical pressure, and the next after-noon, on a table in his dressing room, he was given

---

* Ironically, Treves himself died of peritonitis – a ruptured appendix – in 1923, shortly after publishing his memoirs, which included the famous story of his friendship with the Elephant Man.

chloroform and opened up. Apparently Treves had to cut through about four inches of royal flesh before finding the cause of Bertie's pain – not an inflamed appendix but an enormous abscess around it. Good, if somewhat repulsive, news. Treves drained the pus – a full pint of it – and closed the incision, hoping for the best. Not everyone in Bertie's physical condition woke up from the primitive anaesthetic, or survived post-op infection, especially when the operation had been performed in an ordinary dressing room by a surgeon in shirtsleeves and an apron. But by next morning the King was sitting up, chatting to the nurses, writing a note to his mistress Alice Keppel, and – of course – smoking a cigar.

Only six weeks later, on 9 August, his coronation finally went ahead. It was a glittering occasion, with all the pomp and ceremony that one would expect of Bertie, as well as a few moments of comedy. The actual crowning was performed by the ancient, half-blind Archbishop of Canterbury, Frederick Temple, who placed the crown on backwards. Bertie had to reach up and swivel it himself. And some members of the congregation noticed that the King could not help occasionally letting his eyes stray upwards to a gallery above the altar, where, like a string of pearls, sat a row of his mistresses, past and present, none of whom should really have been invited. Alice Keppel was there, of course, along with Winston Churchill's mother Jennie, and – to add the French touch that coloured every aspect of Bertie's life – Sarah Bernhardt, who was dressed as unconventionally as ever, all in white.

IV

Bertie's determination to take an active part in the daily business of monarchy did not flag after his coronation. He quickly gained a reputation amongst all his ministers for his swift and efficient replies to all of their requests. He prided himself on dealing with every note and despatch the day he received it.

Characteristically, one aspect of the country's affairs interested Bertie much more than all the rest – foreign affairs. Not only did he make sure that he read every communication from his ambassadors (and being a friend or relative of practically every sovereign in Europe, he regarded them as *his* ambassadors), Bertie also asked them to give him private briefings, too. These could be notes passing on inside information about the mood in a country or its royal palace, or, when he was travelling, short briefing sessions about the political situation, the economy or even the state of the local railways. Then, suitably informed, Bertie would hold private meetings with foreign leaders to gauge the temperature of Britain's relations with the country. Bertie regarded Britain's international relations as his personal mission. As Benjamin Disraeli put it: 'He really has seen everything and knows everybody.'

What Bertie was doing, of course, was putting his past life of pleasure and social flittering to good use. He had always chatted with monarchs and leaders about their countries – and incidentally discussed the local racecourses, casinos, theatres and females – and now he was having exactly the same conversations in the explicit service of his nation.

At one point, Bertie's government requested that he should differentiate between personal and political visits from foreign sovereigns, so that the nation would not have to pay to entertain Kaiser Wilhelm, for example, if he rowed over to Bertie's yacht for drinks during Cowes Week. But Bertie refused to differentiate and, as the years of his short reign went on, he would be proved increasingly right, because in his case any opportunity to sit down and chew the fat of European politics counted as a state visit. As he had shown in the past, good relations between countries could be maintained just as well – in some cases better – with a cosy dinner as a tightly worded treaty.

The proof of all this is that Bertie was genuinely respected by foreign diplomats. In 1907, the Belgian Chargé d'Affaires in London said that: 'The English are increasingly getting into the habit of seeing international problems as coming almost exclusively under the remit of King Edward, whose profound political instinct and productive diplomacy they very rightly respect.'

Bertie had even grown detached – some would say mature – enough to make a few key gestures towards the French to remind them that his love affair with them needed mutual respect. As early as 1889, when he was still Prince of Wales, he had declined the official invitation to attend the Paris Exposition Universelle because of its political symbolism. It had been organized to coincide with the centenary of France's anti-royalist revolution, and it was of course impossible for Bertie to lend his name to the wholesale guillotining of monarchs (even if they were French). Many of the crowned heads of Europe and even their ambassadors refused to attend Paris's centenary Expo, citing prior engagements or sudden illnesses.

However, Bertie decided that if he couldn't go as a prince, there was nothing to stop him attending as a private Francophile, so he took Alexandra and the children to Paris to see the new Eiffel Tower. In fact he was given the honour of being the tower's first official visitor, and got a two-hour private tour from Gustave Eiffel himself, who took the royal family to the summit. According to a report in *Le Figaro* newspaper of 11 June 1889, Bertie was 'very interested' in the English restaurant on the first level, but after that 'the ascent proceeded to the third floor with no interruptions except the change of lifts'.

It must have been a literally dizzying experience because the tower was the tallest building in the world, and made not of solid stone but a latticework of apparently slim girders. What was more, the lifts had not received their final security clearance. Even so, according to *Le Figaro*: 'It was with the most complete peace of mind and perfect confidence that the Prince and Princess of Wales insisted on taking their place in the lift with all their children, the hope and future of the throne of England.' In short, it was a bit like going on the test flight of a new aeroplane, and was proof yet again that Bertie was game for a thrill whenever he went to Paris.

At the top of the tower, Bertie was delighted with the view. He congratulated Eiffel on his 'incomparable work' and 'shook Eiffel by both hands on several occasions'. Back down on *terra firma*, Bertie and his family were greeted by the 'enthusiastic cheers and hurrahs of the crowd'. It was yet another public-relations triumph for Paris's favourite Englishman. One British newspaper quoted Bertie as quipping that 'the Eiffel tower is an awful tower'. but this sounds like the writer's own feeble attempt at a joke.

Bertie's double standards – boycotting the 1889 Expo as a royal but enjoying it as a man – could be interpreted as proof of his weak character. Which it probably was in some ways. But it was also a sign that, unlike so many politicians, he was capable of taking the long-term view. So the French wanted to celebrate their revolution? Why not? No one could deny that it happened. For now, the most important consideration was for monarchist Britain to get on with republican France.

So, ever the ambassador, even when he was on a supposedly private visit, in 1889 Bertie also paid a courtesy call on President Sadi Carnot – and received one in return. Five years later, when Carnot was stabbed to death by an anarchist, Bertie went in person to the French Embassy in London to offer his condolences, a gesture that was also typical of him. It was these private marks of respect that would later win him the trust of so many European leaders, and not only in France.

However, Bertie's 1889 trip to the Paris Expo was a temporary high point in Anglo-French relations of the time, mainly because of both countries' determination to be the world's most efficient colonizers. As the century came to an end, diplomatic tensions grew steadily worse, and finally flared up in an incident that has been long forgotten by the Brits, but which remains firmly stuck in the French historical gullet.

This confrontation was so serious that it would have seemed inconceivable, when Bertie came to the throne in 1901, that he could be only three years away from one of Britain's greatest diplomatic triumphs of the twentieth century, the Entente Cordiale. In 1901 it looked much more likely that France and Britain would go to war again . . .

V

If you ask any French patriot to list the low points in Anglo-British relations, they will probably begin with recriminations about Joan of Arc and St Helena, before spitting out a strange word: 'Fashoda'.

This is the name of a diplomatic incident that still rankles with the French, all the more so because hardly any Brits have ever heard of it. Even in Christopher Hibbert's highly detailed biography of Bertie, Fashoda merits just two-and-a-half lines. From a French perspective, however, this is one of the most serious diplomatic incidents in Franco-British history. It is as if we had come to a dinner party in France's home, insulted its food, its furniture and the intelligence of its children – while totally sober – and then forgotten all about the incident. In short, to French minds, Fashoda* represents all that is worst about *les Anglais* – not

---

* Even more annoyingly to the French, the Brits can't even spell its name right. In French, it's 'Fachoda'. But then the Brits can't spell 'Azincourt' or pronounce 'Waterloo', either.

just their arrogance, but most of all their failure to take French grievances seriously.

The Fashoda incident (in French it was a 'crisis') took place in East Africa in 1898. As a colonial incident it was (sorry, France) a bit of a non-event, a mere showdown at a time when bloody battles were being fought all across the continent, and when the conflict between Britain and the Boers was about to explode into war.

Fashoda was the name of a fort on the Nile in southern Sudan, a strategic point in both French and British plans for Africa. Britain wanted to realize its dream of owning a string of colonies from Cairo to Cape Town, linking Egypt to South Africa via its East African territories, including Sudan. France, meanwhile, wanted to open up an east–west corridor from Senegal to Djibouti, also through Sudan. The French therefore launched three expeditions to occupy the as yet unconquered Fashoda, one from Brazzaville on the Congo River in the west, the other two from the east, across Ethiopia. The Brazzaville party was led by a 24-year-old solder called Jean-Baptiste Marchand, and comprised 120 Senegalese soldiers, a dozen French officers and hundreds of African porters. They sailed upriver in a borrowed Belgian steamer and a small fleet of rowing boats, dragged and floated them across marshland to the Nile, and finally arrived a year and a half later to find out that they were on their own: the other French expeditions had been halted by the Ethiopians. This depleted French force settled into the fort on 10 July 1898 and renamed it Saint-Louis to make it clear who now owned it.

They weren't alone for long, however, because six weeks later General Horatio Kitchener arrived. He was in the process of establishing a military career that would peak at the Battle of Omdurman in the Sudan that same year, but he did no more than demand (politely) that the French leave the fort. The French (just as politely) refused. Wishing to avoid a battle that might spark a war, the two men agreed to differ and asked their governments for advice.

Back in Europe, the French took one look across the Channel at the jingoistic Brits, who had been riding on a wave of patriotism since the Diamond Jubilee, and decided that a colonial war was a strong likelihood. This idea was confirmed when Royal Navy warships began, rather unsubtly, to perform manoeuvres outside the ports of Brest in Brittany and Bizerte in French-owned Tunisia. And when France's Foreign Minister Théophile Delcassé asked the British Ambassador to Paris, Sir Edmund Monson, whether Fashoda could be 'the cause of a break-up between us',* he received the blunt answer 'oui'.

Poor Jean-Baptiste Marchand was duly ordered by his government to quit Fashoda and make for Djibouti, leaving Kitchener's men to move in. Kitchener himself, meanwhile, had gone north to fight at Omdurman and seal his reputation as a national hero.

---

* No doubt thanks to Bertie's influence, Delcassé used the language of lovers, and referred to 'une rupture', the common word for a lovers' split.

La crise de Fachoda poisoned the French psyche. To cover its humiliation, the French government played down the affair. Delcassé said that the 'patriotic sensitivity' of the British was 'overexcited', and 'if the English had said one friendly, conciliatory word, the problem could have been solved'. As he said it, he was probably shrugging as if to suggest that it was all a big fuss caused by those crazy *Anglais* whipping up a storm in their *tasse de thé*. The French also announced that their withdrawal from Fashoda was caused by ill health: Marchand and his men had been too sick to hold out. But no one really believed all this, and France was hit by a wave of Anglophobia, which grew to a positive tsunami when Britain went to war against the Boers in October 1899.

Even a relatively restrained French newspaper like *Le Figaro* quoted speeches by 'Uncle Paul' Kruger, the Boer president of the Transvaal, and reported that: 'The Boer soldiers march away, gravely singing their psalms as they pursue, across the mountains they know so well, their sublime epic voyage.' One Boer soldier was quoted in the same newspaper as saying that Kitchener, was 'good against savages but not against us'. French sympathies couldn't have been clearer.

It could be said that France's support for these Dutch colonizers was only a mark of anti-British jealousy. After all, if France could have occupied South Africa, it would have done so, and kicked the Boers off the Cape of Good Hope. At the time, just about every western European country except Luxembourg, Liechtenstein and Switzerland were scrabbling for any scrap of African land they could get.

This ill feeling over Fashoda and the Boer War troubled
Bertie, not least because for once the French seemed to
have forgotten how much they loved him, and had become
openly insulting.* The anti-British articles in the French
press were not only aimed at the politicians and soldiers.
Some were directed at him. A leftist journal called *L'Assiette
au Beurre* (the *Butter Dish*) printed a cartoon of Britannia
mooning to reveal that her buttocks were tattooed with a
portrait of Bertie. A bit of a change from the fan articles
in the *Courrier de Cannes*.

Bertie had spent so many years living in loving sin with
France, and now it was all going wrong, not least because
there was a new generation of Parisian thinkers who had
not been raised on Anglomania. As Bertie's biographer
Philippe Jullian describes it, they had 'learnt their
manners in the brasseries of the Quartier Latin'. For
them, Bertie was fair game. On one of his trips to Paris
in the 1890s, he planned to go and see a theatre group's
revue of the year, only to be told that if he did so, they
were going to have to edit out several sketches about his
gambling debts and his mother's infatuation with her male
servants.

Because of all this, Bertie refused outright to visit
Paris's Exposition of 1900, the first he had missed since
1855. And when he came to the throne in 1901, he knew
that he had lost the automatic respect that the city's
people and politicians had always had for him. He was

---

* It has been suggested that the original version of a certain proverb
was: 'Hell hath no fury like a Frenchman scorned.'

still popular down in Cannes, where his presence was good for the economy, but his beloved Paris had turned decidedly frosty.

What was worse from Bertie's perspective was that Britain had turned its back on the French, so a reconciliation was going to be difficult. In 1899 the newspaper baron Lord Northcliffe, founder of the *Daily Mail* and the *Daily Mirror*, wrote that: 'England hesitated for a long time between France and Germany, but she always respected the German character whereas she has come to regard France with contempt. An *Entente Cordiale* cannot exist between England and her nearest neighbour. Enough of France, which has neither courage nor political sense.'

Poor Bertie. At the precise moment he became king, he saw his life's work as a prince sink like a holed Channel steamer. As he sat in Buckingham Palace with his Foreign Office papers, any *entente* between Britain and France, let alone a cordial one, must have seemed like mission impossible.

VI

As we have seen, Bertie had never been afraid of going on solo missions to France. And his mother and her various governments had spent decades keeping secrets from him. Now it was his turn.

By 1903, arguments about Fashoda and the Boers had lost their vicious edge, even if 'patriotic sensitivities', as the French called them, were still running high. Bertie knew that Lord Lansdowne, his Foreign Secretary, felt that the main obstacle to peace between Britain and France (apart from the fact that they had been enemies for the best part of a millennium) was a lasting dispute over Morocco, which sat opposite Gibraltar at the gateway to the Med and was therefore one of the keys to naval mastery of the region. Many people in Britain wanted to get their hands on this southern gatepost and dominate the entrance to the Mediterranean.

Lansdowne didn't think that the time was right for any compromise with the French. But Bertie, who had spent his whole adult life getting himself compromised in France, had other ideas. So without telling anyone, he planned a trip to visit France's President Émile Loubet in May 1903. Difficult, one might think, for a king to slip across the Channel unnoticed – even though French monarchs like Louis XVIII, Louis-Philippe and Napoléon III had done exactly that in the other direction. But Bertie had a cunning plan – he was due to sail down to Lisbon to see King Carlos of Portugal, and then steam through the Med to Rome to say *buon giorno* to King Victor Emmanuel of Italy. This much was public knowledge. But what Bertie didn't tell everyone was that, as he had so often done in his younger days, he was planning a quick stopover in Paris.

It's easy to imagine Bertie's glee as he plotted this single-handed intervention in his country's foreign policy. In the past, his stopovers had been fun but frivolous affairs, frowned on by his mother and her ministers. Now he was going to use the same tactic, but in the cause of world peace. If the term had been invented in 1903, he would have been murmuring, 'Payback time.'

Of course his secret mission wasn't without its dangers. If it went wrong – if for example the French decided to use his attempt at diplomacy to score political points against the Germans by leaking the information – he would look an interfering fool, and might get sidelined from active politics again, as he had been when he was Prince of Wales. But Bertie was a gambler who got bored if the stakes were too low. What's more, he knew that he was the only man whom the French trusted enough to play this dangerous game. And if it worked, if it worked . . . Victory would be as sweet as any he had enjoyed in the casinos of Cannes or Monte Carlo.

So Bertie informed neither Lansdowne, nor Alexandra (though she had rarely been completely *au fait* with her husband's trips to France anyway), nor even his private secretary Francis Knollys. He also left the reliable Sir Edmund Monson, the British Ambassador to Paris, in the dark. The only man Bertie trusted with the truth was a junior undersecretary at the Foreign Office called Charles Hardinge, who was married to the daughter of an old friend of his. Again, when it was necessary, Bertie could always call in help from his private connections.

The problem was that the French have never been experts at keeping secrets, and in Paris rumours were soon rife that *le roi d'Angleterre* was on his way. Bertie got wind of this – no doubt friends of his were asking him which *belle Parisienne* he would like on the list of dinner guests – and he felt obliged to let Sir Edmund Monson in on the secret.

Monson took up Bertie's cause, went to see President Loubet, and reported back that Loubet:

> . . . could not lay too much stress on the influence which the King's presence in Paris would have on friendly relations between the two peoples . . . His Majesty, while Prince of Wales, had acquired an exceptional popularity; and he would find when he returned that this feeling was as warm as ever.

Again, if it hadn't been a hundred years too early, Bertie would have smiled to himself and murmured, 'Game on.'

Then came Bertie's real master stroke. He went on his cruise to visit the Kings of Portugal and Italy and, as the *Victoria and Albert* entered the Mediterranean, it was announced that President Loubet was in Algiers. As a mark of respect, Bertie sent a small flotilla of gunboats to salute him,* and in reply the courteous Frenchman quite naturally invited the King to visit him in Paris – *pourquoi pas* a quick stopover en route from Rome to London? *Quelle bonne idée,* Bertie answered, and informed his government that he had accepted. After all, given the tensions about the Mediterranean, this exchange of courtesies was a sign that the French wanted to negotiate. So the King couldn't very well refuse, could he? Lansdowne tried to argue, but Bertie put his foot down and the Foreign Secretary had to give

---

* Given that it was just coming up to the centenary of Nelson's death at nearby Trafalgar, the British guns probably had to be double-checked for 'accidental' live rounds.

in. The politician didn't know it, but he had been outflanked by the new King of European diplomacy. Bertie the meddling Prince had been replaced by Edward Double-O VII.

As it turned out, Loubet had exaggerated Bertie's 'exceptional popularity' in France. Just before he arrived, an anti-British paper called *La Patrie* (*Homeland*) published two special issues commemorating every Anglo-French conflict since Joan of Arc, ending of course with Fashoda. A similarly inclined publication called *L'Autorité* (*Authority*) declared that Bertie's visit 'shocks, offends and revolts us patriots'. Postcards went on sale showing Bonaparte shaking his fist at Bertie and President Loubet, and growling, 'Oh, if only I were still alive.' Even the cabaret singers turned against their old star client. One of them had a big hit with a ditty that went 'Edouard sept, gros et gras': literally 'Edward VII, fat and fat' – *gros* is a word describing the shape of an overweight person and *gras* the actual fat content of their flesh. Another wrote a song with an obscene pun in the title: literally, 'Les Anglais Débarquent' means 'the English disembark' but it is also a vulgar euphemism for the start of a woman's period (because of English soldiers' scarlet uniforms).

On May Day 1903, the date of Bertie's arrival in Paris, *Le Figaro* admitted that people always 'worry what is hidden in the thoughts of kings'. But, toeing the official presidential line, it reassured its readers that 'le roi Edouard' had:

. . . no other idea, no other desire, than to ensure world peace. He is related to all the sovereigns of Europe, most of them younger than he is, and you can be sure that he will use the authority of his age and the familiarity of his family ties to smooth away any obstacles, if there are any, and live in perfect understanding with everyone. It is a great role, a beautiful role.

Unfortunately, the Parisians in the street either didn't read *Le Figaro* or didn't agree.

At 2.55 p.m., Bertie, dressed in a British general's scarlet tunic, arrived by royal train at the now-defunct Bois de Boulogne station, to be met by President Loubet who was, the papers noted, sunburnt after his recent trip to Africa. The two men shook hands, but – unusually – made no speeches. They were clearly nervous about the reception they might receive. They climbed aboard the President's state carriage, and five minutes after Bertie's arrival they were driving into Paris, with crowds lining the route. *Le Figaro* noted that these spectators had been waiting 'for two hours' – in the past the Parisians would have been out at dawn to be sure of catching a glimpse of their favourite monarch.

Driving along the Champs-Élysées, there were cheers, but also shouts of 'Vivent les Boers!', 'Vive Fachoda!' and even the old bugbear 'Vive Jeanne d'Arc!' When one of Bertie's staff grumbled that 'the French don't like us', he retorted, 'Why should they?'

In general, though, the crowd seemed well disposed. Plenty of buildings along the route had been decorated with British flags and 'Welcome' signs in English. So Bertie would not have been put off by a few hecklers.

Besides, he must have been glowing in the satisfaction that his covert operation was actually being enacted. And he understood the French character – they were always at their most aggressive just before letting themselves be seduced.

At 5 p.m., Bertie paid a very short visit to the President at the Élysée Palace, and half an hour later he was at the nearby British Embassy to receive members of the British Chamber of Commerce. There, he gave a carefully worded speech about Anglo-British friendship that had been prepared for him by Charles Hardinge and that was released to the French press to be reprinted next day. It spoke of his wishes that Britain and France could end all hostilities and work together as 'champions and pioneers of civilization and peaceful progress'.

After a twelve-course dinner at the Embassy that included a diplomatic mixture of dishes – cream of asparagus soup *à la Reine*, fillet of beef *à l'anglaise*, *petits pois à la française*, peaches *à la Montreuil* – Bertie went to the Théâtre Français to see an aptly named play, *L'Autre Danger*. In fact, though, it was not about the danger of world war but a comedy by a writer of witty boulevard farces called Maurice Donnay in which a man meets up with an old flame after she gets married and has an affair with her, only to fall in love with her daughter – the perfect choice of show for Bertie.

There were few laughs at the start of the evening, though. Unlike past outings to the theatre, when Bertie would be cheered merely for his choice of mistress, there was virtual silence amongst the audience. *Le Figaro* reported nothing more than a 'murmur of curiosity' as he took his seat. This lack of enthusiasm might be explained by the fact that much of the audience that night was made up of French bureaucrats, not the most extrovert of people. In any case, Bertie laughed his way through the first act and then, during the interval, as he had so often done in the past, he strolled out into the corridors with the rest of the audience, followed by his nervous police bodyguards. There, he saw someone he knew (a pretty safe bet in Paris). It was the former star of the Paris stage, and his former lover, Jeanne Granier, now a *grande dame* in her early fifties. Probably the last time he had seen her was in a Monte Carlo hotel room some fourteen years earlier. Bertie went over and kissed her hand affectionately. According to the police report of the *soirée*, he told her in loud French that could be heard by everyone in the vicinity, 'Ah, mademoiselle, I remember how I applauded you in London, where you represented all the grace and all the wit of France.'*

Next day, everyone who was anyone was repeating this little piece of theatrical dialogue, and all the French newspapers printed Bertie's speech to the Chamber of Commerce, which was hailed as a 'great sensation'.

Suddenly the atmosphere cleared. It was the good old days in Paris again. Bertie, the world's greatest and most sociable Francophile, was back. On the morning of Saturday, 2 May 1903, the British royal standard was cheered as it

---

* Note the brilliant piece of discretion about their frequent meetings in Paris and the Riviera.

313

was raised above the Hôtel de Ville, a building more renowned as the scene of anti-monarchist insurrections in 1789 and 1870. Bertie arrived just before noon, dressed in his red uniform and feathered hat, and was cheered by a large crowd. He was welcomed as 'an old friend' by the President of the Municipal Council (the city mayor) in a reception room decorated from floor to ceiling in flowers, and in reply he stood up and gave one of his trademark spontaneous speeches. Bertie told the assembled councillors in his fluent French:

> It would have been vexatious not to have been able to stop at the Hôtel de Ville for a moment while I was in your beautiful city. I thank you sincerely for the welcome you have afforded me today. I will never forget my visit to your charming city, and I can assure you that it is always with the greatest pleasure that I return to Paris, where I am always treated as if I were *chez moi*.

In short, it was almost fifty years of pleasurable returns to Paris summed up in two or three elegantly constructed sentences. And as the culmination of Bertie's private plan to salvage Anglo-French relations, it was the moment when the apparently frivolous Prince turned into a true monarch on the world stage.

Le Figaro said that this was 'not only a visit from the most Parisian of Princes . . . The royal words that we have just heard rang in our ears as the promise of a new era in relations between our two peoples.' Even London's sceptical *Times* recognized that this was no flash in the pan, conceding for once that it had been Bertie's 'Parisian way of living in Paris that won influence for him'.

On his third day in the city, Bertie was cheered wherever he went. At dinner with the President, he gave a speech of thanks reminding everyone that 'I have known Paris since I was a child. I have returned many times and I have always admired the beauty of this unique city and the spirit of its inhabitants.' At the end of his short address, he diplomatically proposed a toast to 'the prosperity and the greatness of France'.

As he sat in his carriage to the Opéra that evening, crowds of Parisians jostled to get a view of Bertie and were heard to shout 'Vive Edouard!' and even 'Vive notre roi!' When he left for England on 4 May, dressed for his Channel crossing in a black admiral's uniform, he was given an *au revoir* as loud and affectionate as anything he'd known in 1855, 1878 or any other of the high points in his French love affair. The crowds were 'enormous' and 'joyous', and hawkers were selling miniatures of the King, calling out: 'Who hasn't got his little Edward?'

At the station, Bertie and Loubet said farewells like old friends, and as Bertie's train pulled away, it was to a public send-off that, according to the French newspapers, was 'fervent', 'passionate' and even 'delirious'. Loubet was looking tired, said *Le Figaro*, but 'with the happy smile of a man who has just performed a great duty, and performed it well'. He was cheered all the way back to the Élysée, a rare occurrence for any French leader who hasn't just won a war (and there haven't been many of those).

The British Ambassador Sir Edmund Monson later

reported that the success of Bertie's state visit was 'more complete than the most sanguine optimist could have foreseen'. In the space of a few hours, by making sure that he was in the right place at the right time, by improvising a few key words, and most of all by reminding the French that Britain's ruler was the same well-intentioned man they had known for half a century, Bertie had transformed the French from anti-British republicans to relapsed Bertie lovers.

Within days, the politicians got to work and hammered out the text of the Entente Cordiale which, when you look at it closely, is not such a friendly document after all. Rather than promising eternal *amour* and mutual solidarity, it is a slightly sordid exchange of colonialist guarantees – Britain would let France hold on to Morocco if the French stopped trying to grab Egypt. It wasn't a real alliance; it wasn't friendly; it was just a polite agreement by each party not to steal what the others had got their eyes on. But at the time, just after Fashoda and the Boer War, even that was a minor miracle, and its importance is still trumpeted more than a century after it was signed in April 1904 – now that everyone has forgotten what it actually said.

Of course Bertie doesn't deserve all the credit for the Entente Cordiale – diplomats like Lord Lansdowne, Paul Cambon (the French Ambassador in London) and France's Foreign Minister Théophile Delcassé did much of the political preparation for the agreement. But the true spade-work – the laying of the foundations – was all Bertie's. For all its faults, the treaty between Europe's greatest historical enemies would never have been signed, or even drafted, if

Bertie had not secretly engineered his visit to Paris and convinced everyone in France that *entente* with the *Anglais* was a good idea. The French government needed the approval of its suspicious electorate, and, using the tactics taught to him by the Parisians themselves, Bertie seduced the French people into trusting Britain.

Whether they were wise to do this is a different matter.

14

DON'T MENTION THE WAR

~

'I have not long to live, and then my nephew will make war.'
Bertie to his friend Elisabeth,
Comtesse de Greffulhe, 1910

I

With the fractious mood prevailing in Europe at the beginning of the twentieth century, it wasn't enough to be friends with France. All over the continent, alliances were being forged and broken, attempted and abandoned, because everyone knew that it was dangerous to be caught standing alone in the playground.

Bertie was fully aware of all this, and played a vital role in keeping the peace between Britain and a country that both France and Germany desperately wanted as an ally – Russia.

In letters, young Tsar Nicholas called himself Bertie's

'most loving nephew, Nicky' and addressed the English King as 'dearest Uncle Bertie', but in life he was an unstable, isolated character, and relations between the two men were often difficult. Bertie disapproved – often openly – of Nicky's dictatorial attitude to his people (which would later provoke the Russian Revolution), and criticized him for the anti-Semitic pogroms, but always expressed his hope for an official *entente* between Britain and Russia 'similar to the one . . . concluded with France'.

At the time, France already had more than an *entente* with Russia – the two were in an anti-German alliance, and Bertie knew that Britain also had to nurture good relations with Russia if the powerful triangle was to be sealed. However, this fragile stability was rocked when Russia went to war with one of Britain's official allies – Japan – in 1904. Britain declared that it would stay neutral, but the Russians suspected that this was just a ploy and that the Brits were giving the Japanese secret aid. The suspicion ran so deep (especially when Kaiser Wilhelm chipped in, telling the Russians that they should never trust an Englishman) that Tsar Nicholas reacted with Wilhelm-like petulance, calling his uncle 'the most dangerous intriguer in the world'.

Bertie's response was typical. He asked a friend of his in St Petersburg, a hard-living, smooth-talking Scotsman after his own heart called Mackenzie Wallace, to go and reassure Nicholas about Britain's intentions. Wallace was a journalist rather than a diplomat, but this was an advantage, because Nicholas distrusted ambassadors. So Wallace was able to talk his way into Nicholas's confidence and defuse the situation. Yet again, it was Bertie's lifelong sociability and endless chain of faithful friends that saved the day.

However, having found a breach in Anglo-Russian relations, Wilhelm did his best to foment more trouble. In the summer of 1905, he arranged to meet Tsar Nicholas during a yachting holiday in the Gulf of Finland, and the two cousins enjoyed a healthy bitch about Bertie. Wilhelm told Nicholas that their uncle had 'a passion for making "a little agreement" with every country, everywhere'* – not just Japan. The already sensitive Nicholas was easily convinced, and promised Wilhelm that 'he [Bertie] shall never get one from me, and never in my life against Germany'. At which point, according to the legend, Wilhelm whipped out a pre-prepared Russo-German treaty and got Nicholas to sign it.

The two cousins' improvised treaty was ignored by both the Russian and German governments, but in any case, Britain outflanked Germany by signing an Anglo-Russian Convention in 1907. This agreement was forced on Nicholas by France, which offered a loan to Russia on condition that it entered into an alliance with Britain. To prevent any resentment on Nicholas's part, Bertie's personal back-up was needed. Knowing that it was best if he was on hand to consolidate the formal agreement, he paid a state visit to Russia in June 1908, sailing to the Estonian

---

* Ironically, for once Wilhelm was not wrong to be paranoid. Bertie was at that very moment overseeing the marriage of Victoria Eugenie, the daughter of his sister Beatrice, to King Alfonso of Spain. He was also urging Prince Charles of Denmark, husband of his daughter Maud, to claim the vacant Norwegian throne – which Charles did in November 1905, creating a pro-British, anti-German Norway.

port of Reval (nowadays called Tallinn) on the *Victoria and Albert* and holding a series of meetings on board ship.

Again, Bertie showed what a skilled diplomat he was, alternating businesslike discussions with cosy family dinners. He impressed Alexander Izvolsky, the Russian Foreign Minister, with his grasp of Russian and European affairs, and took care to massage Nicholas's sensitive ego. He made the Tsar an admiral of the fleet, an honour dished out frequently to foreign dignitaries, but which flattered Nicholas enormously. Bertie also congratulated the Tsar on his marvellous new railways, told him he looked excellent in the uniform of the Scots Greys – a scarlet tunic with gold braid and an enormous fur busby – that he had donned for the first meeting, and generally avoided all discussion of thorny subjects like Germany. After just a couple of days, the Russian papers were all hailing 'a new era in Anglo-Russian relations'.

This was gratifying and was now becoming something of a habit – wherever Bertie went, the press seemed to end up hailing a new era in Anglo-local friendship. Yet again, peace had been maintained thanks to Bertie's presence. Even in the prevailing climate of intense international distrust, and despite all Kaiser Wilhelm's meddling, it was hard to imagine 'loving' Nicholas ever going to war with his 'dearest Uncle Bertie'.

II

The problem was that maintaining good relations with the willing French and the suspicious but easily influenced

Nicholas was the easy part. Like everyone else in Europe, Bertie knew that the main threat to peace came from a much more dangerous, volatile source. He was going to need all the human-relations skills he had learnt in France to deal with someone more demanding and diva-like than the most temperamental Parisian *cocotte* – his other nephew, Kaiser Wilhelm.

The trouble wasn't all one-sided. The Brits were becoming rabidly anti-German, partly because of the increasing strength of Germany's industry and merchant marine, but mainly because of the fear, whipped up by the popular press, of Wilhelm's expanding fleet of warships. Bertie feared them too, and knew that the only way to keep the German gunboats away from Britain's colonial outposts was to maintain a strong grip on the Kaiser himself.

It would need a psychiatrist to diagnose the exact reasons for Wilhelm's ever-changing emotions towards his British family, but there seem to be three key reasons for his mood swings, the first of which was an inferiority complex caused by his withered left arm, which had been paralysed during childbirth. Because of this, he always felt the need to prove that he was stronger and louder than anyone else. The second was a childish craving for attention: Bismarck used to say that Wilhelm wanted every day to be his birthday. The third, and perhaps the one that he felt most keenly, was a desire to be recognized as Bertie's equal or – when he succeeded to his throne while Bertie was still a prince – his superior. Wilhelm wanted more than anything else to be accepted as a core member of Victoria's immediate family, which he saw – rightly – as the trunk in the European family tree.

Bertie knew that managing these psychological flaws with infinite tact was even more important than any political negotiations if a European war was to be avoided.

Wilhelm and Bertie had some things in common. They could both be very charming company, particularly if beautiful women were around, and they shared an obsession with details, especially where clothes were concerned. But unlike his uncle, Wilhelm had a petty streak, and felt obliged, for example, to force his superior knowledge on people. Christopher Hibbert cites a case when, à propos of nothing, Wilhelm asked Bertie's private secretary Frederick Ponsonby how many councillors served on the London County Council, and how often there were elections. Ponsonby confessed his ignorance, only for Wilhelm to recite the exact figures across the dinner table to impress the guests. He had obviously learnt them by heart just to be able to show off. He was Mr Right, but in the wrong way – a man who hated to be caught out or proved wrong, and who would make sure he retaliated if he was offended.

As soon as Wilhelm had succeeded to his throne in June 1888, Bertie had begun to bear the brunt of these attacks. Once, for example, Bertie – who was still Prince of Wales at the time – intervened in a heated argument between the German Foreign Minister and the British Ambassador about the Franco-Prussian War, and made offensive personal remarks about Wilhelm. When these were reported back to him, Wilhelm immediately began plotting his revenge.

Shortly afterwards, in September 1888, Bertie was in

Vienna visiting the Austro-Hungarian Emperor Franz Joseph, and was told that Kaiser Wilhelm planned to arrive in the city just after he had left. In a spirit of family togetherness, Bertie wrote to Wilhelm telling him that he would wait and be sure to see him. However, Wilhelm replied that he did not wish to see his uncle, and furthermore, he had booked Bertie's rooms, the best suite in the best hotel in town, so Bertie – who was a mere prince while he was an emperor – had better vacate them. With admirable calm, Uncle Bertie penned a pained letter, saying that he felt 'the greatest affection' for Wilhelm and was hurt by his behaviour. When this appeal went unheeded, Bertie packed up and left. He knew that there was no point prolonging the confrontation when his nephew was in this kind of mood.

But Wilhelm's tempers were usually assuaged by a petty victory, and when he visited England the following year, everything was sweetness and light. The Brits put on a big show of hospitality, and gave Wilhelm's ego the dose of love it needed to keep it functioning smoothly. Bertie made him an admiral of the fleet (fortunately it didn't mean that Wilhelm could sail off in a British battleship), the Colonial Secretary Joseph Chamberlain gave a speech saying that Britain's 'natural alliance' was with 'the great German Empire', and Bertie got an invitation for a return visit the following year during which Wilhelm was careful to treat his uncle 'quite like a sovereign', as Bertie expressed it in a letter to his mother.

But, just like Bertie's inflammation of the knee and his chesty colds, Wilhelm's pettiness flared up several times throughout the 1890s. Uncle and nephew had a running battle at Cowes, for example. When Wilhelm bought a racing yacht in 1891, Bertie commissioned his own, *Britannia*, with which he enjoyed frequent success at Cannes Regatta and during Cowes Week. Wilhelm reacted by ordering his own new boat, bigger and faster than *Britannia*, from the same builder, prompting a saddened Bertie to sell his pride and joy and conclude that 'Cowes was once a pleasant holiday for me, but now the Kaiser has taken command it is nothing but . . . [a] perpetual firing of salutes, cheering and other tiresome disturbances'.

Wilhelm had won again, which probably explains why his state visit to Britain in 1899 was marked by yet another show of family friendship. He declared his neutrality about South Africa while other Europeans were plotting a pro-Boer coalition, and bathed in the British affection at the time for anyone not French. The only moment of Anglo-German disharmony came when Bertie had to intervene to stop Alexandra making fun of Wilhelm for bringing a hairdresser whose only job was to curl the imperial moustache.

Good relations were maintained in 1901 when Wilhelm chose to stay on in England as a private citizen between Victoria's death and her funeral* ten days later, despite the protests of his government back in Berlin. As a guest of honour at the huge funeral procession through London, he finally undid the snub of not being invited to the Diamond Jubilee, and returned home talking enthusiastically about an Anglo-German alliance (though he called it *Deutsch–Englisch* – a different order of priorities).

* See Chapter 13.

325

Predictably, family relations were strained to the limit when the Entente Cordiale was signed. Wilhelm's reaction was his usual mix of political menace and petty absurdity. Cruising around the Med in March 1905, he ordered his ship to stop just offshore of the Moroccan port of Tangier, and had himself rowed to shore through a dangerous swell, almost capsizing in the surf, an experience which apparently terrified him. He then rode to the Sultan's palace on a horse that objected to being ridden by a German and bucked so much that he was almost sent sprawling. There, Wilhelm made a speech announcing that he had come to support Morocco's right to independence from France. This must have confused the Sultan, who knew that this madman on a white horse had not brought enough firepower to stand up to the large number of heavily armed Frenchmen who were keen to have a say in Morocco's future. Nevertheless, Wilhelm was so pleased with his troublemaking that he got back on his yacht and sent Bertie an April Fool's joke. In her biography of Bertie, Jane Ridley quotes the telegram: 'So happy to be once more at Gibraltar and to send you from British soil expression of my faithful friendship. Everybody so nice to me. Had a delightful dinner and garden party with Sir George and Lady White and many pretty ladies.' It sounds banal, but this was at a time when an unscheduled stop at Gibraltar, the heart of British naval power in the Mediterranean, by Kaiser Wilhelm and his escort of German gunboats would have had the telegraph wires to London glowing red hot.

It seems almost impossible to imagine the leader of such a powerful nation as Germany mounting a small colonial invasion that threatened European peace, and then blithely having a joke with one of his potential opponents in the resulting war. It was as if Hitler had invaded the Sudetenland and then sent Churchill a photo of a potato shaped like de Gaulle's head. And the sheer insanity of Wilhelm's behaviour shows how vital Bertie was to keeping the peace. Although the Kaiser was a head of state playing on a world stage, most of his provocation, both earnest and petty, was directed at his uncle, and only his uncle's reaction really mattered. In the early twentieth century, Bertie really was the key to world peace.

III

As it was, Bertie was obliged to take the mad Tangier landing seriously and send a message of support to France's President Loubet, prompting Wilhelm to call his uncle a 'devil' and even make a public pronouncement about Bertie's immorality and his adulterous affair with Alice Keppel. Bertie was furious, but confined himself to private fuming – except for an impromptu speech while visiting President Loubet, during which he unwisely announced that he would like to send 150,000 troops to Schleswig-Holstein. It was as close as Bertie ever came to descending to Wilhelm's level.

An international confrontation over Morocco was only averted by a hurried conference at which Britain affirmed its support for France, as promised by the Entente Cordiale. In the face of such solidarity, Germany could only step down, leaving Wilhelm's nose bloodied yet again, and putting him in an even more dangerous mood.

Luckily, as always, Bertie was able to play the family card and keep the peace. On Wilhelm's birthday in 1906, Bertie wrote to him reminding him that they were 'old friends and near relations', and expressing the hope that 'the affectionate feelings that have always existed may invariably continue'. Wilhelm fell for the family sweet talk, reminding Bertie in his reply that they had been together at Victoria's deathbed – 'that great Sovereign-Lady' – and that 'she drew her last breath in my arms'. Wilhelm felt sure, he said, that 'from the home of Eternal Light she is now looking down upon us and will rejoice when she sees our hands clasped in cordial* and loyal friendship'. Wilhelm even concluded that his uncle's letter was his 'most cherished [birthday] gift', though this may be a slight exaggeration given that everyone around him in Germany knew that his egomania would not have been satisfied with anything less than a new racehorse, a sword that was longer than Bertie's, or a new battleship to play with.

And the biggest problem with Kaiser Wilhelm was his battleships. Despite constant inquiries from Britain as to why Germany needed such a huge navy, and coded warnings that the British saw this naval arms race as provocation, the German shipyards kept on turning out new gunboats. Finally, in August 1908, with political discussions getting nowhere, Bertie was sent to visit Wilhelm for a chat – one sailor recommending to another that he might like to tone down his boatbuilding habit.

---

* Note the choice of adjective, doubtless an appeal – conscious or not – for Bertie to be friendlier with him than with France.

The two men locked themselves away in a room in Friedrichshof Castle, near Frankfurt, and talked for more than three hours without any disagreements. In fact, Bertie got the feeling that it was pointless broaching the subject of naval policy with Wilhelm, and kept things light. After this, suitably buttered up, the Kaiser was left to pursue more serious political matters with Charles Hardinge for the rest of the day. Discussions were friendly and as Hardinge stood up to leave, Wilhelm told him 'in a very emphatic manner' that 'the future of the world is in the hands of the Anglo-Teuton race', and that Britain needed to 'lean on a continental power, and that power should be Germany'. He sounded exactly like someone who had been brought back into the family fold. Bertie had done his job perfectly.

The need for Bertie's personal touch became even more urgent on 6 October 1908 when Emperor Franz Joseph of Austria–Hungary – one of Bertie's oldest European colleagues, and until then a reliable friend – announced that he was annexing Bosnia–Herzegovina.

That is one of those sentences that usually scares people off reading anything about early twentieth-century history, and with good cause. Suffice it to say that the annexation of this small Balkan territory set off a chain reaction in European politics, starting with grumbling in nearby Serbia, and continuing with insurgency in Bulgaria, annoyance in Italy, fury in Russia, calls for calm from everyone else except the Germans, and ultimately the First World War. For the moment, though, the key point was that Britain, France and Russia demanded negotiations over the

Bosnia–Herzegovina question, which Wilhelm did everything he could to stall, quibbling about the date, location and conditions of the talks. It wasn't until April the following year that everyone agreed to accept the annexation, by which time most European leaders were aggrieved at almost all the others. The whiff of war was in the air, and Wilhelm's curly moustache was twitching with anticipation.

At the end of that same chaotic month, October 1908, tensions were heightened still further when an interview with Wilhelm was published in England, in the *Daily Telegraph*. In it he swore – in startlingly non-imperial language – his friendship for Britain, saying that the English were 'mad, mad, mad as March hares' not to believe him. 'Have I ever been false to my word?' he asked, knowing full well that he had on many occasions. He went on:

> Falsehood and prevarication are alien to my nature. My actions ought to speak for themselves, but you [British] listen not to them but to those who misinterpret and distort them. That is a personal insult which I feel and resent. To be forever misjudged, to have my repeated offers of friendship weighed and scrutinized with jealous, mistrustful eyes, taxes my patience severely.

He continued with threats that were as thinly veiled as a belly dancer in a Tangier sailors' bar:

> Germany is a young and growing empire. She has a worldwide commerce which is rapidly expanding, and to which

the legitimate ambition of patriotic Germans refuses to assign any bounds. Germany must have a powerful fleet to protect that commerce and her manifold interests in even the most distant seas. She expects those interests to go on growing, and she must be able to champion them manfully in any quarter of the globe. Her horizons stretch far away.

Very similar dreams of world domination – and insincere promises of peace – would be expressed by another German thirty years later.

Fortunately for Britain, the pro-British parts of Wilhelm's interview so incensed patriotic Germans that he was crucified in his own press and called to order by his government. This proof that nobody loved him apparently sent Wilhelm into fits of childlike weeping.

Shortly afterwards, things got even worse, both for Kaiser Wilhelm and his uncle. It was announced that an American magazine called *The Century* was about to publish another interview with the talkative Kaiser. A journalist called W. B. Hale had spoken to him on board the imperial yacht and subsequently had his interview approved by the German Foreign Office. However, because of the *Telegraph* scandal, the Germans withdrew their permission to publish. Unfortunately, there were leaks, and a synopsis was printed in the British press, all of it politically inflammatory and some parts downright warlike. 'If the pan-European war, so much talked about, is inevitable, the sooner it came the better,' the *Observer* quoted Wilhelm as saying. It reported that:

Germany was ready and tired of the suspense . . . King Edward [had] been humiliating His Imperial Majesty for more than two years, and he [Wilhelm] was exasperated . . . The effect of the Zeppelin dirigible balloon would give Germany a powerful advantage in war and she was ready to make use of it to the fullest extent.

Wilhelm was even suggesting an anti-British alliance between Germany and the USA. Britain was, he said, a 'decadent' and 'faithless' nation and, in a section of the interview not quoted in the British press, he made more scathing remarks about Bertie's private morals.

Wilhelm later denied that he had ever said a word of it, but it all rang very true, and if Bertie had been a lesser diplomat and statesman he would probably have decided that his crazed nephew was beyond even his redemption. However, at this crucial time in Europe's affairs, Bertie was able to prove yet again that he was the ideal person to have at the helm, a man who (unlike Wilhelm) had lived enough to gain a balanced sense of priorities. Admittedly, they were slightly French priorities, with the emphasis on pleasure, but they enabled him to weather storms like this and keep Europe on course.

Bertie therefore swallowed his pride in the national interest and went to meet Wilhelm in February 1909, his main mission to impress upon his hot-headed nephew that he needed to stop threatening global war.

Wilhelm's welcome was cordial. He had even arranged for Bertie's suite to be decorated with a portrait of Queen Victoria and a picture celebrating British naval victories.

This was clearly someone wanting approval from his dear old uncle. However, by now Bertie was too ill to make the most of his authority over his nephew. Uncharacteristically, during the official dinners and a ball given in his honour, he sat almost silent and immobile. He couldn't stop coughing. At one banquet, he had prepared a written speech, but he was too breathless and wheezing to deliver it. He even declined the honour that he usually enjoyed so much – distributing gifts of British medals to local dignitaries. And at a performance of a ballet, *Sardanapalus*, the story of an Assyrian king fabled for his orgies and the huge number of his concubines, Bertie fell asleep – a sure sign that he was not a well man.

It was left to Alexandra to broach the important subject, in her own innocent way. She told Wilhelm that he was 'stupid' to be 'making all this commotion about . . . [his] navy'. The kindest thing one could say was that hers was a tactic lacking somewhat in Bertie's subtle touch.

Wilhelm's only reaction to this sorry show was to have a word with his stool pigeon at Buckingham Palace, James Reid, who was now Bertie's principal doctor, and agree on a code in case Bertie fell dangerously ill. Wilhelm was afraid that his uncle would refuse to send for him, just as Victoria had done in her final days. It seemed that Wilhelm was already planning his starring role at Bertie's deathbed. Perhaps he would be able to prop him up, as he had done for Victoria, and share his final moments. Maybe he could even turn the tables and exert some authority on Bertie's successor – his young, inexperienced son George. In any case, Wilhelm clearly sensed that the time was rapidly approaching when he would be free of the last vestiges of family authority. Bertie's sudden signs of weakness brought war a big step closer.

It sounds simplistic, but when Wilhelm was feeling like a beloved grandson and nephew, he really seems to have been at peace with himself, and with Britain. And while he was at peace with Britain, he wasn't going to attack France. It was precarious, but it wasn't war, and it was a state of affairs that had existed pretty well ever since Wilhelm's accession to the German throne in 1888. Bertie had been vital to that twenty-year European peace, and he had been the most stable, reliable and determined person involved. Without Bertie to soothe Wilhelm's savage inner beast, or with a British monarch who was less fascinated by international relations, less willing to stand up to jingoistic politicians, or simply less fluent in the various foreign languages necessary to keep on good terms with the French, Germans and the Russians, there might have been a First World War much earlier. It would have been a very different one, too – an Anglo-German annihilation of France, for example, which, knowing Wilhelm, might well have been followed by an Anglo-German war for European domination, resulting in the destruction of both.

We will never know, but one thing seems certain: if only Bertie had toned down his playboy exploits just a little; if he had gobbled his food with less gargantuan determination; even if he had only applied the same moderation to smoking as he did to alcohol, he might well have lived longer and preserved European peace beyond 1914.

15

C'EST LA FIN

~

'[Thanks to Edward VII] the balance of European powers was less unstable, and peace less precarious.'

Raymond Poincaré,
French politician

I

During the early years of his reign, Bertie's health had declined in fits and starts, more or less in synch with the political ups and downs that Europe was suffering. And sadly for Europe, as soon as he had got over his stomach abscess of 1902, he had immediately resumed his unhealthy lifestyle.

Christopher Hibbert lists Bertie's favourite dishes as king: at home he would have a glass of warm milk in bed, followed if he was going out shooting with a breakfast of bacon and eggs, haddock, chicken, toast and butter. Lunch depended on whether the occasion was formal or not, and could even be relatively light if he was shooting. Tea would consist of poached eggs and cakes, and was followed by a dinner that often involved twelve courses. His favourites were oysters, which he slurped down several dozen at a time, plovers' eggs, caviar, sole poached in Chablis, chicken in aspic, and any game birds that were available – pheasant, grouse, partridge, snipe, woodcock, quail; all of them prepared in thick, creamy sauces. Quails he preferred stuffed with *foie gras*. His favourite style of lunch and dinner was a meal during which he could gobble as much as possible while being amused by gossiping friends or the coy chatter of a pretty woman.

On top of all this, Bertie was still smoking more than twenty cigarettes and a dozen cigars a day, and would sometimes take a cigar break in the middle of a formal dinner.

Not surprisingly, his heart and lungs began to battle it out to see which could finish him off first. The lungs presented his most visible weakness. After a particularly bad bout of bronchitis in the winter of 1905, on doctor's orders Bertie swapped his usual break in Cannes for a trip to Biarritz. He immediately approved: 'Though this place is quieter than the Riviera it is more bracing and I am sure healthier.' What he meant was that the cooler, fresher Atlantic air helped to ease his breathing so that he wasn't so subject to the coughing fits that often cut short his conversations.

In Biarritz, Bertie subjected himself to a health cure of sorts, cutting down slightly on his food. His French police bodyguard Xavier Paoli described his 'reduced' daily intake:

after his glass of milk in bed, Bertie would breakfast on bacon, boiled eggs, fried trout or smelt (a small Atlantic fish) and coffee. Lunch was often boiled plovers' eggs with paprika, grilled fish, and a meat dish (either chicken or lamb). His favourite fruit and vegetables were asparagus and strawberries. He drank very moderately (in the Frenchman's eyes), taking just a couple of glasses of Chablis or champagne with a meal. It wasn't a starvation diet, but Bertie was clearly making some effort.

As his reign went on, he began to make a habit of wintering in Biarritz for longer and longer periods, inviting Alice Keppel with him as *maîtresse-en-titre*. He would travel down on the royal train, while she followed on separately for appearance's sake. Bertie would take up residence in a suite of rooms at the Hôtel du Palais, a new luxury establishment on the seafront. It had been built on the site of the Empress Eugénie's holiday residence, which had been destroyed by fire in 1903. Meanwhile, in a neat piece of symmetry, Alice and her young daughter Sonia would stay at the nearby Villa Eugénie, which had once belonged to the Empress's son.

Together, Bertie and Alice would enjoy something resembling a family holiday. In the morning, Bertie would work on his terrace, dealing with the messages sent over from England. Then in the afternoon they would go out in one of Bertie's claret-coloured cars that had been driven down from England. Speeding through the Pyrenees or along the coast, Bertie would have a bugle sounded so that the drivers of slow carts and carriages would know that his convoy was approaching (an idea suggested to him by

Kaiser Wilhelm). He may also have invented the common British practice of stopping right by the roadside for picnics. At a picturesque spot, he would order his loyal driver and mechanic Charles Stamper to pull over, and then his attendants would get out the picnic basket and some chairs for a quick meal on the hard shoulder. These regular outings along unpolluted roads would probably have been good for mind and body if Bertie hadn't smoked non-stop every mile of the way.

In March 1907, he arrived in Biarritz suffering from a severe cough, and *The Times* printed a short piece that included a description of the morose King walking 'along the shore, where he sat for a long time on one of the benches': a melancholy image evoking a man desperately calling on the sea air to clear his diseased bronchial tubes.

A year later, things were even worse. In 1908, Bertie decided to stay on the ground floor of the Hôtel du Palais rather than the first as usual, to spare him the exertion of walking upstairs. He was only sixty-six, but seemed to be giving up on Biarritz's promise to cure his breathing problems.

Bertie wasn't pinning all his hopes on France, however. He had always been a regular at the German spas, and this didn't change when he became king. Just before his accession to the throne, he elected Marienbad – now in the Czech Republic, then part of the Austro-Hungarian empire – as his summer health resort. It was a fashionable meeting place for royal families and European socialites, and was also conveniently situated for a stopover *chez* Kaiser Wilhelm on the way.

In Marienbad, Bertie would go for brisk walks, wallow in mud baths, drink copious quantities of the healing waters, avoid champagne and eat very sensibly (for him, anyway), sticking to light meals of trout and grouse accompanied by aubergines and peaches. Over the period of a fortnight he could lose about eight pounds.

Of course he would enjoy himself, too, with parties, bridge evenings and concerts, including, on one occasion, a show by Yvette Guilbert, the French *chanteuse* who had been shipped down to perform for him in Cannes a few years earlier. Marienbad had a full theatrical programme, and Bertie was often in attendance. Only once was he disappointed, and walked out of a play called *Hell*, a succession of not-very-stimulating erotic songs in German. Hardly surprising that he was unimpressed – he had been brought up on French eroticism, which was in a league of its own. Bertie was congratulated on this moral stand by the Bishop of Ripon, but he didn't feel that congratulations were in order, and replied: 'I have no wish to pose as a protector of morals, especially abroad.' Possibly Bertie's most accurate piece of self-analysis ever, and proof that, even in relatively old age, he never forgot his inner Frenchman.

II

Perhaps symbolically, Bertie had one of his first attacks of uncontrollable coughing in Germany, while on his last state visit to see Wilhelm in February 1909.

Bertie was, as usual, enjoying a smoke, when he suddenly began choking, dropped his cigar, and had to have the tight collar of his German army uniform hastily unbuttoned by his terrified wife and the Foreign Office representative Charles Hardinge to save him from suffocating. Hardinge's intervention was a neat metaphor – keeping Bertie breathing was synonymous with keeping Britain's foreign policy alive. And on that occasion in Germany it worked, just about.

Tragically, it was a trip to his beloved France a year later that seems to have finished Bertie off. Or, to put it more kindly, perhaps his body chose to say its farewells in the country that had taught it virtually everything it knew about life.

In March 1910 Bertie travelled to Paris. While there, he went to the Théâtre de la Porte Saint-Martin, one of Sarah Bernhardt's favourites, the stage on which Edmond Rostand's *Cyrano de Bergerac* was first performed in 1897. There, Bertie saw Rostand's new play, *Chantecler*, although it's hard to know why it was recommended to him, because it was already a flop. It was a sort of tame, non-political precursor of Orwell's *Animal Farm*, a verse fable about farmyard animals in which the eponymous cockerel (whose name means 'sing clearly') reveals that he makes the sun rise every morning. Bertie, no fan of allegories unless they involved scantily clad nymphs, found the play 'stupid and childish' (as had most of Paris's theatre-going public). He also found the theatre so stifling and airless that he began to sweat, and caught a chill, which quickly developed into bronchitis.

Next day, he confided in a friend, the beautiful socialite

Comtesse de Greffuhle, that 'I have not long to live. And then my nephew will make war.' Bertie's self-awareness seems to have covered his mortality as well as his morality.

He left Paris for Biarritz as planned, but after two days he was feeling so ill that he took to his room. He had a fever, and was breathing very rapidly, coughing all the while. Mrs Keppel wrote a note to a friend saying 'I am quite worried', which was no doubt the English stiff-upper-lip version of 'Oh my God he's dying, what should I do?' Later, when Dr Reid found symptoms of pneumonia, Alice went even further and wrote that she was 'alarmed'.

In any case, the weather was so bracing outdoors that it would have killed Bertie outright. Biarritz is on the same latitude as the Riviera, but the climate is incomparable. The Atlantic breezes that can feel refreshing when they are gentle often turn into gales, and the spring of 1910 was marked by snow, rain and constant wind. Queen Alexandra invited Bertie to come on a Mediterranean cruise, but even in his reduced condition, Bertie didn't want to shorten his holiday with Mrs Keppel. Despite the bronchitis, France was having its romantic effect.

After a few days he actually began to improve, so that the risk of suffering a typical French statesman's death – in a hotel room, alone with his mistress – was at least post-poned for a while. He even felt well enough to start chain-smoking cigars again. A bulletin was issued to the British press announcing that 'His Majesty is now completely restored to health'. Though strictly speaking, that hadn't been true since about 1890.

* * *

Bertie knew that his days were numbered, which might explain one of the outings he made when he felt well enough to go for drives again.

Perhaps as a means of denying his own responsibility for his chronic illness, he was highly superstitious. Attached to his bed at home was a bouquet of herbs that he hoped would help to heal him or at least bring him luck. He hated going into dinner if there were thirteen people present, and once when he did so, he was heard to console himself with the thought that one of the women was pregnant, which added another guest. He also counted the sticks of asparagus on his plate, and was alarmed if there was an odd number.

During Bertie's last stay at Biarritz, perhaps in an attempt to seek metaphysical help for his health problems, he drove to the shrine at Lourdes, the Pyrenean town where pilgrims had been flocking ever since 1858, when a fourteen-year-old girl called Bernadette had had visions of the Virgin Mary and dug a hole that yielded holy waters.

On 20 April, Bertie, Alice and a small party of friends covered the first stage of the journey – a hard, 120-kilometre drive from Biarritz to Pau that would have taken at least three hours, given the conditions of the road. Next day, they drove thirty or so kilometres up into the mountains, slowed by several burst tyres, and didn't arrive in Lourdes until the afternoon. Bertie, an ill man, must have been very determined to get there.

He was greeted by the Bishop of Lourdes and taken into the grotto to see the pool where pilgrims in search of a miraculous cure for their ills dunk their afflicted body parts or have themselves completely immersed. Sadly for Bertie, he couldn't undress and dive in to bathe his chest – not only because a huge crowd had gathered to see him, but also because it would have been an overtly Catholic thing for an Anglican monarch to do. Besides, the water is so cold that it would probably have brought on a fatal bout of pneumonia.

Bertie stayed on in Biarritz until the last week of April 1910 while Alexandra cruised to Corfu, and on the night before his departure, there was a parade of local sailors and the fire brigade, a band playing and fireworks lighting up the stormy sky. It was the town's biggest-ever *au revoir*. Bertie, though, was afraid it was a definitive *adieu* – next day, when everything was packed, he looked out over the bay and said that he was 'sorry to leave Biarritz. Perhaps it will be for ever.'

And for once in his life, he didn't stop over in Paris on his way home through France – an ominous omen.

Back in London, it was clear to everyone that Bertie's French holiday hadn't done him any good. He was quiet, exhausted, coughing incessantly, and had no appetite – except for cigars. He worked on as diligently as ever signing documents, but barely talking as he did so. When he did speak it was to confess to his secretary Frederick Ponsonby that: 'I feel wretchedly ill. I can't sleep, I can't eat.' The enjoyments of life were deserting him one by one.

On Monday 2 May, after a quiet evening of bridge (a game that required little or no conversation), Dr Reid found

Bertie in his dressing room at Buckingham Palace, breathing very quickly and coughing painfully. He had a temperature of 100 degrees. The doctor applied hot poultices to Bertie's chest and back, gave him a shot of morphine and put him to bed. The next evening Bertie still couldn't eat, and found it impossible to talk without coughing.

The following day, Bertie forced himself to conduct audiences, but was coughing too much to utter more than a few sentences. When it was suggested that he might like to rest, he famously replied: 'I shall not give in. I shall go on. I shall work to the end. Of what use is it to be alive if one cannot work?'*

On the last morning of his life, 6 May 1910, Bertie lit a cigar but found that even that was no pleasure any more, and he finally gave up smoking – too late.

He insisted on sitting up in a chair, where it was easier to breathe, and sucked in lungfuls of oxygen from a large bottle, but still looked distinctly blue in the face. Lunch was brought in, but he didn't feel like eating, and stood up to go and play with his canaries, which were kept in a cage by the window. The effort was too much for him and he collapsed. Refusing to go to bed, he was propped up again in his chair and continued his laboured efforts to breathe, while his doctors injected strychnine to stimulate his heart – a risky last resort, because an overdose would have caused asphyxia and death.

By this time, all of Bertie's close family was with him

---

* Here, for once, he was showing that he didn't *always* think like a Frenchman.

– minus Kaiser Wilhelm. Alexandra had returned early from her cruise, and, in a spirit of generosity and resignation that was typical of her despite spending so many years as the betrayed spouse, she called for Alice Keppel. The *maîtresse-en-titre* had visited Bertie the day before and was due to return at 5 p.m., but Alexandra thought that it would be too late to see her lover conscious, and sent news that she should return as soon as possible.

When Mrs Keppel arrived, Alexandra shook hands coldly, but told her sportingly, 'I am sure you have always had a good influence on him,' and walked over to the window to give the *maîtresse* a few moments of privacy. Bertie, though, had fallen into a coma and did not recognize Alice, which sent her into hysterics, so that she had to be removed from the room.

Bertie was finally put to bed at 11 p.m. and died there just three-quarters of an hour later, suffocating from the effects of emphysema. His last words before losing consciousness were to express his pleasure at hearing that one of his horses, a two-year-old called Witch of the Air, had won the 4.15 at Kempton Park. Bertie gasped that he was 'very glad'. History has not recorded whether the dying King had put a bet on his horse.

III

The day before the funeral, with the departed sovereign lying in state in Westminster Hall, Kaiser Wilhelm almost caused a riot. He had decided that he would lay his wreath at 2.45 p.m. precisely, and gave just an hour's notice that the tens of thousands of mourners who were filing past to pay their respects should be kept away.

Bertie's old friend, Charles Wynn-Carrington, was Lord Great Chamberlain, in charge of the lying-in-state. He was afraid that Wilhelm's stunt would cause serious public unrest. When the public mourning had begun, there had been a queue one mile long snaking along the Embankment. By the next day, it had stretched to four miles, with people waiting six abreast, and on the final day, when Wilhelm intended to visit, the line was an unbelievable seven miles long.

Wynn-Carrington described the crowds in his diary: 'People waiting patiently for hours. Hundreds passed the night in the rain. They all went by from 6 a.m. to 10 p.m. quietly and reverently without intermission.' But tell them that the German Emperor was going to halt proceedings for an hour, and the mood might well turn ugly.

So he went to find Wilhelm, who was calmly having lunch, and told him that he would have to enter the hall via a side door so that the long flow of public mourners would not be interrupted. A side door? The tradesman's entrance? Wilhelm was not pleased. Even from beyond the grave, Bertie was making his nephew feel inferior. It may not be much of an exaggeration to say that Kaiser Wilhelm's (delayed) reaction to this final humiliation was, as Bertie had predicted, world war.

The day of the funeral, 20 May, was fine, though it had rained all night and drenched the mourners who had flooded in from all over the country. Amongst the VIP guests were the Kings of Belgium, Denmark, Greece, Bulgaria, Norway, Portugal and Spain, the Archduke of

Austria, the Prince of the Ottoman Empire, the Empress of Russia and dozens of princes and princesses from small European nations like Hesse, Hanover and Schleswig-Holstein. Most of these were Bertie's relatives or personal friends. France was represented by members of its two opposing clans – the republicans and royalists – with Stéphen Pichon, the Foreign Minister who would go on to be one of signatories of the Treaty of Versailles in 1919, and Pierre d'Orléans, the nephew of Bertie's old friend Henri and grandson of deposed King Louis-Philippe.

As this impressive funeral cortège assembled at Westminster, Wilhelm tried to steal the family show one last time, leaping from his horse as Alexandra's coach approached, opening the door for her, and kissing her as she emerged.

Along the route through London to Paddington station, from where the coffin was to be transported to Windsor for the funeral service, people stood silent, their hats off, almost none of them smoking – either as a mark of respect or because they knew what had just killed their sovereign. Many people had laid simple wreaths along the route, and everyone was struck by the dignified calm of the occasion – not one of the 6,000 policemen on duty was forced to make an arrest. There were black-clad spectators at every window, on every balcony and every roof that afforded a view of the long procession of soldiers and dignitaries. Bertie's body was being escorted by a guard of sailors, perhaps as a posthumous message to Kaiser Wilhelm that Britannia still intended to rule the waves after her great defender was gone.

The funeral in Windsor was a confused, badly organized affair that would have infuriated Bertie, the stickler for precision and organization. There was no seating plan for St George's Chapel, so protocol was enforced by mourners being ejected from their pews when a more important guest arrived. It is easy to imagine the mixture of fury and amusement that Wilhelm would have felt as he clung on to his place in the front pew.

The new King George V had sportingly invited Alice Keppel to the service and she was smuggled in through a cloister door. He also broke with precedence and let his mother follow the coffin down the aisle, which should rightly have been his place as the succeeding monarch. But after so many decades when Alexandra had been forced to take a back seat in her husband's life, this was her great occasion, and George let her stand alone by the coffin as Bertie was lowered into his final resting place.

At 11 a.m. that morning, France also said farewell to its favourite *Anglais* with a funeral service at the English church in Paris, in the rue d'Aguesseau, just around the corner from Bertie's favourite hotel, the Bristol. It was attended by the country's top politicians – the Foreign Minister Théophile Delcassé, the former Prime Minister and future war leader Georges Clemenceau, and President Armand Fallières (whom Bertie had met), as well as an old guard of powdered aristocrats – Bertie's friends, his lovers, and failed intriguers from 1870, when France had said *adieu* to its own last monarch, Bertie's mentor Napoléon III. It was a sombre occasion. France knew that it had lost probably its closest and most important British ally in all its history.

IV

The public grief in Britain was deep and real – deeper than when Victoria died, even though she had been on the throne more than six times longer than Bertie, and had overseen Britain's rise to the pinnacle of the world's most powerful empire.

The explanation for this depth of feeling was Bertie's human touch. He brought the monarchy out of the closet. He delighted in public ceremonies and managed to say a kind word to every one of his subjects who met him. It was obvious to his people that he was conscious of the privileges he enjoyed, but that he also understood the duties that went with them. More simply, the nation felt that Bertie loved life and wanted everyone else to enjoy it, too.

What he hated most were people who were incapable of appreciating the pleasures of life: racists, religious bigots and bores. And, of course, warmongers who threatened the peace that allowed him to travel unhindered from one country to the next – from spa to château to hunt to intimate dinner.

Thanks to Bertie's obvious sincerity, the ordinary British people no longer begrudged him his pleasures, and forgave all the sins that the Victorians had condemned him for. When he died, even the British press forgot its past moralizing and talked about the nation's 'deep sorrow' for the loss of a 'common leveller' and 'peacemaker' who had enjoyed 'one of the most brilliant and fruitful reigns in history'. Bertie had come a long way in a short time.

He also got glowing write-ups in all the European press.

The Russian paper *Novoye Vremya* (*New Time*) declared that Edward VII had 'moulded the destiny of his realm'. In Austria he was hailed as 'the most influential man of the present day' and a monarch 'who had been his own Foreign Minister'. Even the German papers praised Bertie in their own way, with the *Rheinisch-Westfälische Zeitung* calling him 'a victorious antagonist' and 'the great adversary, who inflicted inestimable damage upon us' – though that was perhaps less an obituary than a declaration of war.

Fittingly, Bertie received his greatest homage from France. Purely out of respect for him, the Archbishop of Paris cancelled the annual celebration of Joan of Arc day, the patriotic ceremony that reminds the French every year that their traditional enemies have always been the English. Paris couldn't have paid Bertie a greater historical tribute – thanks to him, for the first time ever, the French forgave England for the Hundred Years War, which had of course been started by Bertie's namesake Edward III.*

And since it was France that had enabled him to forget the traumas of his pleasureless childhood and develop into the warm, tolerant and popular man that he became, it is fitting that the most heartfelt – and most accurate – testimony to Bertie's life came from a Frenchman.

On 15 April 1912, almost exactly two years after his death, a statue of Bertie as a relatively young-looking yachtsman was unveiled on the seafront in Cannes. At the ceremony,

---

* The forgiveness was temporary. The French re-instated the celebrations the following year and in 1919 had Joan of Arc canonized as their anti-British patron saint.

which was disrupted slightly by a gusting wind, there was an impressive turnout of dignitaries, including the senator and future president Raymond Poincaré, as well as France's Minister of War and Minister of the Navy. The British Ambassador to France, the aptly named Sir Francis Bertie, read out a speech in French saying that King George V wished to thank the town for this informal statue:

> . . . because it was as Prince of Wales that King Edward came to know and love Cannes, and that Cannes came to know and appreciate him. It was thanks to the King's frequent visits to different parts of France before his accession to the throne that His Majesty was able to see in person the feelings of the French people and the opportunity to establish between our two neighbouring countries relations of cordial friendship.

In reply, Raymond Poincaré's speech was much more personal – and much longer. He gave a brilliant assessment of Bertie the man as seen by the French, who, *après tout*, knew him better than anyone. It was, in essence, a posthumous love letter from France to Bertie. And, like many love letters, it said as much about the recipient as the writer.

Describing the statue, Poincaré said that:

> In the elegant and robust yachtsman astride this pedestal, you will all recognize the magnificent Prince who, beneath the Cannes sun, exuded so much graciousness, wit and seduction. Of all the places where this tireless traveller was led by his all-embracing curiosity, the Mediterranean coast

was one of his favourites. Each one of you will remember his noble ease, the sharp good sense, witty bonhomie and instinctive diplomacy . . . that were the characteristics of his genius . . . No human experience was alien to him.* He raised or lowered himself to the level of deep or trifling questions. He was at home in Cannes, Paris or London, in palaces and in modest homes . . . He adapted himself effortlessly to the varying conditions of a life that encompassed all pleasures, sadness and earthly honours. For more than half a century, he fulfilled, with admirable tact, the delicate role of heir to the throne, and this long preparation for monarchy gave him an incomparable schooling in delicacy and discretion . . . Every time he came to France, he penetrated deeper [ahem] into his examination of our society, our morals, and our institutions. He maintained relationships with our writers, artists, and men of state, and on each of them he practised the art of making them love him, an art of which he was a master . . . When, at the age of sixty he finally acceded to the throne, he transformed all his accumulated resources of prudence, wisdom and skill into brilliant political qualities . . . He was well informed about the financial, military and naval strength of all the European nations and he was determined to use this information, his experience and his natural subtlety to pursue a firm and trustworthy policy of peace and stability. He did not try to break with the past. He did not wrench England out of its splendid isolation. It was with method and subtlety

* When a Frenchman says that about a statesman it is a compliment.

that he prepared the necessary evolution, and with gentleness that he influenced his government to change their position. Sir Edward Grey [Britain's Foreign Secretary] said that the King's visits to the courts and nations of Europe were precious to Great Britain, because . . . he possessed a gift that has never been equalled for inspiring in governments and peoples a legitimate confidence in the good will of the people and the government of England.

Poincaré recalled the signing of the Entente Cordiale and Bertie's successful policy of keeping the peace with Russia and Germany, saying that he had made 'the balance of European powers less unstable, and peace less precarious'. He then went on:

Edward VII was peace-loving by nature, by choice, and by reasoning, and if he referred to France as the best friend of England, he certainly did not give this friendship a meaning that might worry other powers. And it is in the same spirit that France has conducted this policy of *entente* since the death of Edward VII . . . France does not plan to attack or provoke any of its neighbours, but we are aware that, to avoid being attacked or provoked, we must maintain, both on land and sea, armed forces capable of protecting our honour and our interests.

It is a moving speech – a heartfelt lament for a lost friend and ally, as well as a sincere plea from a politician who hopes for peace but is resigned to war now that Bertie, the one man who could prevent it, is gone.

V

It is not always wise to trust a French politician's judgements, but in this case Raymond Poincaré seems to have hit the nail on the *tête*. If Bertie had been alive and healthy when Archduke Franz Ferdinand of Austria was assassinated in Sarajevo on 28 June 1914, he would almost certainly have been able to 'calm the spirits', as the French say.

Bertie would have assembled Emperor Franz Joseph of Austro-Hungary, Kaiser Wilhelm of Germany and Tsar Nicholas of Russia – on a yacht, at a spa or in a *Schloss* somewhere in central Europe – handed out the cigars, and talked firmly but amiably about the danger of a pointless, disruptive war.

What exactly was the problem? Ah yes, a nineteen-year-old Serbian student had shot the Archduke, heir to the Austrian throne, and his wife, Sophie, and now Serbia's assorted allies and opponents were at each other's throats. It was very regrettable, Bertie would have agreed. But was Franz Ferdinand really worth a war?

Before he could be shouted down with complex political arguments about alliances and the balance of power, Bertie would have played the trump card he knew best – family.

Even Franz Ferdinand's own relatives disliked him, Bertie would have reminded the assembled gentlemen. For a start, he was a bloodthirsty maniac. Everyone enjoys blasting a few animals to kingdom come (nods and grunts amidst the cigar smoke), but Franz Ferdinand was a psychopath – he boasted of having shot 274,889 animals in his lifetime. Yes, he insisted on having every corpse counted, and kept an exact tally. The man was a serial killer.*

Not only that, Franz Ferdinand was unreliable. In 1900, four years after becoming heir to the Austrian throne on his father's death, he had ignored the traditions of his family and the instructions of his dear uncle Franz Joseph and married a non-royal woman – entering into what is known in royal circles as a morganatic marriage (cue shudders around the table). This had resulted in Franz Ferdinand's children automatically being removed from the line of succession. All in all, Bertie would have concluded, what use was he as an heir?

His wife was not much of a loss, either. Apart from being a mere countess, Sophie was by all accounts an unsmiling, dull-witted religious crackpot. And people were saying that this unlikeable couple were worth a world war? Bertie would have guffawed (and coughed) at the idea.

By now his audience of royal males would have been stroking their decorative facial hair. At least half won over, they would have been ripe for Bertie's clinching argument.

There was, as everyone seemed to have forgotten, an ideal successor to Franz Ferdinand – his nephew, the young

---

* A German historian, Emil Franzel, would later coin a brutally accurate name for Franz Ferdinand's bloodlust: 'feudale Massenschlächterei', or feudal mass butchering, thereby suggesting what was likely to happen to any political opponents he might have had when he became emperor.

Karl Franz Joseph Ludwig Herbert Georg Otto Maria. Admittedly his name was a bit of a mouthful, but in all other respects he was perfect. In June 1914, he was twenty-six years old, married to a princess (Zita di Borbone-Parma, granddaughter of a Portuguese king), and had recently produced a male heir. Even better, since his uncle's morganatic marriage in 1900, Karl had been groomed as an eventual emperor. He was the dream candidate.

In a cruel way, Bertie might have suggested, it was almost a relief that Franz Ferdinand had been removed from the line, just as Bertie's own eldest son, the uncontrollable Eddy, had been, by flu rather than a bullet. Because the most important thing, surely, for all of them – Franz Joseph, Wilhelm, Nicholas and Bertie himself – was the survival of their royal lines. And young Karl Franz Joseph Ludwig etc. was the best Austrian for that job. Why, then, would anyone bother to go to war on Franz Ferdinand's account?

And while the others were all puffing thoughtfully, and Kaiser Wilhelm was wondering what to do with all his new battleships – a cruise past Cowes, perhaps, or artillery practice off the coast of Schleswig-Holstein? – Bertie would have closed his speech by bringing all his years of experience into play.

It wasn't just about Austria. Were they sure, he would have asked, that a war between major powers was the best way of ensuring the survival of their dynasties? Bertie had seen at first hand the result of the Franco-Prussian war, when one of the two emperors involved had lost his throne. Were Franz Joseph, Wilhelm and Nicholas willing to throw their crowns into the ring? Were they certain that if

Germany, Austro-Hungary, Russia and Britain, along with all the minor monarchies still dotted about the continent, went to war, all those countries would emerge from the conflict with crowned heads of state still in place?

Bertie had ridden the waves of republicanism in Britain while France had been tossed about between régimes. He had seen his mother put her throne at risk merely by becoming a recluse, and he had become the people's King precisely in order to protect the stability that he cherished so much. Now his two nephews and his oldest surviving friend in Europe were at risk of throwing away their futures – and the future of Europe as a group of interlinked monarchies (with the exception of France, but they were harmless if you left them alone) – all for the irrelevant madman Franz Ferdinand, and a quarrel over tiny Serbia?

Bertie, peacemaker and lover of all the good things in life that prolonged peacetime had to offer, simply would not have let it happen.

All of which points to perhaps the most tragic thing about Poincaré's eulogy: just two years before the start of a conflict that would kill 16 million people and wound another 20 million, the Frenchman completely disregards the new English King. There is no sense that George V will be able to follow in his father's footsteps. The King is dead . . . period.

If Bertie had one failing as a statesman – leaving aside any criticism of his morality as a man – it is precisely this. For some reason, he failed to prepare his son to take on the role as European peacekeeper. George could speak almost no French, only semi-coherent German, and had rarely set foot outside England except to visit the colonies. To most European leaders, including his own relatives, he was a stranger. And, most importantly, in the eyes of his cousin Kaiser Wilhelm, George was the embodiment of the inward-looking, jingoistic Englishman. And weak to boot. Wilhelm wasn't afraid of what his cousin would say if he declared war on him or anybody else.

But perhaps Bertie's failure to prepare for the future was predictable. He was a self-made man. His mother didn't teach him much at all, apart from the need to stay close to his family and the importance of not turning into a recluse, as she had done. Starting in his teens, Bertie had learnt the real priorities of life on his own, letting himself be guided by the experienced hands of the French. And he must have sensed that it was this unique, personalized, life-long education that had made him the only man in the world capable of doing his job as the peacemaking uncle of Europe.

Most of all, though, right up until the last few days of his life, Bertie always lived as if he felt immortal – or as if he could not conceive that the pleasures of life would ever end. This was why he hated being bored. There was always something amusing to be done somewhere, and he couldn't understand why anyone would want to miss out. Protecting world peace was simply his way of getting everyone to join in the fun instead of squabbling about politics. He had an intense appetite for the here and now, and the future – including, sadly, his heir and Europe – could wait. His personal presence was the spark that kept the flame of peace alight.

Appropriately, there is no exact English word for this quality that made Bertie such a popular man and successful diplomat. You have to say it in French – what had guided Bertie ever since his first visit to Paris in 1855, and stayed with him until the end of his life, was pure *joie de vivre*.

Afterword

~

LIFE AFTER BERTIE . . .

Nowadays, Bertie's role in keeping the First World War at bay is generally underestimated or even ignored. Most people seem to see the conflict as a machine that was gaining momentum throughout the first decade of the twentieth century, and would have broken loose whatever anyone did. I hope that this book has shown that things could have been different. Bertie really could have cooled the hotheads, and convinced the world not to go to war over so trifling a matter as the shooting of an Austrian Archduke who was unpopular with his own emperor.

Bertie hardly even gets much credit for the Entente Cordiale, which in most minds seems to have happened by magic, or at the very least been dreamt up jointly by the British and French governments to annoy the Germans. In truth, though, as we have seen, the agreement that changed the whole balance of European politics would never have been conceived without Bertie.

He does get some acclaim for creating his own era at home. Today, when we think of the Edwardians, we generally imagine big hats, brass bands and garden parties, people enjoying the last few years of peace and innocence at the start of the twentieth century. Bertie's reign saw the flowering of a rich cultural life that seemed to reflect his personality – George Bernard Shaw's comedies, Rudyard Kipling's uplifting 'If—', and P. G. Wodehouse's eternally fun-filled country houses, where the only problem was who would marry whom and which poor soul might actually have to get a job. In the popular memory, Bertie's nation truly was Elgar's 'Land of Hope and Glory'.

Life was by no means rosy for everyone in Britain, as the Suffragettes tried to show. And Beatrix Potter and Kenneth Grahame's almost-human rabbits, moles and toads seem to suggest that some of the pervading optimism was in fact a child-like pre-war naïvety. But if we remember the Edwardian era as generally positive, it is largely thanks to Bertie's own joviality.

He should also be credited with creating the modern British monarchy. It was Bertie, the people's King, whose taste for pageantry turned the monarchy into one of Britain's national treasures. The makers of mugs, tea towels and documentaries owe him a huge debt – as do his royal descendants. If modern English princes are celebrities, and have their weddings televised worldwide, it is largely thanks to Bertie.

Though it is another country that seems to have benefited most from his legacy. Bertie wasn't the first, or the only, Brit to go to France in search of earthly pleasures, but for fifty-odd years he was the most famous. It was his fun-seeking in Paris, Cannes and Biarritz that established France's image as a place where good food, sophistication and erotic delights are a way of life. He was the Englishman who helped to turn France's *fin de siècle* into a *belle époque*, and who ensured that its fame would spread all over Europe, first amongst the upper classes, and then with everyone else.

Before Bertie, France was an enemy, to be despised, distrusted or at least disdained. After him, it was sexy, fashionable and alluring – and still is today.

What's more, Bertie seems to be responsible for a phenomenon that continues to make me laugh after twenty years of living here in France. For some reason, even now, an Englishman who speaks French is regarded as the poshest life form in the universe. You may not know how to open a bottle of champagne, you may never have read Proust, but if you can get your irregular verbs right, you will be welcomed into France's most snobbish social circles as an equal. It can only be thanks to Bertie. The liberating troops in 1944 made English-speakers popular here; the Beatles made everything British trendy; but it was Bertie who made Englishmen inherently chic, and his memory lives on in France's subconscious.

For this, and for being such a fascinating – and attractive – subject for a book, I for one would like to say a big *merci*.

SELECT BIBLIOGRAPHY

There have been countless biographies of Bertie, and the proof that he is a complex character is that they are so very different. But what interested me more were the opinions of him while he was still alive, and descriptions by his contemporaries of the people and places he knew, especially by the French, who knew him best. By hunting around in newspaper archives, it is also possible to get a direct insight into how Bertie's contemporaries saw him and talked about him.

Below is a selection of the books that have been most useful to me, or simply the most entertaining about Bertie's times. Most of them have been cited in the text. The out-of-print French books can mostly be found on the Bibliothèque Nationale's website: gallica.bnf.fr.

All English translations of excerpts from French sources are my own.

Biographies of Bertie

Gordon Brook-Shepherd, *Uncle of Europe: The Social and Diplomatic Life of Edward VII* (1975)

Virginia Cowls, *Gay Monarch: The Life and Pleasures of Edward VII* (1956)

Émile Flourens, *La France Conquise: Edouard VII et Clemenceau* (1906)

Christopher Hibbert, *Edward VII* (1976)

Philippe Jullian, *Edouard VII* (1962)

André Maurois, *Edouard VII et son Temps* (1933)

Jane Ridley, *Bertie: A Life of Edward VII* (2012)

Giles St Aubyn, *Edward VII: Prince and King* (1979)

Stanley Weintraub, *Edward the Caresser* (2001)

H. E. Wortham, *Edward VII: Man and King* (1931)

Memoirs

James de Chambrier, *La Cour et la Société du Second Empire* (1904)

Henri Château & Georges Renault, *Montmartre* (1897)

Jacques Debussy, *L'Impératrice Eugénie* (1913)

Gaston Jollivet, *Souvenirs de la Vie de Plaisir sous le Second Empire* (1927)

Adrien Marx, *Les Souverains à Paris* (1868)

Comte de Maugny, *Souvenirs du Second Empire: la Fin d'une Société* (1890)

Xavier Paoli, *Leurs Majestés* (1911)

Irène de Taisey-Chantenoy, *À la Cour de Napoléon III* (1891)

Emma Valadon, *Mémoires de Thérésa, Écrits par Elle-même* (1865)

Horace de Viel-Castel, *Mémoires du Comte Horace de Viel-Castel sur le Règne de Napoléon III* (1883)

Other sources

A. C. Benson & Viscount Esher (editors), *Letters of Queen Victoria, 1837–1861* (1907)

Catalogue Officiel: Exposition Universelle Internationale de 1878 à Paris (Volume 4 has all the details of British exhibitors)

Ludovic Halévy & Henri Meilhac, *La Vie Parisienne* (libretto, 1866)

Napoléon III et Eugénie Reçoivent à Fontainebleau (exhibition catalogue, 2012)

Paul Reboux, *Le Guide Galant* (1953)

Lytton Strachey, *Queen Victoria* (1921)

Émile Zola, *Nana* (1880)

PICTURE PERMISSIONS

Plate Section 1

1. Victoria and Albert in 1894. Getty Images
2. Bertie as a teenager. Getty Images
3. Painting of Empress Eugénie and courtiers by Franz Xaver Winterhalter. Roger-Viollet/Topfoto
4. Emperor Napoléon III of France. Getty Images
5. Bertie in 1865. Getty Images
6. Bertie. Getty Images
7. Princess Alexandra. Getty Images
8. Royal family. Getty images
9. Prince Bertie. Getty Images

Plate Section 2

1. Hortense Schneider. Getty Images
2. Jeanne Granier. Author's (very) private collection
3. Louise Weber. Getty Images
4. Pauline Metternich. Getty Images.
5. Sarah Bernhardt. Getty Images
6. Yvette Guilbert. Getty Images
7. Caroline 'la Belle' Otero. Author's (very) private collection
8. Cora Pearl (Eliza Emma Crouch). Getty Images
9. Théresa cartoon. Roger-Viollet/Topfoto
10. 'L'Impudique Albion' cartoon. Roger-Viollet/Topfoto
11. Cover *Le Petit Journal*. Getty Images
12. Edward in Biarritz. Roger-Viollet/Topfoto
13. King Edward and Kaiser. Getty Images

The author and publisher have made all reasonable effort to contact copyright holders for permission and apologise for any omission or error in the credits given. Corrections may be made to future reprints.

INDEX

The entry for Bertie is under Edward VII. Otherwise he is referred to as Bertie throughout. Where women are marked as 'mistress' without any other specifications, they were mistresses of Bertie himself.

Stephen Clarke lives in France, where he divides his time between writing and not writing. His first novel, *A Year in the Merde*, originally became a word-of-mouth hit in Paris in 2004, and is now published all over the world. Since then he has published four more *Merde* novels, as well as *Talk to the Snail*, an indispensable guide to understanding the French, *Paris Revealed*, his insider's guide to his home city, and *1,000 Years of Annoying the French*, in which he investigates what has *really* been going on since 1066. A *Sunday Times* bestseller in hardcover, *1,000 Years of Annoying the French* went on to become one of the top ten bestselling history books in paperback in 2011.

Research for Stephen's books has taken him all over France. For *Dirty Bertie* he delved into French archives to hunt out nineteenth-century newspapers and kiss-and-tell autobiographies. He also visited the venues of Bertie's French escapades, from grand chateaux to dingy cabarets. He has now returned to present-day Paris, and is doing his best to live the Entente Cordiale.